AUTHOR
IN
PROGRESS

D1400575

WD

WRITER'S DIGEST
BOOKS

WritersDigest.com
Cincinnati, Ohio

For more resources for writers, visit www.writersdigest.com.

20 19 18 17   5 4 3

Distributed in Canada by Fraser Direct
100 Armstrong Avenue
Georgetown, Ontario, Canada L7G 5S4
Tel: (905) 877-4411

Distributed in the U.K. and Europe by F+W Media International
Brunel House, Newton Abbot, Devon, TQ12 4PU, England
Tel: (+44) 1626-323200, Fax: (+44) 1626-323319
E-mail: postmaster@davidandcharles.co.uk

ISBN-13: 978-1-4403-4671-2

Edited by Rachel Randall
Designed by Alexis Estoye
Production coordinated by Debbie Thomas

DEDICATION

For authors in progress everywhere

ACKNOWLEDGMENTS

Every writer reflected on these pages played a significant role in actualizing *Author in Progress*, but a few were especially helpful when I first conceptualized the book. Additional thanks to Tracy Hahn-Burkett, Donald Maass, Vaughn Roycroft, and Heather Webb for their enthusiasm over and confidence in this concept, and for shared wisdom that helped to evolve the narrative. This book is better because of you.

—Therese

TABLE OF CONTENTS

 **PART ONE: PREPARE**

PART TWO: WRITE

PART THREE: INVITE

PART FOUR: IMPROVE

▌▌▐▐▌▌▌▙ PART FIVE: REWRITE

▌▌▐▐▌▌▌▙ PART SIX: PERSEVERE

PART SEVEN: RELEASE

FOREWORD

JAMES SCOTT BELL

Back when I started out in the writing game, youngster, we had it tough. There wasn't any Internet thingy, by thunder. We had to hunt down books and magazines printed on paper. If we wanted to learn the craft of writing fiction, we had to travel by covered wagon to the bookstore or order books delivered by Pony Express.

We didn't wake up every day to writing advice delivered to us through a computer monitor or (who'da thunk it?) on a phone! Yessir, and I used to walk ten miles to school, in the snow, right here in Los Angeles. So don't tell me about tough!

Times change.

Now we've got blogs and websites and lots of knowledgeable writers and teachers sharing their expertise in a variety of ways. On my own group blog, Kill Zone, I do that each week. Why? Because I love the craft of fiction. I love to learn and grow, try new things, and teach others what I discover.

I've always considered myself a fiction writer first. My main goal is to write the best novel I can, every time. Which is why, even after making a living as a writer for twenty years, I still read craft books and *Writer's Digest* and blogs on writing.

My favorite blog is Writer Unboxed. Therese Walsh and Kathleen Bolton made this a quality site from the get-go. It has stayed that way, which is no easy task. But you'll see why it's been so good when you read the contributions in *Author in Progress*.

I like that title. It tells me the book is not just for newbies trying to get published. It's for the vets, too. Because real writers never feel like they've got everything nailed. They don't assume they can take it easy on their yachts as they "mail it in." Readers can smell that attitude a bookshelf away.

Real writers, even if they've reached a nice level of success, keep trying to get better. They experiment. Take risks. Go deeper.

I tell my workshop students to imagine they need brain surgery (and if you want to be a writer, maybe you do). You go in to meet the surgeon, and he's playing Angry Birds. On the floor, in the corner, you see a stack of medical journals. The top one has a cover article titled "NEW DISCOVERIES ABOUT THE CEREBRAL CORTEX."

"Have you been reading those?" you ask.

"Um, not yet. That's my to-be-read pile."

"When was the last time you read a medical journal?"

"Oh, not since I started here at good old Carver Memorial Hospital. I know what I'm doing! Now which part of your brain am I removing?"

We want our surgeons to keep up on their craft, do we not? Why should writers be any different? Readers expect us to deliver the goods. They're laying out money for a return, primarily in entertainment. If you disappoint them because your characters are flat or your story stale, they're not going to want to give you any more money.

By the way, writing for a fair exchange of money is what every writer wants to do, whether they admit it or not. So just admit it, and attend to the wisdom in this book.

Author in Progress has craft and method instruction, but also much more. It is nourishment for the writer's soul and motivation for the writer's heart. What all the contributors to this volume share is a love of what we do and a generous spirit toward their storytelling fellows.

You'll find, as I did, that the material here inspires you to get to your keyboard and write.

So write! Apply what you learn. That's how you make progress.

JAMES SCOTT BELL is the author of the number one bestseller for writers, *Plot & Structure*, and numerous thrillers, including *Romeo's Rules*, *Try Dying*, and *Don't Leave Me*. In addition to his traditional novels, Jim has self-published in a variety of forms. His novella *One More Lie* was the first self-published work to be nominated for an International Thriller Writers Award. He served as the fiction columnist for *Writer's Digest* magazine and has written highly popular craft books, including *Write Your Novel from the Middle*, *Super Structure*, *The Art of War for Writers*, and *Conflict & Suspense*.

INTRODUCTION

THERESE WALSH

After I got my publishing deal, the question I received most often from not-yet-published authors was this: *How did you do it?*

The pithy answer? *You put your butt in a chair and write.*

Don't you want to punch that answer in the face? It's like hearing someone with great hair say that she simply rolls out of bed in the morning and fluffs it a little. You know she has a cabinet filled with gels and sprays and various anti-frizz products, but she doesn't want to share her secrets or admit to the mirror time required. She just wants you to admire the final product.

Well, *butt in chair* is only part of the story, and the least fantastical part at that. So let's try again.

How did you do it?

I spent several years writing and editing a version of the manuscript that would become my debut novel, but it wouldn't *become* my debut until after I gutted all of that polished prose. I tore the story to the ground and then built it back up with a new (more innovative) structure, new (shades-of-gray) characters, new (layered) storylines, and a new (stronger) voice. I finished the manuscript for a second time, and *that* version is what finally sold. The "formula," in broad strokes, was this:

1. Write.
2. Receive feedback with an open mind.
3. Improve myself to improve my story.
4. Repeat.

These steps contained fine brushstrokes, of course, as well as dozens of questions: *What do you write? How often should you write? Do you need to take classes, read books, get an MFA? What barriers might you face, and how do you* overcome them? How do you receive feedback, and where do you find it? How do you process it all? Which changes do you—and don't you—make? What if you want to quit? How long must you go on? When is enough enough?

The purpose of *Author in Progress* is to answer those questions. This book offers guidance for the evolution of your manuscript and for yourself as a writer. We'll walk you through the stages every novelist must face, whether you want to obtain a traditional publishing deal or self-publish, and we'll introduce you to the stumbling blocks you might encounter before writing, while writing, when asking for feedback or seeking instruction, through rewriting, and beyond.

That said, this is not a book that will teach you everything you want or need to know about writing. Rather, it will *keep* you writing by validating your experience. It will help you develop the myriad skills you'll need to work as a professional novelist and overcome the most challenging hurdles. Because unless you're a superhero, as you travel the road with your story, you're going to get weary. You're going to feel defeated by, even betrayed by, the words. You're going to wonder if your experience is normal.

I can tell you with 99 percent certainty that it *is* normal.

It's our goal with *Author in Progress* to help you find yourself in the pages, home in on your current struggle, discover a comrade, and persevere. You'll come to understand that many of us have been or currently are on the road with you. And you'll feel less alone.

Writing a novel is as much a mental exercise as it is a physical and intellectual one. So we suggest that you consider a new rule—an addendum, if you will—to *butt in chair: author aware.*

The author who is aware of the road ahead is much more likely to succeed in an increasingly competitive industry than one who stumbles blindly in the dark.

The author who is aware that other writers travel that same road sees that she is not lost, has no reason to feel hopeless, and is among friends.

The author who is aware begins to see a pattern—how each book takes its writer on a similar journey, whether that book is his first or twenty-first—and takes comfort in those parallels while learning more lucidly from each step.

The team at Writer Unboxed has provided a guiding light on that well-traveled road for more than a decade now, publishing more than 3,500 essays and interviews about the craft of writing and the writing life. It's our pleasure to shine that same light for you here, and it's our hope that you'll join us on our website (writerunboxed.com) and our Facebook group (writerunboxed.com/facebook) whenever you need to be reminded that you do not walk the road alone. So often Writer Unboxed community members say they read exactly what they needed to read, exactly when they needed to read it, on our site. We hope you get that sense time and again as you read these pages.

Welcome to the tribe. Write on.

Therese Walsh
Editorial Director, Writer Unboxed

PART ONE

PREPARE

It's easy to underestimate what it takes to write a novel, especially if you've never completed one before. Blissful ignorance can only get you so far, though, before you start to question if you have the necessary skills and drive, or if the job is easier for everyone else. Better to know now what the journey ahead will be like so you can prepare—and succeed.

WHY WRITE?

Understanding Your Deepest Motivations

BARBARA O'NEAL

I had a friend early in my career who published her first book at the same time I did. Her novel was well received, but she never wrote another. Years later, I asked her why. She said, "I went shopping for author dresses instead of writing another book."

She wanted the life of an *author*, not the life of a *writer*. She wanted the attention gained from book events and reviews, not the solitary and sometimes lonely existence of a working scribe. In the end, the reality wasn't compelling enough to hold her interest, and she headed in another direction.

Another writer began her career writing romances. She did very well, but after seven or eight books, she changed direction and started writing literary historical novels. She thought she didn't care what she wrote as long as she earned money, but it turned out that she wanted the respect of the literary community as badly as she wanted the financial benefits.

What motivates you to write? Is it money? Fame? Do you want to change the world, make someone laugh, entertain the masses, see your name in lights, or make your mark in the literary world? Do you want to live a different life than that of your siblings? Do you want to model your experiences after those of your literary heroes?

Maybe it's all of the above. My own motives are a big mix. But I think it's important—crucial, even—to understand your core motivation as a writer, the one hidden beneath the surface motivations of making a living, earning respect, or leaving a legacy.

CONSIDER WHY YOU DO THIS

Why do *you* write? Maybe a more accurate question is: *Who* are you writing for? Who is your reader, that one person you imagine as you write? The answer is different for all of us, and it can change over time. Perhaps you begin writing for your brother, then for your writing teacher, and then for a critique partner.

Here's what I think: More than writing for any one person, you are writing to share a story.

Humans are universally driven to tell tales. The members of ancient civilizations painted symbols on the walls of their caves to record their hunts. Can you picture that prehistoric man haunted by his epic battle with a bison or a woolly mammoth? He might have tossed and turned on his furs as the firelight flickered, remembering and reviewing the danger and the triumph of his day—until he was driven to share it, to mark the event. "I lived," he declared to the world with his story painting, "and this is what I saw."

All these centuries later, his story remains. We are still moved by it, still awed.

In the dark ages of Ireland, the people were clannish and suspicious. Only bards were given free reign to travel. They carried stories from hearth to hearth, bringing news and entertainment. Their status was almost as high as that of kings and queens.

The monks of medieval Europe spent their time transcribing the Bible into illuminated manuscripts of exquisite beauty, preserving the holy stories for all time.

When you embrace the need to share a story, surface-level motivations like fame and fortune begin to melt away.

EMBRACE STORIES

When I was nineteen or twenty, my friend had a baby. It was the first time I'd witnessed the process of pregnancy and birth, and when the boy was born, I wrote a letter to him, celebrating his arrival in the world. I was so filled with emotion that I could not talk about it; I could only write. I wanted to mark this simultaneously fresh and ancient, unique and common event. I didn't want it to be forgotten.

We see the same drive to record even the most mundane events in the overwhelming number of selfies that surround us and in the Instagram, Tumblr, and Facebook accounts that chronicle a single everyday life—multiplied billions of times. We chronicle both major and minor events: births and deaths and big hunts, our freshly pedicured toenails, the pile of dishes in the sink. The record has become like the debris left behind after a great storm—it carries no narrative.

In a world so inundated with data, records, and the minutiae of daily life, writers play an enormously important role. No matter our field, we are charged with the duty of forming a narrative out of that hectic data. We are asked to take a multitude of details and tie them together to form a story that makes sense; a story imbedded with a lesson, perhaps; a story that might uplift, give peace, or prod the reader to think or laugh.

We come to the page for many reasons—for the hope of glory, for the promise of fame, to take revenge, to prove we are more than our families, school bullies, or ex-wives think we are. We want money and validation, honor, recognition … all those things.

So we say.

In truth, it's all about the story. You might be writing an exposé, the story of business or government wrongdoing. Or maybe you're developing a nonfiction tale of how rich guys got rich (and there's more to the story than meets the eye) or capturing a single moment's observation in the music of a poem. Or you might be crafting a rage-filled tome meant to declare war on an unjust society, or a gentle romance to give relief to a weary woman.

Regardless of what you write, and regardless of your surface reasons, your motivation is rooted in the drive to say, as that caveman did, "I lived. This is what I witnessed."

Story is why writers exist, and story is why you are driven to the page. In a world so overwhelmed with everyday trivialities, we need writers more than ever to sift substance from the noise, to make sense of a chaotic world.

HOW TO GET IN YOUR OWN WAY, METHOD 1: WRITE FOR FAME AND FORTUNE

This'll hamstring your writing, but not because filthy lucre taints your artistic vision or whatever. It's because you have *no idea what will actually sell.* You struggle to buy birthday presents for your own kids; do you think you'll magically know what book will appeal to a million strangers?

—BILL FERRIS

SETTING REALISTIC GOALS

Gain Power by Sidestepping the One-Size-Fits-All Mind-Set

ERIKA LIODICE

When it comes to setting goals, writers are commonly told to make them "SMART"—that is, specific, measurable, attainable, realistic, and time-bound. While that's great guidance, no one ever explains how to tell if your goals are indeed realistic.

I know this because setting unrealistic goals used to be a specialty of mine. In fact, next to my computer is a greeting card that pictures a little girl pushing with all her might against a boulder twice her size. Inside, my dad wrote: "This made me think of you."

I've been setting unrealistic goals for as long as I can remember. Take, for example, the time I was ten and tried to organize a carnival in my backyard: Only one kid showed up, and I spent more money than I earned. Or consider the time I was thirteen and was cast in a Great Adventure amusement park commercial that I hoped would be the stepping-stone to my movie career—that was my first *and last* onscreen appearance. And then there was the time I was twenty-five and thought that I could crank out my first novel in a year; it took three.

For me, it took *not* running a marathon, *not* starting an organic vegetable farming operation in my backyard, and *not* finishing my second novel faster than my first to realize that setting realistic goals begins with being realistic about who you are—and, more important, who you are *not*.

ACCOUNT FOR YOUR U-FACTOR

Have you ever noticed how writers' goals tend to sound similar? *My goal is to write 2,000 words a day. My goal is to write every night after work. My goal is to finish my novel by the end of the year.* The problem with these one-size-fits-all goals is that they don't account for your U(nique)-factor: the special blend of strengths and weaknesses, talents and limitations, and preferences and aversions that make you uniquely *you*.

If all of my *un*-achievements have taught me anything, it's that realistic goals should harness your natural strengths, talents, and preferences to propel you forward while preventing your weaknesses, limitations, and aversions from tripping you up.

BEGIN WITH SELF-ASSESSMENT

To better understand your U-factor, consider the following questions and then evaluate how your answers align with your writing goals. Be on the lookout for misalignments, as they are a good indication that you've set an unrealistic goal.

WHEN ARE YOU MOST CREATIVE? If your creativity engine kicks on in the morning, then your goal to exchange your nightly TV show for writing time may set you up for disappointment. That's because your goal (nightly writing sessions) isn't aligned with your U-factor (morning creativity). Instead exchange those TV shows for sleep so you can wake up early and get cracking on that manuscript.

However, if your creativity rises after the sun sets, aiming for early-morning writing sessions may leave you with lackluster results. In this case, shift your goal—and your schedule—to harness the power of those dark, quiet hours.

DO YOU PREFER TO CONCENTRATE ON A PROJECT FOR LONG PERIODS OF TIME OR IN SHORT BURSTS? If you produce your best work when you have plenty of time to immerse yourself in the project, then your goal to steal away for several mini-writing sessions throughout the day may prove frustrating and unproductive. That's because your goal (mini-writing sessions) doesn't align with your U-factor (a long attention span). You might consider the more realistic goal of scheduling fewer writing sessions that encompass bigger blocks of time and allow you to maximize your steadfast focus.

On the other hand, if you tend to lose interest quickly, then vowing to devote your entire Saturday morning to your manuscript may fill you with dread. You might have greater success with shorter, more frequent writing sessions.

DO YOU APPROACH LIFE WITH A PLAN, OR DO YOU PREFER TO TAKE THINGS AS THEY COME? If you're a structured person who approaches life strategically, then your goal to write your novel by the seat of your pants may leave you feeling adrift. That's because your goal ("pantsing" your novel) isn't aligned with your U-factor (planning and organization). Your organized nature can be a major strength; tap into it by approaching your plot with a plan.

However, if planning cramps your style, your goal to outline your book chapter by chapter might feel like torture. This doesn't mean you couldn't (or shouldn't) work from an outline; it simply means that you should create a goal that caters to your free spirit, like creating a macro-level outline that gives you a general idea of where you're headed while allowing you to explore new ideas as they arrive. (For more on plotting and pantsing, see the "Plot It, or Pants It?" essays by Ray Rhamey and Anne Greenwood Brown.)

DO YOU TEND TO ABANDON LONG-TERM PROJECTS IN FAVOR OF SOMETHING NEW AND EXCITING, OR DO YOU TYPICALLY SEE THEM THROUGH TO COMPLETION? If you enjoy starting projects more than finishing them, then your goal to complete your novel by the end of the year may feel daunting and out of reach. That's because your goal (completing your novel) isn't aligned with your U-factor (the need for new and exciting challenges). Rather than working toward one big goal, try tackling your novel chapter by chapter or scene by scene, breaking down your goal into a series of smaller challenges that fulfill your desire to constantly begin anew.

On the other hand, if you have a proven track record of seeing long-term projects through to completion, smaller goals might not pose enough of a challenge and could cause you to lose interest. Set a more realistic goal of focusing on bigger milestones that take longer to reach but allow your perseverance to shine.

BELIEVE IN THE POWER OF "U"

If you've ever *not* met your daily word count goal, *not* finished your novel, or *not* used your writing time for writing, don't despair. These *un*-achievements aren't a reflection of your capability (or lack thereof); more likely, they're a symptom of setting an unrealistic goal.

By taking the time to first understand your U-factor, you've armed yourself with the information you need to set a realistic goal that motivates and inspires you rather than one that makes you feel like you're pushing with all your might against a boulder twice your size.

 HOW TO GET IN YOUR OWN WAY, METHOD 2: DEPEND ON NEW YEAR'S RESOLUTIONS

How many of last year's resolutions did you keep? Thought so.

—BILL FERRIS

 PRO TIP

Getting words on the page is not as important as getting the right words on the page. Don't get so caught up in meeting word goals that you don't give yourself enough time to think about the story you want to tell, to play with it, explore it, daydream about it.

—ROBIN LAFEVERS

STOCKING UP ON LITERARY GATORADE

How an Early Dose of Reality Can Help You Succeed

MARGARET DILLOWAY

So you're thinking about writing a book. Welcome to the club! Think of me as your coach, cheering you on from the sidelines, providing you with a big swig of literary Gatorade. Writing isn't a spectator sport, and you'll need a healthy dose of eye-opening electrolytes to stay in the game and put forth your best performance.

To a newbie, the path to publication seems like an almost unreachable goal, sort of like a lottery win. In part this is because, most of the time, we hear only the hypersuccessful stories: the people who quit their regular jobs, write their first book in two months, have agents knocking down their doors, and then cart a wheelbarrow full of money away from New York.

I thought I'd be one of those juggernaut authors my first time out of the gate. I was wrong. My first book—nonfiction—got canceled before publication. My first novel never sold, and I had to find a new agent for my second book, which became my debut.

What authors don't hear about are the struggles, though they are far more common than the megasuccesses. Knowing how to deal with them is as reassuring as having Band-Aids with you in the backcountry. And, hopefully, your path will be a bit easier because of it.

IGNORE THE STOPWATCH

Like home improvements, writing projects tend to take a lot longer than you first suspect. You've learned how to plot, and you know who the main character is and what she wants, so it should be easy after that, right?

Think again.

When I started writing my first kids' book, I thought it would take only a couple of months. I'm not quite sure why I thought this, considering I had spent about three years and fourteen or so drafts writing my debut novel. I guess I thought practice made perfect and that I now knew what I was doing.

Instead I found it difficult to get the voice right. I knew I had a strong concept, and I knew the gist of the plot, but my execution wasn't great. Thus my son was in third grade when I started, and when the book comes out, he'll be in eighth grade. I finished the final edit last year, so if you're keeping tabs on the math, that's four years of writing, plus an additional year between final edits and publication (the typical turnaround time in publishing).

Often the first draft (or two or twenty) of a novel comes slowly as a writer struggles to find her voice. Maybe she chooses the wrong point of view, or a meddlesome minor character proves to be more heroic than the original protagonist. Perhaps past tense isn't lending itself well to the story and must be switched. This is all part of the process.

Above all else, serve the needs of the novel, not your desire to finish the manuscript or keep up with changing market trends. Remember that J.K. Rowling wrote the first Harry Potter book in five years and Donna Tartt took eleven for *The Goldfinch*. You're not alone.

FIGHT THROUGH THE DOWNS

Every writer has down days, when their words behave like boulders forced through a flour sifter. This doesn't mean you should give up. Remember: You can't edit a blank page. So any words, even poor ones, equal progress.

Besides, those words are rarely as bad as you think they are.

Later on, when your draft is polished and shiny and sent off to an agent, you will inevitably face some rejections. Allow yourself to wallow for one day—no more—and then move on.

KEEP WORKING

Unless you've got a superhealthy nest egg or your significant other actually makes enough to support you in a fashion Suze Orman would approve of, keep your day job. Most writers I've spoken with report that having a day job provides them with structure and makes them eager to get home and get writing.

Besides, writing in a heatless garret may sound romantic, but in practice it's not. Worrying about where your—or your kid's—next meal is coming from will stress you out in ways that make it hard to be creative. A Princeton University study found that constantly having to think about money, or the lack thereof, dominates your consciousness.

RESEARCH RETREATS

Now is also a good time to begin researching and applying for reputable writing retreats (another reason to keep your job—so you can pay to attend them!). Retreats accept applications months in advance, so keep a list of deadlines handy and apply well before those dates.

Why are retreats important? Besides providing a way to hone your craft, you will have an opportunity to form long-lasting friendships with other writers and find mentors to guide you through your career. You'll also get several days of uninterrupted writing time away from your usual routine.

Apply for those in your region or, if time and budget allow, farther afield. Most require a writing sample and are highly selective, so you may have to apply more than once before you get in.

Retreats like Bread Loaf in Vermont, Squaw Valley in California, and Hedgebrook in Washington (for women), all have excellent reputations. You could even go abroad to the Iceland Writers Retreat, which attracts instructors like Cheryl Strayed. If you've always dreamed of visiting a particular place, see if a writing retreat is held there.

No matter which retreat you choose, make sure the instructors are published writers whose work you admire.

READ

Read a lot. If you're new to a genre, read its classics and bestsellers before you even start writing so you get a feel for the appropriate tone, voice, and pacing.

I tend to read *outside* my genre while I write because otherwise I find myself accidentally grifting portions of other authors' work. But reading great novels, no matter the genre, helps the words flow.

KNOW YOU'RE NOT ALONE IN THE GATORADE CLUB

Authors call the first book the "practice book" because most of the time, the first manuscript you ever write doesn't sell. This may be true for your second and third and fourth and fifth books, too.

Author Michelle Gable's debut *A Paris Apartment* was a huge international bestseller and led to publishing deals for several of her other books. Of course, her "overnight success" came after some false starts. She says, "I had a book that was supposed to go to a five-way auction (then they all dropped out on the day of the auction because they said, 'It's too hard to sell a debut author'), as well as a canceled contract. I think I had at least four other books that my agent shopped that didn't sell … perhaps there are others I am blocking out! So that'd be six total that didn't happen."

Plain old persistence is what separates published authors from unpublished ones. Many people give up at some point during this long process. Although the path may be hard, not one author I've ever spoken to has said, "I wish I hadn't written a book."

Neither will you.

 ## HOW TO GET IN YOUR OWN WAY, METHOD 3: WAIT UNTIL YOU HAVE MORE TIME

I know—your life is *crazy* right now. Writers are crazy by definition, so you'll always feel like you're running a cat ranch. You won't have 'time to write' until you attend your local cemetery's Eternal Writing Retreat, and that's not what ghostwriting means; I looked it up.

—BILL FERRIS

YOUR UNIQUE STORY

Become Your Novel's Secret Ingredient

ROBIN LAFEVERS

One of the most important—and difficult—tasks of writing is to identify and then tell a truly unique story—a story only *you* can write. That can seem especially daunting when you consider all the books that have already been published. How can yours fit in? Stand out? Be fresh?

Here's the answer: Bring your own unique take to the stories you write. Let your stories, full of your obsessions, interests, and truths, influence and shape your work in ways no other writer's experience can.

 **PRO TIP**

A personal connection to the story you want to tell can help you create engaging promotional material when your novel is published.

FIND YOUR MOST AUTHENTIC VOICE

Your voice is an essential and powerful aspect of your creative vision. It encompasses not only the words you choose and how you string your sentences together but also the very subjects you are compelled to write about and how you view them. In fact, your entire worldview—hopeful or edgy, tragic or matter-of-fact, and so on—is a key component of your voice.

Voice embodies an author's core emotional truths and personal wisdom. Take time to learn your core truths. What personal wisdom do you bring to the human experience? Look under the rocks and stones of your own soul, and write as raw and real as you can. How does one get at this invaluable material? Start with these exercises:

- Reconnect with the sorts of stories that first awakened your love of reading and provided you with your greatest reading pleasure. What blew your mind? Showed you the full scope of what was possible? Shook the foundations of your world? The seeds of your own voice and most powerful stories are likely hidden in those books.
- Experiment with your voice, not just by trying first-person over third-person POV but by trying on different aspects of your *self*. Think about how your voice changes when you talk to different people—your closest friend versus a casual acquaintance, a beloved sibling versus an overbearing cousin. Play with those different voices, and strive always to uncover your most unique, authentic voice and core stories.
- Force yourself out of your comfort zone, not only craft-wise but subject-wise.
- Experiment with different genres and forms.
- Allow yourself to become creatively restless. Whether in your personal life or your creative practice, restlessness often tells you something important. It might mean you are ready for new challenges—something harder or less conventional. It could mean that your muse feels stagnated by the tasks you've assigned yourself and that you should experiment. Try something you've never considered before: present tense, writing from multiple points of view, or writing a novel in verse. Let restlessness push you to color outside the lines.

DIG DEEPER

Think you've nailed your artistic vision? You aren't done yet. Now it's time to dig deeper. This involves exposing yourself (are you beginning to sense this recurring theme?), but you'll do so by degrees rather than all at once. You will peel back a little skin, one layer at a time; see how much it stings; acclimate to the new sensation; and then start over and reveal a little more.

To do that, you must be willing to explore your own heart. What are your issues? Really think about this for a moment. These are the issues you don't like to face, the ones that make you squirm, that you're reluctant to admit even to your therapist. I hate to be the one to tell you, but these issues will be the springboard for some of your most powerful stories. It's not only a matter of following your weirdness but also of exploring *why* you're weird in the first place. What need is that weirdness, quirkiness, or avant-gardism fulfilling? Yeah, you have to look *there*. Then you have to find a way to get some of that rawness into your story.

Consider the complex relationships in your life. Will your characters have equally complex and dynamic relationships and as rich and varied emotional lives as the one you possess? Do some timed writing exercises—spend twenty minutes max—on the following topics: your first kiss, your first loss, your first experience with shame, your first betrayal, your first major mistake in judgment. Your responses to these prompts will help shape your worldview and how you interact with everything around you, and will therefore play a large part in shaping the story you are trying to tell.

You need to have the same depth of consideration for your characters. You need to understand the defining moments in their lives. (For more on this topic, see Lisa Cron's essay "Story First, Plot Second.")

IDENTIFY YOUR UNIQUE SPIN

Just because you are writing about a subject that has been tackled before—many times, even—doesn't mean you can't bring something fresh and unique to the story, something that will not only make it stand out but also allow it to shine. Consider again those books you loved best and all of your writing to date. Do certain themes resonate with you time and again—redemption, forgiveness, self-discovery, or the triumph of the human spirit? Do particular stylistic choices, such as taking the protagonist to the mat emotionally, having her experience a powerful catharsis, or encouraging transformative growth, draw you in?

Ask yourself, *Why am I compelled to tell this story?* If the answer is that you're *not* compelled and are just playing around with a cool idea, you may encounter problems as you progress. Maybe you simply haven't dug deep enough to know how to weave your own literary bone and sinew through that cool idea or premise. *Why* does the cool idea appeal to you? *Why* are you itching to play with this premise?

Still coming up blank? Consider your setting. Since one of the roles of a setting is to echo and enhance a theme, chances are that the setting or premise that appeals to you has left a trail of bread crumbs that will lead you to a deeper connection with your story and thematic elements. Drill down, and identify the elements of the setting that call to you. Is it the thin veneer of civilization? The usurping role of technology? The brutality of the times? The contrast between social façade and teeming personal ambition? A distrustful or conspiratorial atmosphere?

You can also use setting to compare and contrast thematic elements. If your core story is somewhat familiar, a fresh setting allows it to shine in an entirely new way. Or what if you took all the elements of a particular setting you loved and created something new with it? Excavate and identify the elements that draw you to that setting, and consider creating an alternate world with them. What would that newfound freedom allow you to express within the context of your characters' lives yet still let you touch on resonant chords with your readers?

Does your genre or story lend itself to common tropes or conventions? Another way to rejuvenate your work is to identify those tropes and conventions and then turn each on its head. Play with reader expectations. You should still fulfill them—especially if they are genre conventions and therefore the very reason readers pick up those books in the first place—but do so in unexpected ways.

Getting your unique creative vision on the page is pretty much that simple, though it is far from easy. But being a writer isn't about doing what comes easy—it's about finding what you love to do and giving yourself permission to take the time you need to wrestle your truest, most compelling stories onto the page.

 ### COMMUNITY CONVERSATION: FINDING AN AUTHENTIC VOICE

The Writer Unboxed community weighs in online. Please consider adding your voice by visiting Writer Unboxed via this QR code or link to the site. Join the conversation at writerunboxed.com/your-unique-story, and use the password "aip" (all lowercase).

Writer Unboxed is a moderated community, but comments that evolve a conversation in a positive manner are always welcome.

CG BLAKE: For a writer, finding one's authentic voice is perhaps the most essential, yet difficult, skill to develop. It can be a multiyear process that requires a deep personal commitment.

I was always attracted to family sagas. Anne Tyler's work, in particular, resonated with me. Years ago, I did what Robin recommends here and asked myself why. The answer was personal. I was blessed to come from a loving family, but we didn't do well when it came to sharing our deepest feelings. This can lead to misunderstanding and hurt, something I've explored in my own writing. I realized after completing my first novel that subconsciously the book was about me and my hopes, dreams, and fears, though the story doesn't resemble my own at all. A writer's voice must be his own. As Judy Garland said, "Always be a first-rate version of yourself, instead of a second-rate version of somebody else."

ROBIN LAFEVERS: CG, thank you for providing such an elegant example of exactly what I was talking about! And we are *so* in agreement about the multiyear deep commitment.

I am struck by your journey to find answers to these questions and how hard it can be to identify our own issues when we come from a happy family background. It can feel like digging up dirt on people we love—but it's not. It's exactly as you said—a way to find why certain themes and issues resonate and a way to see how those issues color our worldview and personal journeys.

VAUGHN ROYCROFT: I've received feedback in the past about my wordiness or the density of my prose. And although my gut told me it was correct and that I needed to simplify, a deeper part of me mourned the possibility that I would somehow lose an essential component of my voice. I've been working on a rewrite with this in mind, but at the onset I'd decided that I would focus on the essence of the story itself, voice be damned.

Now, with the illumination you offer here, I'm starting to see so many elements of my voice that extend way beyond wordiness. I can see how my setting embodies both my hope for the enlightening power of civilization as well as my almost primal desire to withdraw from it. It reveals my faith that there is something real and pure in "legend," that something fundamentally true can be found in ancient cultural lore.

As for theme, I'd known I was delving into issues of finding loyalty and honor even amongst the ugliness of an era. I'd kept a one-eyed side view on what I call "rescue love"—the deepening of romantic love for someone who's somehow rescued you. But after reading this, I'm seeing a throughline of issues for my protagonist that I know are born in the dark stuff I normally hide, from bearing high expectations to then feeling lucky (and thereby a fraud) and finally to feeling undeserving. This brings one back to a need to prove oneself worthy of those original expectations—a wonderfully vicious circle for series work.

ROBIN LAFEVERS: Vaughn, I think you've identified one of the key epiphanies about voice: realizing that it is *not* just the words we use and our syntax but so very much more. And, as you're discovering, the words might even be the least of it.

I am struck by the voice elements you've discovered in yourself, as they are elements that speak to me as well. And I know I've said it before, but it bears repeating: Writing will frog-march us, kicking and screaming, to the very edges of our soul and back. I'm not sure whether to apologize or wish you bon voyage!

PAULA CAPPA: I was struck, Robin, by your comment: "Think about how your voice changes when you talk to different people." Is that ever true! But that's me as a person. In fiction, I, the author, tend to vanish. I feel like voice comes from and is created by the character's vision and style on the page. Your piece makes me wonder if I have a voice outside of my characters. Maybe there are two parts to voice: the character's voice and the author's voice. Then there's writing style.

ROBIN LAFEVERS: Paula, this flummoxed me for a long time because I wrote such distinctly different books, for different age groups and with wildly different tones. I couldn't understand how I could have an author voice when my story voices were so different. And that's when I realized that our voices change radically when we talk to different people or when we talk about different subjects, relaying a joke versus conveying a painful childhood memory.

I think there are three distinct layers to voice: the author's voice, the story voice, and the character's voice.

The author voice is our universal voice, the one that infuses everything. Even though I think I write wildly different stories, people who know me well can always "hear" me in all of my work, although it sounds invisible to me.

Story voice is the type of story we're telling and to which audience. The thing is, we all have many aspects to our personality: funny sides, serious sides, dark sides, places where our deepest fears reside. To me, it makes perfect sense that our body of work will cover more than one side of ourselves; thus, we're able to produce different flavors of stories.

However, while we might vary in whether we want to focus on humor or seriousness or hope or despair, *what* makes us laugh or cry or hope or despair is part of the essence of who we are, and that will very likely remain constant throughout the body of our work. Whether it is center stage or part of the backdrop is the variable.

Then, lastly, there is character voice, which I think is probably the most conscious voice we're aware of, at least initially.

DEE WILLSON: If I am not enthralled by the characters, if I can't hear their distinct voices or *feel* their plight, their story, then how can I expect someone else (a reader) to feel it? Life is too short to spend countless days, months, or years writing a story you aren't so deeply invested in that the only way out is to get it down on paper. Love every minute of it.

ROBIN LAFEVERS: Yes. So very much yes to that, Dee! In fact, that needs to be quoted and shared and posted and tweeted.

DONALD MAASS: When I ask editors what they're looking for, the most common response is "a strong voice." It's a vague term, but it means style, strength of prose, and distinctive storytelling that remains consistent from book to book.

For writers in our age of intimate point of view, though, voice in a practical sense means characters' voices. Like everyone, characters can be lazy. Their voices can be like easy-listening radio, lulling and unchallenging. Thus, it's wise to push not just yourself but your characters out of their comfort zones.

Same goes for making a story personal. Like authors, characters will avoid what is uncomfortable to reveal. What are they failing to see or accept about themselves? What do they not want to admit or own? We have layers to peel through. So do they.

Also, an author's reasons for telling a story may not be a character's reasons for being in that story. Writing the story can, in a sense, be a dialogue between author and characters, each arguing points and insisting on the story's meaning. What do you need your protagonist to understand? What is your protagonist trying to tell you that you don't want to believe?

ROBIN LAFEVERS: Wow. *Wow.* This is something I've been in the process of recognizing for the last couple of years. It is one of the most fascinating aspects of writing, and the most terrifying: to realize the journey you created is not precisely the one you'll end up going on. And, yes, the discovery of that as it unfolds on the page between you and the characters—characters whom you were *supposed* to be in complete control of—can create some very interesting revelations.

VIJAYA BODACH: Robin, while reading your analogy of peeling layers of skin, I kept thinking how this applies also to each revision I make. I am bolder, truer in my writing. I have a story that is in its seventh draft, and although all the elements were there, now it has a depth that wasn't in the exploratory draft. And it was during revisions that I was able to cut to its core.

I discovered my voice by writing a lot. It began early in childhood because of our fractured family, but thus began a lifelong habit of writing letters, sharing myself, and clarifying my thinking through writing. I wonder if that is why I am afraid of giving words to a story in my head that frightens me. Perhaps I do not want to discover something dark and horrible within myself, and whatever it is can stay buried if I never write it.

ROBIN LAFEVERS: Or, Vijaya, perhaps it's a searchlight, showing you where you have some deep personal work to do in order to truly free yourself of something and begin to move forward. That seems to me to be one of the functions of engaging in a creative form like writing. The act of creating changes us and makes us stronger, draws us closer to wholeness.

 **PRO TIP**

Be authentic. Write what you are meant to write, the way it pleases you to write it. Our chemical wiring programs our attraction response to others. In this same way, we are attracted to the books we love, the programs we watch, and the colors we wear because we are meant for them. The same is true for the art we produce.

—ERIKA ROBUCK

BEING UNBOXED

How Faithful, Confident, Boundary-Pushing Writers Rise Above the Noise

DONALD MAASS

For thirty-six years, I've been a literary agent specializing in fiction, and my agency has sold many hundreds of titles around the world. We've seen careers flourish, stall, fail, and meet every fate in between. We've helped our clients not only publish their work successfully but also survive every publishing crisis you can imagine.

I've also studied the techniques that result in effective fiction. I've written six books on the subject, focusing on the advanced methods that make fiction feel large and great, and that meld storytelling and art into twenty-first-century novels that transcend genre and sell like crazy. I teach all that stuff every chance I get.

You could say I've learned a thing or two.

One of the primary lessons I've learned is that a successful fiction-writing career is not dependent on factors that authors often imagine are important: connections, an agent, an editor, the deal size, the cover or back-panel copy, blurbs, reviews, publicity, series potential, the season it's released, timing, trends, or luck. Even writing well doesn't guarantee success, as we know from the sometimes weak sales of both exquisite stylists and mile-a-minute plotters.

Success as a fiction writer is rooted in something much more slippery, a factor that's hard to define, harder still to talk about, but nevertheless real. We know it when we see it, and when we see it we say, "Of course!" But then we struggle to pin it down and fail to use it to our advantage.

The factor I'm talking about could be called originality, but even that is too general to be useful. Original fiction can also fail. Clearly it's not enough to say, "Be original!" and be done with it.

Beyond originality lies a realm of art that utilizes the best methods available, honors its roots yet feels contemporary, delivers what we need as well as what we didn't know we wanted, entertains us even while it challenges us to think, involves us in a life much like our own and yet unlike anything in our experience, affirms our values while changing our lives, causes us to feel deeply when we'd rather relax, and dazzles our eyes without causing us to look up a single word in the dictionary.

The common factor among the authors who work this magic is that they are all *unboxed*. They are free.

That doesn't mean they ignore the rules of storytelling or that they can get away with writing unsatisfying novels. It does mean that they can wear many hats at once, juggle contradictions without despair, tell stories that are both universal and personal, and marshal the methods of their craft for their purposes. They turn rules into tools and life into something greater.

Unboxed writers are uncomfortable if their thoughts are too similar to everyone else's. They appreciate the box in which they arrive but then kick out its sides and build a house of their own. They seek to be unsafe, but they also constantly improve their craft and learn about themselves. They make a high-wire act look easy because they have their feet on the ground.

Unboxed writers are free, yes, but they are also smart. They know the rules but also know themselves. They please readers but aren't happy if they're not pleasing themselves first.

Let's take a look at what it means to be unboxed, the traps that prevent it, the outlook that fosters it, the opposites it embraces, the methods behind it, and the faith it celebrates. Every writer can be unboxed. You just have to believe … and know how.

AVOID SNARES, TRAPS, AND BOXES

Why do fiction-writing careers stall, stumble, and collapse? Pre-published writers may enviously wish to have that problem, but believe me: As difficult as it is to get published, it is even more agonizing to enter the game only to get suspended for a technical foul.

What causes careers to go south can often be traced back to the very beginning. Why does a rational human being start writing fiction in the first place?

Most simply love writing. It's a universal pleasure, a relief from the rest of life. There's promise in writing, too: the promise of a livelihood built on creativity, of independence, of wearing pajamas to work, of the satisfaction of holding a book in your hands that you—*you!*—wrote.

But days of writing stretch into months and then years. Many writers labor over multiple drafts and eventually realize that writing a publishable novel isn't easy. Rejection and the confusing etiquette of an opaque industry erode the pleasure of the process. The good response to those frustrations is to become a professional. Serious writers get online, get connected, learn the terminology, and strengthen their skills.

Still, that is not enough. Rejections continue, albeit with a bit more reward. A personal response, encouragement to resubmit, and positive feedback from peers all deepen the writer's resolve to persist. As persistence stretches into still more years, though, doubt creeps in. *Is publishing really possible? Am I fooling myself?*

At this stage, some writers fall away, giving in to envy, believing publishing is a game more rigged than the stock market, falling prey to hucksters who dangle magic keys, buying into schemes to get noticed, or simply giving up. Smart writers double down, though, and work hard to understand what they don't understand about writing publishable fiction.

Here is where the path grows crooked and treacherous. Writing publishable fiction isn't wrong, but it isn't wholly right, either. "Getting it right" easily becomes "write for the market, learn the rules, jump on trends, catch the wave, and do as you're told because the powers that be know what they're talking about—and anyway they need to be satisfied if you're going to get a shot."

Most of all, though, the late stages of breaking in are directed by a single, primary imperative: *Get your plot right!* Writers at this point often are fixated on the requirement to be perfect and fearful that a single misstep on the page will spoil years of work. I see this in submissions when a requested manuscript is followed the next day by an improved version and the plea: "Read this one!" Story structure becomes the focus and end-all.

There is nothing wrong with a tight plot, but often that solid intention turns into a safe novel, perhaps even a novel that can be marketed and sold to a publisher. This might seem like fulfillment of the dream, admittance to the club, and it's common to see a swell of confidence in the bearing of debut authors. Safe storytelling, though, is not a guarantee of success; in fact, it can lead to the technical fouls (read: poor sales) that later sideline rookie starters.

The truth is that safe novels satisfy readers only a little. Readers don't want what they've read before or what feels effortless to consume—when reading unchallenging fiction, reader brain scans register only dull gray. Readers do, of course, seek the comfort of characters they care about, the affirmation of their values, and happy endings, but they also seek novelty and challenge. When a novel is too safe, it cannot provide that experience.

Following the rules is not wrong, but *only* following the rules is not right, either.

Fiction writers can fall prey to a number of psychological traps, too. Creative blocks, exhaustion, and despair lead to unfocused stories, unfinished manuscripts, scattered goals, and getting stuck like a perpetual student in graduate school, which in writing terms means bouncing from one project or genre to another, never taking a novel to the finish line.

Published authors encounter their own set of traps and snares. When careers stall, crash, or cause anxiety or envy, authors sometimes begin to focus on ephemera, feeling that they need more publicity, flashier price promos, better covers, bookmarks, a movie deal, or any number of other things that make little difference in sales. (Certain retail factors like front-of-store displays do help sales, but the biggest help of all is something no publisher can buy: word of mouth.)

There are plenty of remedies for career woes: everything from inspiration to writing retreats to mood music. Don't get me wrong—a spa treatment is never a bad thing, but by itself it won't spring writers from the trap into which they've fallen. Indeed the biggest trap of all is the hardest to see because you are willingly locked inside it.

It's a box.

It's the box of conforming to expectations, playing it safe with characters, relying on easy plot tropes, writing in an "acceptable" style, adopting a familiar voice, presenting easy themes (or none at all), and challenging neither your readers nor yourself.

Getting published may seem to require safety, but success requires something more.

UNBOX YOUR THINKING

What is story? The fundamentals of novel structure are well known and easy to discover. Sooner or later every serious fiction writer also gets a handle on scene structure, middles, and microtension. Voice, inner journey (or *arc*), backstory, theme, and the development of the story world come naturally to some—rarely all together—but most fiction writers must figure them out.

The complex craft of novel writing can be learned.

Mostly.

Story spinning contains another dimension, though, that is harder to pin down and (almost) impossible to teach. It's a magical gift for developing premises that intrigue. It's an inborn awareness that what goes into a story emotionally is not what's happening in the plot but what's happening inside characters. It's a gut instinct that somehow just knows which narrative threads to pursue and which to drop, when to summarize and when to slow down. It's the voice that says, *Right now that protagonist of mine needs a shot to the head because, well, just because.*

Where do storytelling instincts come from? Lots of reading? Hard knocks from critique groups? The unfair bestowal of native genius? Getting in a zone, in a groove, or in touch with the Force? Trial and error?

Who the hell knows?

Just because some aspects of novel writing aren't schematic, taught, or even well understood does not mean that we shouldn't think about, study, and steal them. Embracing the immaterial and relying on unreliable aspects of the art is part of being unboxed.

Take pacing. Almost everyone gets this wrong. If you skim portions of published novels, you know that's true; yet the work of certain authors is almost impossible to skim. Even material notoriously labeled "slow"—scene setting, exposition, and so on—is absorbing and compelling when penned by these authors. In their hands, dark and dull characters become not a drag but a joy.

What are such authors doing that the rest aren't? They know, somehow, how to make everything on the page matter. Does that sound vague? It is, until we break it down and see that the urgency that underlies the words comes not from the plot situation but from the author.

Beneath what goes down on the page is the author's feeling while writing: *I absolutely need to tell you this. It matters to you because it matters to my characters. It hints at and anticipates things I haven't yet told you. It's full of mystery or foreboding or false joy. It's telling you to stay on your toes, pay attention, watch out for what's coming.* In short, such authors play games with our heads and have a great time doing so.

That takes confidence, and while confidence is a quality, not a craft, it's something we must consider. Indeed, it's the secret behind what seems like magic. Giving yourself confidence is one way to become unboxed.

Another way is to add the *extra thing* to a premise. The extra thing is the element that throws a twist into a familiar plot, gives a character a unique trait, reverses what we expect, adds a dimension that elevates a story, opens a world to our wondering eyes, or in any other way adds some intrigue that makes us want to read and gives you more to write. When an extra thing requires explanation, changes the way things happen, mashes up genres, raises lots of questions, or simply adds length to a story, well, that's good. If you're not afraid of that, you're unboxed.

Still another way to be unboxed is to have both a healthy respect for and gimlet-eyed suspicion of genre requirements. Readers expect romances to tell a love story, mysteries to offer solutions, horror to frighten, thrillers to thrill, inspirational novels to uplift, and literary fiction to capture life. They are not wrong. What they do *not* want are plot tropes, character stereotypes, and re-treaded themes. When they get those, it's the author who's wrong.

How, then, in a practical sense, do you go about honoring a story type yet also make it your own? It starts with having your story type serve you rather than you being a slave to your story type. Focus on characters wholly yours, on a place that you know better than anyone, on your own definition of justice, on danger that feels especially dangerous to you, on magic that you know is real, on values that vary from the orthodox, on what is unusual about ordinary life. In short, focus on what everyone else misses, fudges, and gets wrong—and that you can set right.

Working within a framework while also working against reader expectations is the sweet spot that makes novels not just enjoyable but surprising. Readers aren't moved by what has moved them before, only by how you can move them in new ways now. They want familiar ideas put together in fresh ways. They want to feel like they're in on the joke even though they haven't heard the joke before.

That high-wire balance is possible when it's a balance you hold within yourself. To be unboxed is to dwell in an in-between place and be happy there.

LEARN TO LIVE WITH CONTRADICTIONS

Pascal wrote, "Contradiction is not a sign of falsity, nor the lack of contradiction a sign of truth." Goethe wrote, "What we agree with leaves us inactive, but contradiction makes us productive." Schrödinger wrote, "If a man never contradicts himself, the reason must be that he virtually never says anything at all."

WHY ARGUE WITH PHILOSOPHERS?

Clearly the ability to accept contradictions, or even embrace and enjoy them, is a sign of maturity. That's true for fiction writers, too. Being unboxed means living with contradictions like these:

- The more I love my characters, the more I must hurt them.
- My readers love my characters because they are good; I must make them do things that are wrong.
- Antagonists are justified in their beliefs but not in their actions; protagonists are right in their actions but wrong in their beliefs.
- Villains are delightful when they have fun; when heroes have fun, they are boring.
- The more unique my protagonist, the more universal she becomes.
- The more plot driven my story, the more hidden its message; the more urgent my message, the more hidden its story.
- The more I argue an obscure point, the more my readers will grasp the obvious.
- The lowest stakes are in saving the world; the highest stakes are moral and personal.
- No one cares about me or my story, but the more I care, the more they will pay attention.
- It's urgent that my story be told, but there is no rush whatsoever to get it published.
- To get published requires me to satisfy reader expectations; to get published requires me to violate reader expectations.

To reconcile contradictions and turn them into assets, you must find balance between them and determine what matters to your story. The unboxed writer is content to live with ambiguity and does not depend on anyone—readers, reviewers, agents, editors, or other people in the industry—to determine whether a story works. The unboxed writer knows what works. The rest is just editing and feedback.

Criticism is just advice. Rules can help but can also be broken. Change is the norm, but constant is the writer's vision. The unboxed writer is untroubled and focused because what matters is story, and story has a purpose. Momentary despair with the process passes quickly for the unboxed writer because at the end of the day, he is grounded in an enduring faith.

HAVE UNBOXED FAITH

What is that faith? It's the certainty that your story matters. Your story is not just persuasive but needed. Readers are resistant and guard their hearts, but deep down they want to be engaged and challenged, just as the world wants to be changed.

The unboxed writer doesn't worry about publication because the more she stays true to a story's heart, the more publication will take care of itself. Writing what no one else is writing might make a story harder to sell but in the end will make it more successful.

The unboxed writer has a toolbox full of craft, a proven process, support in a lonely profession, and a bottomless well of ideas. Most of all, though, the unboxed writer is free because he has a mandate: He has been chosen to tell stories and does not doubt that calling. The stories he has to tell are important, and the more personal they are, the greater the impact they will have.

The unboxed writer has faith. It's a faith reinforced by effort, tempered by experience, honed in front of the keyboard—all of that, certainly—but it's a faith grown strong because it's not a gift from others but a conviction about himself.

I matter. My story matters. The more it's mine, the more I will change the world.
Is that you? It can be. Believe it, and you're there. Welcome to being unboxed.

Big books take big chances. The best plan is to get into that mind-set now.

 FAQ

Should I write to trend?

Donald Maass: Chasing trends makes it hard to win the race. For one thing, you can be sure that a hundred other novelists are thinking just like you. Not the best odds. Some of the biggest clients at my literary agency are those who created trends.

Should I be able to envision my book on a shelf early on—or is that being too "boxed"?

DM: While it's helpful to select a category for pitching (and perhaps shelving) purposes, I prefer when authors envision their stories rather than their packaging. Thinking about the finished product is getting ahead of the game.

I'm working on several manuscripts in several genres. Which should I focus on?

DM: Write what's burning hot in your brain. The market will eventually tell you what it's ready for—and where your strengths lie. My only caveat is to avoid writing too many titles in a series until you have a publisher or publication plan.

PUT A RING ON IT

How to Know If Your Story Idea Is "The One"

ERIKA ROBUCK

When you sit down to write, do you stare at the blank screen or page with a sinking feeling of dread, as if you were about to enter unexplored tundra? Or do you have so many ideas clamoring for space in your mind that it's as if a murder of crows has taken up residence there? Wouldn't it be nice if a dating site for writers existed where we could plug in our passions and get paired with a series of perfect story matches?

Inspiration comes to us in different forms: a difficult childhood, an overheard conversation, a news story, a historic tour. Often these experiences are the catalyst for the greater work, but in a process fraught with insecurity and self-doubt, how do you know which subject is the *right* subject? How do you know when you have found "the one"?

Selecting your next book idea—or validating the one you have chosen—can be as complicated as finding true love. But if you follow these guidelines, you can make the process quite a bit simpler.

PLAY THE FIELD

Have you finished the exercises Robin LaFevers posed in her essay "Your Unique Story"? That's a great place to start. If you still need more ideas, try making a list of subjects about which you are passionate. The ideas that get your heart pumping, your breath quickening, and your mind racing are worth further consideration. If an idea wakes you at night, distracts you from the business of everyday living, or encourages you to daydream—without care for your personal comfort—you might have found one worth pursuing.

Now that you have your list (and it could be anything—the history of fruitcake, kayak anglers, flesh-eating bacteria, zombies, Caligula), it's time to start dating. Spend a few days with each subject, luxuriating in the research process. Court your idea. Explore it by searching for it online or checking out its Wikipedia page. Read everything you can on the topic. Watch every related YouTube video. Practice stream-of-consciousness journaling.

Based on what you find and what it inspires, you should quickly be able to decide which subjects have been tackled to death (zombies); which are unworkable because of an inherent lack of tension (fruitcake, kayak angling); and which provide the greatest potential conflict (bacteria, Caligula). More ideas may equal multibook deals, so stay open to possibilities and keep your research organized.

PICK A PARTNER

Often a romantic relationship begins with infatuation. You obsessively check your messages, feel like you never spend enough time with your partner, entertain fantasies of future meetings, and feel a primal urge to be with the other person without consideration of the consequences. Though this level of intensity can lead to quick burnout in a real-life romance, it represents ideal conditions for a writer working with a new idea. If you are not consumed, you cannot pay the proper attention.

Alternately, if you don't feel compelled to continue the book you have started, then you probably should cease production. A relationship of this caliber requires love and sacrifice, and if your feelings are lukewarm, you will not have the appropriate level of passion necessary to see the process through.

 SPACE IN TOGETHERNESS

If you want a career in writing, you must think of yourself as separate from the work. You have to be able to approach it with a clear head, an intellectual mind. Your book is not you. More specifically, it is not *all* of you. Even if you write memoir—to paraphrase Stephen King—the first draft is for you; the rest are for the readers. Your life's work, your heart and soul, your magnum opus will one day become a product. While that product came *through* you, it will no longer *belong* to you once it is out in the world. Understanding this early in the process will help you later.

Consider using a pen name. It will remind you that your identity is separate from your business.

When you go through the process of switching your status to "in a relationship," it sends a clear signal, both to the object of your attention and to those seeking it. Some have the audacity to remain persistent. Write down these story ideas on a piece of paper. Put them in a file in case things don't work out with your "main squeeze." Even when we have the best intentions, sometimes we must break up with our ideas.

Just be sure to remove any new ideas from the noise of *now*. You must be here with the one you chose.

UNDERSTAND IT WON'T ALWAYS BE SUNNY

For those of us who live in climates that offer the fullness of the four seasons, we have a cellular understanding of the nature of cycles. Early love—the beginning of the relationship—is like summer: hot, burning, intense, colorful. You can be lazy because you know it's vacation time—you're on the honeymoon. But we all know what awaits us when the holiday is over: the dying off. The planting of bulbs that need time to germinate for future regeneration—the bleak season.

After your initial burst of creative energy, it is normal, and arguably necessary, for a staleness to enter your work. You can sometimes see to distant shores where the journey will end and take you back to fulfillment, but more often all that looms is the endless road.

The middle.

Now is not the time to give up. If you allow it, this is where the magic happens. As we must put our selfishness aside to understand and complete our partners, we must put *ourselves* aside to ask the work what it needs from us to reach its fullness. You might be tempted to pull out the file of other ideas at this time, but don't—not yet. You committed to *this* idea. Stick with it.

Writing—like life—is a symbiosis. We must allow it to act upon us, as we act upon it. But we must show up to do the work. Doubt will creep in and will try to distract you. It will lead you down other paths, telling you the work is beyond your capabilities. Hold tight to the hand of the idea that took you this far. Walk through the fire together. You might be consumed, but if you make it to the other side, you will experience a glorious rebirth.

Just as spring follows winter, enlightenment will emerge after the dark and doubting season. A deeper understanding of the idea will take hold. This understanding will rekindle your initial passions because you will learn that though you might not have been worthy, you were willing. This willingness has allowed the art to flow through you, growing to its full potential. You have learned something, and now you must share it with others.

You might find that the idea you thought was specific to you shows up in others' work. Do not be afraid of this. Your openness has allowed Jung's "collective unconscious" to do its work. You might even become part of a trend. You should never chase the trend, but if you are fortunate enough to be a part of it, allow the larger interest to feed your success. If you were faithful to the work, no one will have written it exactly as you have. No one will have seen it the same way. It will round out a total portrait to reveal a truth.

Pockets of collective genius have arisen over time: Hawthorne and his contemporaries, the Lost Generation, the musicians of Woodstock. These communities flourish when the artists allow what is aligned to their natures to emerge in the most authentic ways possible. Artists reveal the struggles and feelings of society. The work is important. Do it.

START YOUR JOURNEY

If you feel you've reached a block or if you have such a surfeit of ideas that you cannot concentrate, I hope I've given you the tools you need to find "the one." We can never be fully prepared for a journey. If we could foresee all the challenges, the twists and turns that lay ahead, we wouldn't begin. But with the right partner—the right idea—you will be equipped, willing, and courageous enough to embark.

 THE MAGIC OF A PERFECT FIT

A wise person once said that fixing your sights on a goal starts the machinery of the universe that conspires with you to help you achieve it. (It will also work hard to convince you that you are not worthy, but more on that later.) The more you train your eye to see signs of affirmation, the easier it will be to recognize them.

In my own writing, I've had many strange, wondrous, and unexplainable occurrences—winks from the universe, as I've come to refer to them—that have validated my writing choices. Once when I completed a novel about Zelda Fitzgerald and was filled with that terrible emptiness and doubt that comes after a book is written, I decided to go to her grave. I was seeking something ... permission, forgiveness, closure perhaps? I had told my writing partner how sad I was to be done with Zelda and how I wished I could ask

---

Zelda if she felt I had represented her fairly in the work. When I pulled into the graveyard, a song Zelda danced to when she met her husband (one that I'd mentioned many times in my novel) came on the radio. I do not believe it was a coincidence.

Have you ever heard a pregnant woman say that everywhere she looks everyone is pregnant? It's true. If you trust the process, once your eyes and heart and mind are fixed on a topic, all the tools you need will rise to meet you. These experiences will flood your consciousness, overwhelming you. It will be a signal that you have chosen well.

 PRO TIP

Write a love letter to your story and characters. Capture the feeling so you can use it later for fuel. You'll need it.

DO YOU NEED AN MFA?

How an MFA Can Make You a Stronger Writer

JAEL MCHENRY

Question: Do you need an MFA?

Answer: No.

Oops. As you can guess from the title of this essay, I'm supposed to take the "pro" side of this debate. So let's phrase the question a little differently.

Question: Could you *benefit* from an MFA?

Answer: Almost definitely.

Here's a little background on me: My senior year of college, I applied to the most selective MFA programs in the country. One by one, they all politely rejected me.

The following year, I cast my net a little wider and was accepted to American University's MFA program. Success! I spent the next two years attending writing workshops and graduate-level literature classes, devoting my days and nights to becoming a better writer. I wrote a novel as my thesis project, I graduated with a shiny new degree, and I went out into the world.

Ten years later, I still hadn't published a novel.

I'd successfully submitted a few short stories and poems to literary magazines, including the pretty darn reputable *North American Review*. But novelwise, I had near miss after near miss. I got an agent with my thesis novel; he didn't sell it. I wrote another book and got another agent; she left the business. Despite working diligently toward my goal, and despite all those near misses, I still hadn't sold a novel.

Getting an MFA will not get you published. Period.

But it can do a thousand other things for you, almost all of which will make you a better writer. So let's talk about those things.

HEAR IT LIKE IT IS

Feedback is the most important thing an MFA program can give you. Not that you can't get feedback from trusted readers outside the MFA system, but the intensity of critiques in the graduate-degree environment absolutely can't be matched. The difference between a beta-reader and an MFA workshop is the difference between a match and a flamethrower.

In each semester-long workshop, I submitted three pieces of writing to twelve or so classmates, all of whom were deadly serious about the art of feedback, as well as a professor who provided input and guided discussion. They scrubbed and scrutinized each piece for everything from plot plausibility to the characters' names, and they discussed their findings in an open forum that pulled no punches. It wasn't always comfortable, and it wasn't always fun. But there's nothing like a critique to teach you a few important principles:

- It doesn't matter what you *meant* to write; it matters what the reader sees.
- You can't please every reader.
- "But that's how it really happened" is not an excuse for lousy fiction.

What you learn from having people read your work is only half the lesson. I learned just as much, if not more, from critiquing other people's work. You learn how to recognize and express when something is not working. Once you see that in other writers' manuscripts, it gets a lot easier to see it in your own.

GET THE DEADLINE YOU CAN'T IGNORE

During the second year of my MFA, I finished my first novel. Before that, I'd started and abandoned at least five of them for various reasons. My focus pre-MFA was split between writing and college classes and writing and working full-time. Finishing the first book in grad school taught me I could do it.

Later I learned how better to balance writing with other demands on my time, but I needed that first novel under my belt to know what I was shooting for. It turns out that a thesis committee of three professors waiting for you to produce work is a pretty big motivator. It isn't the only impetus, but it's a darn good one.

LEARN THROUGH DIVERSE OPPORTUNITIES

Not all MFA programs are created equal. I'm not talking about selectivity, the talent level of your fellow writers, or what they publish afterward. I mean that the actual composition of the program and how you spend your days in it makes a huge difference. Some MFA programs are pure workshop, which I wouldn't actually recommend—there's more to being a writer than writing. Others combine writing with literature classes, teaching opportunities, required lectures, and even internships.

During my MFA years, I did so much more than practice writing fiction. I took workshops in poetry (with a Pulitzer Prize winner) and playwriting to round out my perspective on language. I wrote a one-act play that was later performed onstage. I edited a literary magazine, selecting and refining other students' work. I took classes on everybody from Dante to Toni Morrison, guided by experts in the field, and I delved deep into the study of words in all their beauty. I read my work in public at a bookstore, performing for a crowd. I had incredibly positive and incredibly negative workshop experiences, and both kinds taught me things I needed to know. Had I chosen *not* to earn my MFA and simply dedicated my days and nights to writing for two years, I might have learned a lot about craft. But I learned a lot of other things—things I've needed since—that I wouldn't know without the opportunities the MFA program afforded me.

CONSIDER WHAT'S RIGHT FOR YOU

Here's the question: Could I have done all of these things without paying tens of thousands of dollars in tuition? Some yes, some no. You can take night classes, go to weeklong or weekend workshops, and participate in online critique groups. You can pay brilliant freelance editors to provide honest feedback on your work. But an MFA program sets up the buffet so you can dish out exactly what you want to eat. Opportunity abounds.

The MFA has a gigantic price tag. Whether that price is worth it is a completely personal decision. Most of the published writers I know don't have one, and plenty of MFA grads I know aren't published. In my mind, the only bad decision is to draw a line between the two groups and look down at the people who make a different decision than your own. I've heard a lot of rancor on both sides of the debate, and it's nearly always misplaced.

Do you need the degree? No. Can you benefit from it? Definitely. Will you pursue it? That's up to you.

 HOW TO GET IN YOUR OWN WAY, METHOD 4: WORRY ABOUT PREREQUISITES

We've all got lists of stuff we think we need to get started—a new laptop, an MFA, a home office—but all we need is a pen, some paper, and a lifetime's worth of untreated psychological disorders.

—BILL FERRIS

DO YOU NEED AN MFA?

How to Learn Your Craft—and Get Published—Without the Degree

CATHERINE MCKENZIE

I'll admit I wasn't aware of the MFA program debate until after I'd gotten a book deal. It's not that I didn't know about master's degrees in writing—I had simply never considered getting one because writing a novel wasn't on my radar. I'm often asked whether I've always been a writer, and my stock answer is: "I've always written." I think that's why the idea of a writing *career* never entered my thought process. I wrote—it was who I was, not what I was going to do.

Then I wrote a novel. I wouldn't exactly say I did it by accident, though I certainly hadn't meant to write one when I first sat down and began typing ten years ago. But that is what it became: a 90,000-word story that had a beginning, a (saggy) middle, and an end. I spent some time trying to fix it, realized I had put too much of me on the page, and eventually put that book in a drawer and started again.

Would that first novel have been better if I'd earned an MFA (or, in fact, taken any writing courses at all)? Undoubtedly, though this notion will only ever exist as a thought experiment. Absent the invention of a time machine, I'll never know what I might or could have written if I'd chosen that path. Conversely, those who did choose to pursue a graduate degree in writing won't ever know how their MFA program influenced what they might have written otherwise.

CONSIDER THE ARGUMENTS FOR AND AGAINST

MFA programs are often criticized for being too focused on literary fiction and producing a generation of voices that sound similar. I'll admit that its bent toward the literary rather than the commercial has made the MFA feel exclusive. *Would I even be admitted to a program?* I've wondered, not because I don't think my writing is good enough but because I'm not sure it's the "right" kind of writing.

I do think there's something to be said for the concerns about voice as well. Belonging to a group influences you both consciously and unconsciously. When I sat down to write, I didn't think about whether it was fashionable to write in first-person present—I just *did it.* That was how my voice came out. And though that voice has shifted and, I hope, improved over the years, it is *my* voice. Would I have lost it with more formalized training? I will literally never know.

On the other hand, I can understand how those who did go through formal training might be frustrated with writers like me. You can't become a lawyer, a doctor, or an architect without a degree. But the arts, for whatever reason, seem more accessible. Anyone with a pen or a computer can write the next great novel, or so they think. MFA programs act as a filter; you need some talent to get in, though being accepted is no guarantee of publication or success.

Does a formal writing education help you become a bestseller or win literary awards? Perhaps, although it's unlikely that the three to four thousand MFA students who graduate each year (according to *The New York Times*[1]) publish the majority of the novels released.

And consider this: The first MFA program was established in Iowa in 1936, so every book written before that—from the worst to the best—was published without its benefit. Austen, Dickens, and Shakespeare were all self-taught.

LEARN YOUR CRAFT, AND PUT IN THE TIME

Of course, writers who choose *not* to pursue an MFA still need to study and train. I don't know if Malcolm Gladwell's ten thousand–hour theory (the idea that you must practice something for approximately ten thousand hours to master it) is true, but I'm fairly certain I've spent at least ten thousand hours reading, which I think is crucial for anyone who wants to write. And once I started writing novels, I started reading novels differently, trying to figure out the mechanics. I remember consciously doing this with *Gone Girl* by Gillian

---

1 "Why Writers Love to Hate the M.F.A." (www.nytimes.com/2015/04/12/education/edlife/12edl-12mfa.html?_r=0).

Flynn. I read it once for pleasure and then immediately went back to the beginning to figure out how the author had pulled it off. I've also read craft books, though I didn't read my first craft book until I was in the middle of writing my fifth novel! (It said I was doing it right. Whew!)

Then, of course, you must do the writing itself: the hours and hours and hours of it. It usually takes me six months to produce the first draft of a novel by working, on average, an hour a day. That's roughly 180 hours to a first draft—and that's just *my* pace. It takes many writers far longer. By the time the book hits the bookshelf, it's been through multiple drafts and edits and proofreading—another year's worth of work, easily a thousand hours. That might be a bad billing year for a lawyer, but it's a lot of time to spend on one project. And each step of the process focuses on improving it, making it faster paced, smoother, and more vivid and unexpected. I learn something with each book and set challenges for myself, too.

ASK YOURSELF A FEW KEY QUESTIONS

So should you do an MFA program? I didn't, but it didn't prevent me from becoming an author. Ultimately the choice is yours. Before you apply (or write it off) consider:

1. What do you expect to get out of the program?
2. Are you a self-starter or someone who needs prodding to get things done? If you are the latter, a more structured program might be right for you.
3. What kinds of stories do you want to write? Will you have the freedom to do that in the program you choose?

And remember: There is no right or wrong answer. Both formal and informal training can lead you to a successful career as a novelist. Pick the path that's right for you.

MINING FOR DIAMONDS

Strike It Rich with Research—
Without Getting Buried Alive

DAVID CORBETT

Before becoming a novelist, I worked as a private investigator. My job required, among other things, that I knock on lots of doors and ask lots of questions of lots of strangers. Not all the people I approached reacted cheerfully. I was often yelled at, routinely cursed, frequently threatened, and once almost run over. (The man who tried to kill me, ironically, was a doctor.)

My job taught me the three key elements of any successful attempt to gather facts, and they've served me well in my fiction:

1. **PREPARE AND ORGANIZE.** Begin by developing a fundamental understanding of what you believe you need to learn. This means knowing enough about your basic story and its world, specifically the era and locale of its events and the action you foresee taking place, to have a working idea of the kinds of information and areas of inquiry you lack.
2. **REMAIN OPEN TO THE UNEXPECTED.** Once the research begins, keep an open mind (and eye and ear), taking note of unexpected revelations. Make sure the assumptions made during your initial preparation don't blind you to discoveries that lead in unforeseen and potentially valuable areas, even if they fundamentally change key elements of the story.
3. **REASSESS, ADAPT, AND FOLLOW UP.** Remain flexible yet disciplined. Always ask new questions shaped by what you've learned, to the point of rethinking the whole enterprise, without losing sight of the core inspiration that excited you in the beginning. This is a continual back-and-forth process of assimilation, reevaluation, and discrimination.

As you can imagine, these three guidelines are easier to state than to follow. But if you exhibit self-control and abide by them wisely, they really can help you know when you're straying into the fascinating but unnecessary.

CONSIDER THE ROLE OF FACT IN FICTION

The first question to answer in determining what to research isn't *what*, but *why*. Consider for a moment this quote from Albert Camus: "Fiction is the lie through which we tell the truth." Dozens of great authors, from Ralph Waldo Emerson to Doris Lessing, have expressed similar notions. Which raises the question: If fiction is lying, why bother with facts at all? The answer lies in recognizing that, like magicians, storytellers create illusion. Though the purpose may indeed be to reveal a deeper truth, the fact remains that the focus of our effort is to *convincingly deceive*.

Research serves this purpose. Through credible detail, we establish a fictive world that convinces the reader it's worth her while to suspend disbelief and invest emotionally in our tale. The purpose of research, then, is to establish *authority*, not veracity. It's like misdirection in a magic act. By focusing my reader's gaze on *this* (the details I've supplied), I draw her attention away from *that* (the material I'm obliged to invent).

KNOW WHEN TO STEP AWAY

The peril of research lies in not recognizing its limited purpose and instead pursuing more information than necessary because it's just so darn fascinating. This is why so many novelists confess that the problem with research isn't digging in, it's digging out.

Worse, after so much investment, they feel obliged to shoehorn all the neat stuff they've learned into the book. Nothing stops a story in its tracks as effectively as a wall of needless information.

Research need not become an ever-descending mine shaft from which only the lucky return. All you need is enough information and detail to convince the reader you know your business. The degree of effort necessary to accomplish that end will depend on the sophistication of your audience. (Note: One should never underestimate the intelligence of readers.)

As a general rule of thumb, I try to nail down fundamental details that tell me how life is lived at the time and place of my story. That includes (but by no means is limited to) the following:

- **CLIMATE:** including standard precautions against the elements, from flood levees to parasols
- **CLOTHING:** from necessities to ornamentation, with an eye for the varieties of style within a given social or economic class and between classes
- **MANNER OF SPEECH:** with, again, an ear for variety (letters and newspaper accounts, if available, are invaluable—especially for historical settings—as is the simple act of listening if your story takes place in the present)
- **WORK:** such as who does what and why (this will dovetail with era and geography) and the physical details of that work, the wages, and the dangers
- **CLASS, RACE, SEX, AND POWER ARRANGEMENTS:** such as who feels free, who feels constrained or oppressed, who manages the money, who raises the children, how quickly the children reach adult status, who has leisure time, who inherits property, who cares for the sick, and who goes to war
- **ARCHITECTURE:** specifically the nature of the homes (and households) of the powerful, the powerless, and those in between
- **FOOD, MUSIC, ENTERTAINMENT:** the things that make daily life "lively"

You can see at a glance how this kind of research can easily get out of hand. Understanding your specific story needs permits you to exert some control. And yet wandering off in the dark for a bit may avail unforeseeable gems that automatically enhance your authority as storyteller, such as:

- the inviting honey color of certain varieties of whale oil used in lamps (as opposed to colorless kerosene, which replaced it)
- the class-tinged tension in the Old South between Methodism ("deeds not creeds") and Presbyterianism (which claimed salvation was predetermined and virtuous acts were irrelevant)
- the ethereal interpretation given to consumption (tuberculosis) before its contagious nature was discovered, especially among writers and poets such as Elizabeth Barrett Browning and Emily Brontë (it supposedly "purified the patient and edified her friends"[1])

Balancing the expected and commonplace with the surprising and unique creates the verisimilitude that perfects the illusion of truth.

---

[1] Sheila M. Rothman, *Living in the Shadow of Death: Tuberculosis and the Social Experience of Illness in American History* (New York: Basic, 1994), page 16; as quoted in Gary L. Roberts, *Doc Holliday: The Life and Legend* (John Wiley & Sons, Inc., 2006), page 60.

DEFINE THE EDGES AND THE SHAPE OF THE UNIVERSE

The British novelist Tom Rob Smith follows what he calls a "four-month rule." He permits himself sixteen weeks of unlimited but intensely focused research before even considering putting fingers to keyboard in service of story. To make the best use of that time, he also narrows his research to "best sources." To the greatest extent possible, he tries not to get caught up in scholarly debates that will require him to investigate everything from two (or more) opposing perspectives. For example, in researching *Child 44*, though there were sources on the Soviet Union that viewed the Stalin regime favorably, even triumphantly, he early on decided that this didn't serve his purposes and he didn't waste time reading them.

Similarly, if you find in your research that scholarship has gone through stages of revisionism, you'll most likely want to use the latest sources available. For example, during the mid-1970s, research into nineteenth-century correspondence between women friends (and lovers) led many scholars to believe that women developed deep interpersonal bonds at least in part because their connections to brothers and fathers were emotionally wanting, to the point that it seemed as though men and women existed in mutually exclusive spheres.[2] But then Karen Lystra, a professor of American studies at Cal State University, discovered a treasure trove of correspondence between husbands and wives from this same period, archived at the Huntington Library in San Marino, California. These letters revealed profound intimacy between married couples, with spouses who often considered each other their closest, most trusted companion.[3]

The point is that knowledge, even of the past, isn't fixed. It's constantly evolving due to new discoveries and fresh interpretations. Not only that, contemporary records are often wildly at odds. Newspapers from the 1800s often provide irreconcilable views of events due to the highly factional nature of reportage at the time. It may be true that newspapers are indeed "the first draft of history," but this only underscores the necessity of further revision and correction.

There's also a creative way to address this fluidity of fact. The irreconcilable views of married life or Stalin's regime certainly represent a challenge in

---

2 See, for example, Carroll Smith-Rosenberg's seminal study, "The Female World of Love and Ritual: Relations Between Women in Nineteenth-Century America," *Signs: Journal of Women in Culture and Society*, 1975, Vol. 1, No. 1.

3 See *Searching the Heart: Women, Men, and Romantic Love in Nineteenth-Century America*, 1989, Oxford University Press.

your research. You can choose one faction or the other to believe, or you can use these antagonistic opinions to provide conflict within your story. Tom Rob Smith may not have wasted time poring over pro-Stalin texts, but he understood the need to ground the Stalinist functionaries within his novel in the truth as they saw it.

However you establish the preliminary boundaries for your research, the need to keep an open mind about unforeseen discoveries remains one of the key elements of the work. These discoveries will not only provide details of daily life and animate conflicting perspectives, but they will also generate ideas for scenes and characters you did not anticipate at the outset. But this open-mindedness cannot be open-ended. Something like Tom Rob Smith's four-month rule is valuable because it forces you to begin writing.

Sometimes the time to stop researching and start writing is obvious—for example, when you realize you're encountering the same basic information, with only minor differences, over and over. That indicates you've learned enough. Now write. Another endpoint often comes when you gain a solid sense of what isn't or can't be known—authorities and sources are silent on a particular issue or fact. These omissions in the official record can actually open avenues of creative speculation and invention, which are natural starting points for stories.

But even if you don't encounter either of these natural transitional junctures—or set a time limit, or create some other cutoff—at some point you need to turn away from the research and toward the blank page. That said, nothing obligates you to curtail all research. In fact, you can continue to read and explore as you write your story—as long as the compulsion to learn doesn't dominate the need to meet your daily word count, become an inquisitive tic, or cause a block. You can always update details and scenes as you go along. Writing is rewriting. But you can't revise what you haven't written.

BEWARE OF FUSSING OVER THE FUSSY

Certain areas of expertise attract a devout, rabid, even unbalanced following. One ventures into the Civil War, for example, at some risk, since it forms such an area of intense obsession for many buffs and armchair experts. If writing within the framework of such a jealously guarded arena, it's sometimes best to read the best-available survey text or general history in order to avoid obvious errors, and then focus on some smaller, singularly focused, even idiosyncratic source for a more unique view on events.

In researching his brilliant novel *City of Thieves*—in which two prisoners face execution if they can't find a dozen eggs for a wedding cake—David Benioff relied not only on Harrison Salisbury's *The 900 Days*, the most authoritative text in English on the siege of Leningrad, but also acknowledged his debt to Curzio Malaparte's *Kaputt*, a "work of strange genius" that provided "a completely different perspective."

Even thoughtful precautions can prove fruitless, however. The crime writer G.M. Ford no longer refers to any weapon in a book as anything other than a "gun" because he wearied of the letters from handgun enthusiasts who insisted the sidearm he'd mentioned couldn't perform as described. "And never, *never* put a Harley-Davidson in a book," he added.

It's not just weapons and machinery that inspire such fierce reactions. A knowledgeable reader—a bookseller, no less—once confided to me that she stopped reading Dennis Lehane's *Mystic River* when a woman character used hot water to rid her husband's clothes of blood. "Any woman knows you use cold water," she said, admitting she put the book down at that point because the author "lost her." Fortunately, he didn't lose millions of others.

Worrying over such nitpicking is pointless. Do your best to get it right by using the most reliable sources you can: knowledgeable people you can interview (see below), official documents and newspapers from the period and locale of the story, classic and canonical texts, biographies, letters, and, of course, the increasingly inescapable, if not always reliable, Internet. Then take the blame for all errors in your acknowledgments, and let go.

INTERVIEW AND OBSERVE

Earlier I mentioned my occasional encounters with hostility when trying to get people to talk to me as a private investigator—small surprise, given the fiercely contentious nature of the issues at stake. In general, however, I enjoyed the exact opposite reaction. If approached in a spirit of humility, respect, and curiosity, people tend to be very generous. We all like talking about what we know.

Often it's best to approach interview subjects with self-enforced parameters: "I have five quick questions." Once you sit down together, the information may flow freely, but take care to respect the interviewee's time. Do your homework, and separate the essential from the merely interesting.

Novelist Donna Levin wanted to visit the San Francisco coroner's office for a book she was writing, but she felt too shy to go alone. Knowing I was a PI (at the time), she asked if I'd come along. Her anxiety proved groundless.

The staff member we met gave her a tour of the whole morgue and sat with her for several hours. This underscores a point I made at the beginning: It doesn't take bravado or cockiness to knock on a stranger's door—quite the contrary. Donna won over her interview subject with her thoughtfulness, intelligence, and self-effacing humor.

Experts also often lead to other experts with better, more precise information. For my novel set in El Salvador, *Blood of Paradise*, in which water rights were a key component of the story, I interviewed a hydrologist who had worked in-country. He introduced me, in turn, to another specialist who'd worked specifically on the issue of groundwater drawdown and well depletion in the region where my story took place. This gentleman also provided maps and reports of incredible value, along with anecdotes about battling the Kafkaesque local bureaucracy. His information not only gave me a bounty of great details; it also convinced me my original story idea wouldn't work. This meant a lot of rewriting, but it also spared me the embarrassment of getting it all wrong.

I traveled to El Salvador twice and employed guides from both an ecotourism company and a surfing outfit. They drove me around the country, identifying the prominent flora, fauna, beaches, and churches. We discussed local history, culture, and cuisine, and they even gave me pointers on *caliche* (Salvadoran slang). But the real find was Claire Marshall, a BBC reporter I met by chance on the beach at La Libertad. She introduced me to Carlos Vasquez, a deported former shot caller for Mara Salvatrucha in Los Angeles, now running an outreach group to help other gang members leave the life. We shared coffee in the Zona Rosa in the capital, and his insights on the *maras*, from both inside and outside perspectives, proved golden.

Such investments of time and money are not available to everyone—or necessary. The Internet, despite its faults, is a great source for preliminary information and can often direct you to people, documents, texts—and, most important, *images*—that can help you visualize and flesh out your story world. It's great to visit the locale of your book if possible, but take a cue from historical novelists: You can't visit medieval Ireland or ancient China or any other land in the past. Story worlds are conceived in the imagination and portrayed in words. Fortunately, both lie near at hand.

The same is true of in-person interviews—they're wonderful if possible, but phone or even e-mail contact is not only acceptable but often preferred for its less intrusive nature. Persistence may be required to get a response, but remember you're searching for diamonds—if they were easy to come by, they wouldn't be so valuable.

HOW TO GET IN YOUR OWN WAY, METHOD 5: OVER-RESEARCH

Research is like author time travel. You pause writing for just a sec while you look up the average weight of an American black bear. Suddenly, it's an hour later, and you're reading the Wikipedia page on P.T. Barnum.

—BILL FERRIS

GO PUBLIC

Why Creating the Story Behind Your Story Begins Now

DAN BLANK

Commitment is a terrifying thing. The choice to write your novel is no less of a commitment than any other relationship in your life. It is, perhaps, the most delicate and insidious commitment of all. So much of the work happens in your head that you can easily become your own unreliable narrator.

Perhaps a writer's greatest fear, after being termed a hack, is to become that spammy self-promoter who shamelessly plugs her work in a desperate attempt to find a readership. Still, I would encourage you to make a *public* commitment to your book as soon as possible and share your intentions with the world. Why? Because it *is* difficult to find a readership for your book, and a strategic audience development plan can work wonders.

TALK ABOUT IT—NOW

Too many authors wait to talk about their books until they're published. Their intentions are good; they want to bring their story into the world with grace and elegance. They hope that it naturally finds a fit in the literary landscape and that those who find the story share it with others as one shares an heirloom between generations.

But doing so wastes months of opportunities when you might be seeding knowledge of your upcoming book in the minds of potential readers. Seasoned marketers know that it takes repeated exposure to a product before a potential customer remembers it. Yet too many authors rely on the few short weeks during the book launch to develop a sizable customer base. Then, suddenly, we feel we have one shot: the launch. We hope that word-of-mouth marketing takes hold before we have to do any promotion ourselves. We pray for buzz.

That rarely happens. I want to encourage you—today—to publicly share your writing process before the book is published.

COMMIT ALL THE WAY

What does it mean to commit all the way? When you make a commitment to your novel, you do the following:

- **PROCLAIM IT PUBLICLY.** This can be via a blog post, an announcement on your website, or a Facebook status update, but it can also be through conversations you have with others in the many facets of your life. Too often we compartmentalize our identities (e.g., day worker, night writer, soccer mom, choir member), perhaps thinking that each "audience" is unique, that the people who know us at work are wholly separate from potential readers, when in fact they are the same people.
- **PROVIDE UPDATES.** Don't view your professional life as a series of press releases cataloging big milestones. Don't announce your book and then go silent for months because you feel there is no use in talking about a book that no one can buy yet. People value what they co-create, and sharing your journey brings your audience along and allows them to buy in early.
- **SHARE YOUR "WHY."** Simon Sinek made the phrase "share your 'why'" famous in his book *Start with Why*, and I think it applies here. So many authors remain mute through the months and years it takes to develop a book, and they never get around to sharing the "why" behind a creation. Because of this, would-be readers don't see their evolving and lasting passion for a story or character, only the slick sales pitch that arrives at the launch.
- **SHOW HOW THE SAUSAGE IS MADE.** How a book is made can be a very interesting process to other writers, but readers also find it fascinating. This is an entirely different way to have your readers learn about, understand, and care about what you're creating.
- **FIND COLLABORATORS.** All books are group efforts, period. Don't isolate yourself as a means of protection. Involve others as soon as you possibly can. This can take shape in a variety of ways, from accountability groups that will keep you honest about your writing goals to building a future fan base from your first readers and those who already know you.

 **PRO TIP**

Consider early on who your ideal readers are, and think about ways you might learn more about them. Visiting message boards, blogs, and local groups can help imbue your work with realism and may provide you with a supportive readership once you're published.

DON'T LET THIS BOOK DEFINE YOU

Look, chances are this one book is not going to fulfill all of your dreams. Rather, it will be a stepping-stone to help you develop your craft and understand the process of publishing while establishing a small base of readers.

In all likelihood, your debut won't be a bestseller. You won't get three hundred reviews on Amazon. You won't appear on television or radio shows or see a review in a huge national publication. You won't win any awards.

I can't even tell you how many authors I've talked with who are wildly disappointed in the results of publishing their first novel. Ask yourself: Will disappointments crush you? Will you use them as justification to stop writing, to avoid the topic in conversation, to justify how someone screwed you over in the process, robbing you of "your big shot"?

If the answer is yes, try to focus on the *experience* you want to create.

Have you ever gone to an author reading and been blown away by how the author engaged the audience? She made you laugh and cry. She told stories, used props, or interacted with the audience rather than remaining at the speaker's podium. This author focused on crafting a wide range of *experiences* for readers. The impact of her work might be measured in decades, not just the weeks around a single book launch.

Too often, we count the success of a book with these numbers and highlights:

- book sales
- the number of reviews on Amazon
- Amazon ranking
- prominent blurbs
- prominent media attention
- speaking events
- awards

There are ways to optimize the success of your book, and you may be surprised to learn that you can do many of them before your book comes out. Consider:

- **THE NUMBER OF PEOPLE YOU CONNECT WITH WHO LIKE BOOKS SIMILAR TO YOURS.** Homework: How aware are you of the places readers congregate, both in person and online? How present are you in these communities? This is a number you can control, based on your own habits.
- **THE NUMBER OF COLLEAGUES YOU DEVELOP IN THE MONTHS AND YEARS PRIOR TO PUBLICATION.** Homework: Get to know your fellow authors, librarians, booksellers, media members, and anyone else who supports books.
- **SUCCESSFUL AUTHORS WHOSE WORK IS SIMILAR TO YOUR OWN.** Homework: Study other book launches, and ask other authors about theirs. Take the useful advice, and adjust your own plans accordingly.
- **A LIST OF THINGS TO CELEBRATE.** Homework: Capture every kind word and mini-milestone.
- **A LIST OF PEOPLE WHO KNOW ABOUT YOUR BOOK AND SUPPORT IT.** Homework: Consider your personal address book and your social media influence. Social media is not about getting more followers but about organizing those who support your work so they feel connected to it and can take action when the time is right.

Writing a book is terrifying. Not only is it an enormous and complex task, but it inherently gets wrapped up in our sense of identity and self-worth. This creates a minefield of emotional triggers. The result is that we often try to protect ourselves. We tell ourselves that quality takes time. That we have writer's block. We avoid accountability because we feel it sets ourselves up for failure. We lean too heavily on proclamations of being an introvert. We romanticize "how it used to be," among false perceptions of how it used to be. (Writers in the fifties, sixties, seventies, and eighties schmoozed just as much as writers do today; it was simply limited to a tiny group of exclusive people who had access to those who could connect writers to an audience.)

If you seek a traditional publishing deal, you may tell yourself to wait for the publisher's announcement before saying anything to the world.

Stop.

Take authority not just in crafting your novel but in shepherding it into being. Commit now to learning how to communicate what this book is and why a reader should care. That will take time. The sooner you go public, the more powerful all of your launch efforts will be down the road.

 **PRO TIP**

Ever wonder how some authors post reviews before the book even comes out? Or how, on launch day, dozens of reviews appear on online retailer sites? It is often because they organized and prepared their core audience in the months leading up to the launch. It may not matter if you have forty followers on a social media channel, but it *will* matter if those forty fans leave an Amazon review for your book on launch day.

PART TWO

WRITE

Working through a first draft can be equal parts exhilarating and daunting. Having determination and knowing the most effective sources of your writerly fuel are key. So is flexibility. You may plan to do things one way, only to have that plan obliterated by your own biology (your best time to write), self-doubt (an affliction aided and abetted by perfectionism, imposter syndrome, or "neighbors will judge me" worries), or even your characters (stubborn creatures who refuse to be painted two-dimensionally or who veer away from your painstakingly constructed plot). All of this is normal. Keep going.

THIS IS A TEST

Why You Should Allow Yourself to Explore in the First Draft

GREER MACALLISTER

The beginning is just the beginning.

I suppose some writers get ideas that translate to the page perfectly, and some find no gaps between the concept they have of their book before it is written and the reality of the book after it is written. Except I don't know any of them. And I know a lot of writers.

The first draft can be so frustrating. You know what you want: a page-turner that also develops character, realistic situations that don't get bogged down by unnecessary detail, a story that unfolds with no unnecessary information, and a dénouement that can't be guessed from the start. The problem is, when you lay down those words on the page for the first time, they aren't flawless. They don't cooperate. They are unwieldy and shifty, clumsy and blunt.

EMBRACE THE FLAWS OF THE FIRST DRAFT

This American Life host and NPR luminary Ira Glass agrees. In an interview about creativity, he says:

> What you're making isn't so good, okay? It's not that great. It's trying to be good, it has ambition to be good, but it's not quite that good. … But your taste is still killer, and your taste is good enough that you can tell that what you're making is kind of a disappointment to you.

If you doubt that your work is any good, there's a chance it could be great. Terrible writers, after all, never doubt themselves. That juxtaposition Glass talks about—between your taste, which is great, and your work, which isn't necessarily great on the first try—is why revision exists.

LET YOURSELF GO WILD

Whether you plan your book with a fifty-page outline or wing it completely from beginning to end, a gap will exist between what you want and what you write. You might as well benefit from that gap. You might push the voice further than you have in the past, nail your characters to the wall instead of letting them off easy, or just write without editing for the first time in your life. The first draft is the time for experimentation.

You aren't wedded to your first draft; you're barely even dating. The first draft is really just the first step, where you begin to explore what your book might become. And as such, the best thing you can do with your first draft is take advantage of its shapelessness. Use it to go wild. That's what first drafts are for.

ACCEPT THE GAP—AND MANAGE IT

So your first draft isn't going to be everything you want it to be, but you want to do more than just tolerate this gap. How can you put it to use? Setting a secondary goal for the first draft—besides writing or finishing it—is a great idea to help ensure that the gap won't be a vast chasm in every single way.

What should you spend most of your time and effort on?

I know people who hate to throw out any words they've written, so they agonize over the first draft word by word, sentence by sentence. This is a hard way to go. But if you write this way, my advice would be to write your first draft short and then build on it rather than writing everything that comes to mind and expecting to trim later. Then your gap is one you know how to deal with, instead of the thing you most fear.

If it's important to you that your plot is watertight—certainly an essential quality for mysteries and thrillers, which tend to set up a lot of dominoes in the first two-thirds of the book before setting them loose in a torrent in the last third—then you may need to acknowledge that you'll have a gap in your characters' development and your sentence-level writing in that first draft. And that's okay.

But in a way, the draft itself will highlight its strengths and weaknesses. This is where the exploration comes in. Write and write and then write some more, and accept what comes out in the first draft. It won't be perfect, but it could be very illuminating.

LET THE BOOK FAIL

Sometimes, partway through a first draft, you realize that things aren't working out. Odd as it may seem, failure is also success. It's just like having your query rejected by an agent who wouldn't have liked your novel; as painful as rejection is, a query has done its job if it gives the agent a true enough sense of the work that he can decide between "Hmm, I might like this" and "It isn't for me."

I started several novels before I finished one, and it wasn't just because I didn't have the discipline to stick with it. It was because not all my ideas were novel ideas—novellas, maybe, or long short stories. Some turned out to be plays. But it takes a certain type of idea, a certain plot and set of characters, to sustain interest—both your own and your readers'—for 80,000 or more words. You might not know whether an idea can be a book until you try to write it.

And if you have to abandon the project, well, you learned something in the process, so getting partway through a first draft and realizing that it isn't a novel also counts as a success. Really! It's not a waste. Every word you write helps you learn more about how to use words in the future.

Whether it's your first book or your 101st (congratulations!), there's a lot to be learned along the way.

 FAQ

Is it normal to consider quitting on a story after drafting the first few chapters? What's going on?

I have started at least five and, like many, chucked a completed one that was "meh." As for short stories, I have close to one hundred that I couldn't finish.

—ROBIN BLACK, AUTHOR OF *LIFE DRAWING*

I am so compulsive and struggle so much with getting words on paper that I only very rarely abandon a project. It takes me too much work to even get to fifty pages. I just sort of blunder my way through it.

—LISA BRACKMANN, AUTHOR OF *GO-BETWEEN*

It's not only normal but healthy. I've quit writing probably five times the number of novels I've completed, and usually after just a few chapters.

—BRUCE HOLSINGER, AUTHOR OF *THE INVENTION OF FIRE*

I have at least two books that have gotten to the fifty-page stage and then been abandoned. I always worry at that stage whether the book has legs. Ultimately that is where the hard work of the novel begins: getting from the setup to the payoff, which has been called the "saggy middle" for good reason.

—CATHERINE MCKENZIE, AUTHOR OF *FRACTURED*

I've left many half-finished stories in the drawer, sometimes because I chose a story or character without sufficient legs. Often it's that I've approached an emotional topic that I'm not ready to confront. And sometimes I chose something too facile and I recognized my laziness.

—RANDY SUSAN MEYERS, AUTHOR OF *ACCIDENTS OF MARRIAGE*

 **PRO TIP**

Be willing to produce a lot of material that won't make the final cut, whether in multiple drafts or a journal. Because here's the thing: We writers don't have so much as a block of marble or lump of clay or even paints with which to create. Writers are required to produce the material from which they will then craft the book. So recognize that your early drafts and story journaling are essentially creating the material, rather than writing the story you will be telling.

—ROBIN LAFEVERS

 **PRO TIP**

Take care with "pretty writing" in a first draft; it's hard to unfrost a cake.

—THERESE WALSH

STORY FIRST, PLOT SECOND

Develop Your Protagonist's Story-Specific Past

LISA CRON

As you start the intoxicating, challenging, rewarding, and, yes, sometimes maddeningly frustrating process of writing a novel, chances are you're wondering, *Where does my novel begin?* Could there be a more logical, obvious, and necessary question?

Actually, yes, there could. Especially since, as it turns out, that's the exact wrong question to ask at the beginning of the writing process. Why? Because it refers to what happens on the first page in the novel, which is when the *plot* kicks in. And what you're *really* writing about—what will capture your readers, make them care, and incite the sense of urgency that won't let them put down your novel—starts long before your plot begins.

The right question to ask is: *When does my* story *start?*

Because believe it or not, your plot and your story are not synonymous.

FIND THE START OF YOUR STORY

All novels start in medias res, a nifty Latin term that means "in the middle of the thing." Thus the first page of your novel opens with the *second* half of your story; the first half creates an unavoidable problem that your plot will catapult your protagonist into. And so, in order for your plot to have a story to tell, a whole lot of relevant things must happen before your novel begins. A specific cause-and-effect trajectory in your protagonist's past has created the problem that on page 1 will hit critical mass, both in the plot and—much more important—within your protagonist herself.

Yet writers are often told to scrupulously avoid backstory as if it will only trip them up, get in the way of the story they're telling, and alienate the reader. This couldn't be further from the truth. Backstory is what drives your novel forward and gives meaning to everything that happens. Backstory is present, in one form or another, on every page you write. As William Faulkner so aptly said, "The past isn't dead. It isn't even past."

If you ignore your protagonist's past and begin envisioning your story on the first page, you're in essence saying, "I don't need to know what happened before this moment in my protagonist's life in order to write about what she'll do from here on out." Or, put more bluntly, "I'm going to write a three-hundred-page novel about the most crucial, meaningful turning point in someone's life who I know absolutely nothing about."

You can't expect to engage your reader with that mind-set. Your protagonist must arrive on the first page of your novel with an internal problem already brewing, *before* the plot problem tosses her out of her easy chair and into the fray. Because that internal problem? It's not what your novel is truly about; it's what hooks your readers, makes them care, and brings your plot to life.

Knowing your protagonist's internal problem is essential for two reasons:

1. Your reader is biologically wired to respond to your protagonist's inner struggle. When we're lost in a story, our brains sync with the protagonist's and her struggle becomes our struggle. This isn't a metaphor—functional magnetic resonance imaging (fMRI) reveals that when a story engages us, we experience what the protagonist is going through as if it were happening to us—because it is. We feel what she feels because her emotions travel down our neural pathways. To hell with those clunky virtual reality visors—humans already come equipped with the most effective VR of all: the ability to neurologically slip into someone else's life, especially when she's struggling with an unavoidable problem, trying to figure out what the heck to do. The unspoken question we're wired to bring to every story is: *What would it cost, emotionally, to have to go through that? What will I learn about what makes people tick that will help me navigate my own life?*

2. Developing your protagonist's internal problem first is crucial because that's what you'll then use to create and spur the plot. In fact, often your protagonist's internal struggle *creates* the external problem. This is especially important when the external challenge around which your plot revolves doesn't, at first blush, seem like a problem at all. For instance, maybe your protagonist just met the love of his life or is about to be crowned the King of England or has just won the lottery. Woo-hoo! While in real life that would be pretty darn good, at the beginning of a novel, the question is: *Why would such apparent good fortune be a problem for my protagonist?* Because if it's not, your reader has no reason to care and nothing to root for.

CREATE THE PAST TO GIVE MEANING TO THE PRESENT

Make no mistake; the answer to the question "Why is this a problem for my protagonist?"—the answer to why *anything* would matter to your protagonist—always lies in her past.

We're not just talking about the external things that have happened in your protagonist's past, because like the plot itself, they're surface events. And no matter how objectively dramatic, a story is not about how the protagonist solves a surface problem. An external problem that doesn't put your protagonist to an internal test is not a problem at all; it's just a chore. That's why the real question you need to ask is: *How did those past events shape my protagonist's belief system, knocking her worldview out of alignment and causing the internal conflict that my plot will then force her to confront?*

Because your novel is not about the plot, nor even what happens in it. The plot is there to serve one master: the story, which is about your protagonist's internal evolution.

The reason this might come as a surprise is that most of us don't actually know what a story is. It's not our fault. It's just that we're so familiar with stories that we *feel* as if we know. After all, we're instantly captivated by an effective story and just as quickly bored by a story that's just a bunch of things that happen. So what don't we understand?

The problem is that there's a massive difference between responding to a story and knowing what you're responding to. As the great Southern writer Flannery O'Connor once quipped, "I find most people know what a story is until they sit down to write one." Turns out that the ability to *recognize* a story is hardwired, but the ability to write one … not so much.

As a result, while we all love stories, most of us don't know what a story really is or what has us riveted when we're under its spell. For readers that doesn't matter one iota; after all, when you're savoring a tasty morsel of chocolate, you don't care why it tastes so good—you just want more (than is good for you, if my experience means anything). But writers who want to engage their readers need to know what lies behind the magic trick. We need to know how it actually works. Because it's not magic at all—we've just been focusing on the wrong thing.

CONSIDER: WHAT IS A STORY?

Let's begin by defining story.

A story is about how what happens externally (the plot, which is the surface of the story) affects someone (the protagonist, your reader's avatar) who's in pursuit of a deceptively difficult goal (the plot problem) and how that person changes *internally* as a result. And that, my friends, is what rivets us: the escalating internal struggle that plot events trigger within the protagonist, compelling her to change in order to achieve her goal.

If you're wondering, *Wait, change from* what? *To what? Why?*, you've also pinpointed why you can't just find your story as you go and get to know your protagonist as you write forward.

The simple truth is that your protagonist must arrive on page 1 with a fully formed story-specific worldview because *humans go through their lives with their worldviews already formed.* We don't find out *later* what happened to us in our past. And once something's happened to us, it becomes part of how we see the world and informs the decisions we then make. Iconic credit card taglines notwithstanding, our history is the one thing we never do leave home without. And they're not neatly tucked away in a trunk of memories that we unpack every now and then when we're in a reminiscent mood. They are actively present every minute of every day as we bravely forge our way through life. They are the yardstick by which we measure the meaning of everything.

When you face a difficult situation—any situation in which you have no choice but to make a decision and take action, whether it's what to order for dinner, when to walk the dog, or whether you should investigate what's making that odd scratching sound in the basement—you make that decision based on what your past has taught you to expect. Chicken is delicious; the dog is doing that little dance by the door, so you'd better grab the leash; you've seen enough horror movies to know that no good ever comes of odd sounds in the cellar! In other words, our past is the subjective lens through which we interpret and assess the present. Without it, how would you *ever* be able to make any decision about anything, short of forever flipping a coin?

How, indeed, would you know anything at all?

Imagine how terrifying it would feel if you walked into a room and someone you don't know but who apparently thinks they're your spouse says, "Listen, dearest, so much has happened. We really have to talk." If you couldn't access your past, you'd be racking your brain, wondering, *Talk about what? Why? And pardon me for asking, but can you remind me who you are again?*

Point being, if you don't know anything about your protagonist's story-specific past—especially what she believes and why she believes it—how will you even know what she *might* do? Or why she'd do it? Or how she got into this situation to begin with?

Again, the answer is simple: You won't.

To be clear, we're not talking about a general overview of your protagonist's past or a lengthy-yet-random list of her heartfelt likes and dislikes, beginning with her love of bread pudding and ending with her fear of flying cockroaches (yes, they do exist; sorry). We're talking about something far more specialized, intricate, and focused: Your protagonist's story-specific backstory has as much specificity and depth as the novel itself because it is *not* separate from your novel; it's the most seminal layer.

T.S. Eliot summed up why backstory is so crucial quite eloquently when he wrote, "The end of our exploring will be to arrive at where we started, and to know the place for the first time." You must create the plot to help the protagonist arrive at that very insight, but in order to do so, you need to know how your protagonist sees the world, in detail, *when the novel begins*. Otherwise, how do you know what that change will be or why it's necessary? The key words, as you might suspect by now, are *in detail*. It doesn't work to hastily sum it up in a line or two, like this: "Ralph must change from being a self-centered jerk into a caring human being. Why? I just told you—because he's a self-centered jerk!"

The shift we're talking about is deeper, way less judge-y, and rife with escalating internal conflict. If that sounds vague and conceptual, let's get specific!

DEVELOP YOUR STORY

The story that leads up to the first page of your novel revolves around two things that have been firmly established in your protagonist's life long before the plot begins:

1. something she has wanted for a really long time
2. a deeply rooted misbelief that's standing in her way; think of this as the fear that holds her back, constantly causing her to misinterpret what's happening

Your novel is about how the plot then gives your protagonist no choice but to go after the thing she wants, and how the only way for her to get it is to face her misbelief and, hopefully, overcome it. That doesn't mean she *will* overcome it, but that's what readers are rooting for from page 1.

It goes without saying (she said anyway) that you can't create a plot that will force your protagonist to confront her misbelief without knowing what that misbelief is, where it came from, and how it's shaped her life.

This does not, however, mean you need to know absolutely everything about your protagonist's past—in fact, creating a soup-to-nuts character bio tends to be just as paralyzing as knowing nothing. If you're writing about a guy who needs to overcome his fear of commitment, you don't need to chronicle everything about him down to his favorite color, his stance on climate change, and the evolution of his lifelong passion for comic book collecting (unless, of course, he spent every waking moment cultivating that collection as a way to avoid commitment). In other words, you're only looking for things that are relevant to the story you're telling.

In order to do that, you need to get specific. Otherwise, how will you know what is relevant to his particular issue with commitment? Thus the first question you'd ask is: *Why, exactly, is he afraid of commitment?* Again, you're not simply looking for a short answer, like: "He's afraid of commitment because he is afraid of getting hurt. Sheesh, who isn't?" That, too, is general and thus too superficial to yield any real inside info. The "who isn't?" is a dead giveaway. We come to a story for fresh insight, for ways of seeing things that *aren't* obvious.

So, digging a layer deeper, the next question is: *What, specifically, triggered his fear of commitment?* Chances are good that this will send you back to his youth, where you'll find the exact moment when his world shifted and this misbelief—that commitment causes pain—was born. His misbelief was something learned through experience, leaving him thinking, *Aha! So this is how the world works. Got it!* In other words, misbeliefs spring up organically as we struggle to master the way of the world, the better to survive—both physically and socially.

That's why a misbelief is not something to judge lightly, nor is it proof that your protagonist is a willful fool, a scoundrel, a cad, or, even worse, a weakling. Instead, misbeliefs—the kind that hold your protagonist back by causing him to misinterpret what's happening around him—are almost always something that *saved* him from pain at one time in his life. But ever since then, it's done the opposite: kept him from the very thing he most wants. As in, that guy who fears commitment really wants connection, but his misbelief keeps undercutting his chances and guiding him away from it, all under the guise of keeping him safe from harm. And here's the rub: He's grateful for that guidance, and he feels lucky to have discovered this truth early in life because damn, look at all the pain it's kept at bay!

Poor fellow, right? If only he knew the *real* truth! Cue the plot.

But the plot doesn't disabuse him of his misbelief by wagging a finger at him and telling him it's wrong like your second-grade teacher would have. Instead the plot pushes him into difficult corners where he does what we all do: calls up his past experience to make sense of what's happening in the present so he can figure out what the hell to do.

Ah yes! His backstory. That's why developing your story first isn't "prewriting" that you will jettison when you begin the "real" writing. Your protagonist's backstory will appear on every single page, from the first sentence to the last, in the form of dialogue, flashbacks, and memories called up in service of navigating the present. His backstory will be the lens through which he'll view—and evaluate—everything that happens as the plot slowly forces him to recognize his misbelief for what it is: wrong.

As he struggles, so do your readers, who are in his skin, rooting for him, hoping against hope that he'll overcome his misbelief and see the world with fresh eyes. And when he changes, so do your readers, who, as they close the novel, now see their world in a new light, too—whether they realize it or not. This is story's superpower: By allowing us to viscerally experience the protagonist's transformation, we are transformed. The plot alone? It's just a bunch of things that happen. Worse, if those things don't affect your protagonist internally, they're a bunch of boring things, and regardless of how much external drama is going on, they'll leave your reader cold.

That's why when you sit down to write a novel, it's really very simple: story first, plot second.

COMMUNITY CONVERSATION: FOCUSING ON STORY FIRST

The Writer Unboxed community weighs in online. Please consider adding your voice by visiting Writer Unboxed via this QR code or link to the site. Join the conversation at writerunboxed.com/story-first-plot-second, and use the password "aip" (all lowercase).

Writer Unboxed is a moderated community, but comments that evolve a conversation in a positive manner are always welcome.

GRACE WYNTER: With my work-in-progress, which also happens to be my first novel, I'm running into the challenge of trying to figure out how much of my character's story-specific past to share in the present day in the form of flashbacks. The "truths" that my twenty-three-year-old protagonist has told herself stem largely from incidents that happened in high school involving her first love. Her backstory is very much "the most seminal layer" of my novel, and there are three scenes in her past that I think have to be told through backstory. But as you said, almost every writing site and advice column on writing instructs us to avoid backstory like the plague. So how do I transport my reader to these intense moments in the past, when those incidents took place, without sharing them? I'm not sure dialogue will do enough to make my reader feel what my protagonist felt in those moments. (I want my ideal reader to be crying after she reads those scenes.) I know there aren't any hard-and-fast rules for incorporating backstory, but I sure could use some help.

LISA CRON: The truth is that backstory is on nearly every page of every novel. It's just that it's done so deftly that you don't notice it at all—unless you stop and look for it, which is hard because it means breaking the biological spell of the story. When a story grabs us, it hacks our brains, and what the protagonist experiences travels down our own neural pathways, creating the sensation that we really *are* there. And the seminal layer of story that keeps us there is backstory, flashbacks, and snippets of memory because they are the lens through which the protagonist makes sense of what's happening in the moment and decides what she should do about it. Backstory is where the current meaning lies; without it, all you have are a bunch of surface things that happen.

So how do you get it onto the page so seamlessly that it facilitates your readers' experience rather than catapulting them out of the story with a big fat info dump? Here's how: You don't stop the story to give us info, nor do you have a character simply state what the reader should know. Instead you tap into a memory because something in the moment has triggered it in the protagonist—not randomly but because she's in a situation in which said memory has become relevant. She's thinking about it because she's grappling with something she can't avoid in the moment.

When you come out of the flashback, the protagonist (or POV character, if it's someone else) needs to draw a strategic conclusion—a realization—that in some way alters her plan of action or gives her a necessary insight into the situation at hand. Sometimes what the protagonist realizes is that she's been reading the meaning of the past wrong.

In a nutshell, the goal is to have the protagonist ferret out a bit of useful information from the memory—info that she then puts to use in the current situation. Remember: Backstory is only an "info dump" if it's done unartfully. Done right, backstory is what gives your novel the power to hack your reader's brain.

MIKE SWIFT: Lisa, your essay couldn't have crossed my eyes at a more appropriate time. My work-in-progress—my debut novel, which needs to be Martha Stewart perfect—relies heavily on backstory. An internal problem (my protagonist's lifetime of discourse with his father) escalates as he finds himself catapulted into moving back home, causing many external problems. Working through the external eventually helps him with his internal struggle, and he sees his father not as the unforgiving authoritarian he'd always known but as a misunderstood human being, full of the same fears and human frailties we all share.

Since the story begins in medias res, the circumstances that caused the move have already happened. I'm concerned that they may be too much. I have to reveal the death of my protagonist's pregnant wife and the subsequent loss of their child, the early relationship between father and son, and the reason the son has to move back home instead of living on his own—all while the two travel across the country—just to catch up to my in medias res point. Thank goodness it's a five-day trip! Any more backstory and they'd have to catch a slow boat to China.

Thus my question: How much is too much backstory? Yes, I have it creatively sprinkled throughout the manuscript via dialogue, flashbacks, and memories, but is there a point where I should simply move page 1— my in medias res—to an earlier point in the backstory? I really like where it starts, and to me it moves rather well—no dumps, a natural flow, compelling dialogue—and it seems to follow your advice above.

LISA CRON: As long as we have an idea of what the story will be about (that is, your protagonist's agenda) from the get-go, you can give us a hell of a lot of backstory. I was just looking over Donna Tartt's *The Secret History* again yesterday, and she gives us a glimpse of the novel's scope in a two-page prologue and the first couple of paragraphs, and then her protagonist, Richard, gives us a ton of backstory to get us up to speed. The difference between her method and an "info dump" is that she does it artfully, in service of the story she's telling. Or *Richard* does, because the novel is in the first person. He's giving us his backstory as he explains how they got to where the novel opens—his arrival at Hampden College. It's not just logistically *what* happened that got him there; it's *why* he ended up there, so we begin to understand what it means to him. Tartt then liberally sprinkles backstory throughout the novel, not in a "time out, let me explain this to you" way but because the past is what we all use as a decoder ring for the present.

So back to the question as it applies to your novel. You say, "I have to reveal the death of my protagonist's pregnant wife and the subsequent loss of their child, the early relationship between father and son, and the reason the son has to move back home instead of living on his own ..." Those things are huge—especially the death of his wife and child. Those events have already happened by the time he crosses the threshold onto page 1. And that means they are things he'd be thinking about all the time, and they'd color how he experiences everything else. Thus the truth is that you can't keep them off the page because to do so would imply either that they hadn't happened or that your protagonist wouldn't ever be thinking about them or be affected by them—i.e., he wouldn't be human. In other words, your protagonist's past history would be the lens through which he sees everything in the present. Snippets of it would constantly inform his thoughts. Ditto the early relationship between him and his dad—especially if he's moved back into his childhood house, which would hold memories at every turn. Memories that would shade how he feels now, what he'd think, and the meaning of which he'd struggle with. Memories that would probably shift in meaning given what he's learning about his dad as the novel progresses.

All of that gives you a ton of room for backstory—all in service of what he's going through now.

BARRY KNISTER: Christopher Isherwood wrote a group of stories about his Berlin experiences between the world wars (*The Berlin Stories*), which inspired a play called *I Am a Camera* by John Van Druten. The idea of the writer being a camera, a clear, unblemished piece of polished glass through which she sees reality and records it, is as nonsensical as thinking that fictional characters—or actual people we meet in life—come from nowhere. The writer isn't a camera. The writer is a prism, refracting what she sees and writes about according to her own experience.

It's the same with characters. They don't just "grow like Topsy." They enter the first page loaded with baggage. It makes me think of the most recent installment of *Better Call Saul*, a hit series about a con-artist younger brother who becomes a lawyer. The protagonist is loaded with backstory, but what most caught my eye this past Monday had to do with a secondary character. He's nebbish, a nerd who works in pharmaceuticals, and he has started selling drugs to actual drug dealers. He's a complete innocent, oblivious to how he's being played by others. The real drug dealers rob his house, including a collection of baseball cards. The character is so frantic about losing the cards that he risks everything by calling the police to help recover them. When his ex-cop friend asks him how he could be so foolish, he says, "Some of those cards belonged to my father."

Backstory, a whole big chunk of it, is captured in that detail.

"If you ignore your protagonist's past and begin envisioning your story on page 1, you're ... saying: 'I don't need to know what happened before this moment. ...'" That won't do. Writers are drawn to write *this* story instead of that one because of their own history. Their characters choose and act on the same basis.

LISA CRON: Well said, Barry. Everything we do is driven by our past history—because said history isn't really past. It's with us every minute of every day, guiding us, not secretly but concretely, in the moment, as we try to figure out what the hell to do (or what story to write). Sometimes it's implicit, but more often than not, it's explicit.

And I loved that moment in *Better Call Saul*, too—it was probably the most meaningful and most honest thing that character said. It was a moment of pathos, a moment that humanized him. And yes, it suggested *so* much in terms of his past.

TONIA HARRIS: You had me at "When does your story start?" I worked on this question for months and thought I knew my protagonist's misconception. I knew there was an instance in her childhood when her father made her watch him drown sick kittens. ("When a thing's sickly and weak, you best put them out of their misery. Life's a rotten chore for the strongest of us. We have no time for what can't fend for itself.")

I don't think I knew until now what this meant to her and how this influenced her life and strongly affects the story. It taught her a misconception I recognize because I've lived it most of my life: You must be strong through anything and everything, or you have no worth. What she wants most is to be considered worthy, no matter her faults or weaknesses.

You speak of specifics, though. Is wanting to feel valued too general a motivator to keep a reader interested beyond the plot?

LISA CRON: I love your question, Tonia, and the answer is yes and no. Here's the thing: You only have the first layer there, the general. And in truth that's the only place to start, so it's a major plus. But now you have to dig down to the specifics because the question is: What do you mean by feeling "valued"? What would have to happen for her to feel valued? We need a glimpse of that from the get-go. If her misbelief is that you have to be strong or show no weakness to be worthy, then what is it costing her to *be* strong? What does she see as weakness, meaning: What is she afraid to show the world that will make her seem weak and thus unworthy?

Chances are this "weakness" is really her strength, and that's what she needs to learn to tap into.

The backstory you're looking for is story specific, and you can find it by digging into her misbelief and asking, "Why? What happened, exactly? What did she believe before it happened, and how did it shift her worldview?" Give us the defining moment when her misbelief took root by putting us in her skin as she experiences it.

The misbelief is something the protagonist is grateful for; it's saved her from a very difficult situation and helped her see the world as it really is, and she feels lucky to have that info. That's why she let it guide her from then on out. Once you've nailed down that scene, try to trace the trajectory of that misbelief through your protagonist's life via turning-point moments—usually when she stood at a crossroads and had to make a difficult, life-changing decision driven by her misbelief. Those moments often support the misbelief and make her even more certain of its truth. In terms of your protagonist, here's where she may think, *Yes, it's only strength that makes us worthy, and showing any weakness (e.g., vulnerability) signals unworthiness and possibly a moral failing as well.*

The story is in the specifics (scenes), and the meaning your protagonist attaches to what happens always comes from her past.

 PRO TIP

Think about the emotional milestones in your life, and then look to your characters. Do you know how they'll react to similar moments in their lives? You should, because the answers to those questions shape our entire worldview and how we interact with everything around us, and will therefore play a large part in shaping the story you are trying to tell.

—ROBIN LAFEVERS

 HOW TO GET IN YOUR OWN WAY, METHOD 6: FRONT-LOAD THE BACKSTORY

Backstory is important, but you have a whole book to explore it. Remember that date you went on where he told you about his crazy ex and how he lived in his car for a week? That's your book when you cram all your characterization and worldbuilding into the first few pages.

—BILL FERRIS

PLOT IT, OR PANTS IT?

Not All Those Who Wander-Write Are Lost …

RAY RHAMEY

Do you "write by the seat of your pants"? Do you create your narrative organically, intuitively? If you aren't sure, here's a terrific definition of a *pantser* from blogger Paul Liadis:

> **pantser** [pant-ser]
>
> –noun
>
> 1. One who writes a novel by the seat of their pants, without an outline, character sheets, or any semblance of planning.
>
> 2. Crazy person.
>
> **See also:** intelligent, witty, and downright sexy.

So what are the hallmarks—or, perhaps, symptoms—that distinguish a pantser from a plotter? How does a pantser write differently from an architectural writer who builds a complete framework before tackling the creation of the novel itself?

1. YOU DON'T OUTLINE OR PLOT AHEAD. You've been known to think, *If I do, then I know what happens and all the fun is gone. Why bother writing it if you already know what happens?* Moreover, the surprises of discovery you encounter when you write are the same ones your readers will feel as they read.

2. **YOUR CHARACTERS SOMETIMES ARRIVE UNANNOUNCED, AND THEY SHAPE THEMSELVES.** You discover who they are as they do what they do on your pages.

3. **YOUR CHARACTERS HAVE THE POWER TO TAKE YOUR STORY IN A DIRECTION YOU DIDN'T FORESEE OR IMAGINE.** You often follow rather than lead. A "disposable" character in the opening of one of my novels, who served as cannon fodder to help characterize the hero, followed the protagonist after their encounter. She became the second-most-important character in the story and has a huge impact on what happens in the novel.

4. **WHAT HAPPENS—THAT IS, PLOT—GROWS ORGANICALLY FROM YOUR CHARACTERS' DECISIONS.** These choices deal with conflict and fulfill their desires, which you then see and transcribe.

5. **YOU WRITE—AND SOMETIMES DON'T WRITE—BY "FEEL."** Certainly all artists make decisions on what *feels* right, but a plotter's methods and reasons for doing so are much different than a pantser's. A plotter might decide a particular plot twist feels right at a certain point, while a pantser might decide whether what a character wants to do feels right.

If you enjoy these same hallmarks in your writing, welcome to the pantser tribe.

MEET YOUR WRITERLY KINFOLK

A number of best-selling writers, both past and present, have managed quite well by pantsing.

ELMORE LEONARD

Leonard once said, "I don't put a lot of time in on my plots. I like to make it up as I go along. No outline at all." Yep, he was a pantser, all right. Did it for thirty years, intuiting his way to more than forty published novels. Leonard described his process this way:

> You'll meet practically everybody who is going to be in the book in the first one hundred pages. And then, for the second act, I have to do a little figuring about fitting in a subplot and what's going to happen next. In the third act, which I usually get to in my manuscript around page 300—my books are mostly 350 pages or so—I think of the ending.

TESS GERRITSEN

Best-selling thriller author Tess Gerritsen says her characters rise up organically. Detective Rizzoli was going to be killed off the first time she appeared, but she survived and became half of the famous duo Rizzoli and Isles. Tess has stayed with those characters because, as she says, "I want to know what's happening in their lives." Note that she *doesn't* say she wants to *tell us* what's happening; she wants to learn for herself. She says her writing process is "completely chaotic."

> I start off with an idea that really excites me, something that I've picked up from newspapers or a conversation, and then I just want to see where that goes. I don't plot out books ahead of time, I just follow this kind of blind path. Sometimes I don't know the villain until the last couple of chapters.

STEPHEN KING

One of the things pantsing can do is relieve the anxiety that can come with facing the Brobdingnagian undertaking of writing "a novel," because you only deal with writing a page or a scene, which are much smaller tasks nowhere near as off-putting as an entire book. King writes massive novels—*Under the Dome* is 1,072 pages, more than 336,000 words—but he doesn't have to deal with holding the whole gargantuan story in his mind. As he says:

> I lean more heavily on intuition … because my books tend to be based on situation rather than story. … I distrust plot for two reasons: first, because our lives are largely plotless, even when you add in all our reasonable precautions and careful planning; and second, because I believe plotting and the spontaneity of real creation aren't compatible.

J.R.R. TOLKIEN

It appears that even Tolkien, the master of immense fantasy, was at least a partial pantser. In his foreword to *The Fellowship of the Ring*, Tolkien wrote, "This tale grew in the telling …" He later clarified, "As the story grew it put down roots (into the past) and threw out unexpected branches: but its main theme was settled from the outset … ."

As I pursue a character's story, the past that motivates what happens also becomes "known" to me. On the unexpected entrance of a character in a story, Tolkien also reported: "A new character has come on the scene (I am sure I did not invent him, I did not even want him, but there he came walking through the woods of Ithilien): Faramir, the brother of Boromir."

If you're a pantser, you're in great company.

LISTEN TO YOUR INTUITION

Do pantsers struggle when they take on the monstrous task of writing 80,000 to 100,000 words (or even more) without an outline? Without a plan? Actually, no, they're probably enjoying the journey because they've learned how to conquer the challenges of pantsing.

MAKING FALSE STARTS

Elmore Leonard once told readers at a bookstore that after drafting one hundred pages or so, he would revisit what he'd written and sometimes decide that a minor character was more interesting than he had imagined and should be the protagonist.

I started one of my novels three times with a male protagonist in the lead, and the story just petered out. After setting it on a back shelf for a while, I realized that the story actually belonged to a different character, a woman. When I switched to her point of view, it took off. The false starts were more like trial runs that eventually led to the best path forward.

SELF-EDITING

As you might guess, organic writers put a lot of stuff on the page during the process of discovery that might not belong in the story. The pantser's first draft requires plenty of editing and rewriting.

Here's a word of advice from Steven James, author of *Story Trumps Structure*, that I follow in my editing and writing: "If it's in the story, it must matter. If it doesn't matter, delete it." (Steven shares more advice in his essay "Letting Go of the Reins" in Part Five.)

Wise words for any writer, whether pantser or plotter. But sometimes the difficulty is in seeing what actually matters. Many writers get their keyboards slapped for all the backstory they include in the openings of their novels. They argue that "the reader needs to know that." Not necessarily so. The way to judge what matters is to see how it affects the story. If taking it out doesn't change the story, well, your keyboard has a handy *delete* key, right?

GETTING STUCK

Organic writers sometimes follow a story's trail into a blind alley. Or perhaps it's not actually blind—it's that the writer just can't see what happens next. In my writing, I've learned to relax and just step away for hours or days—whatever it takes—and let my "back burner" discover what the story's future holds.

But if your back burner seems truly stymied, James offers two questions you can ask of your story that I've found very useful in my own pantsing:

1. What can go wrong?
2. How can things get worse?

When a story confronts a character with the answers to those questions, she reacts and does things that lead to more things going wrong and getting worse. Since those events stem from the character, they are natural, organic evolutions of the story.

KEEPING DETAILS STRAIGHT

Organic writers, hounding after the scent of a character, may become so wrapped up in the hunt that they lose track of what other characters are doing. That might not matter so much in a first-person narrative, but losing track of characters can have an impact in a third-person story with more than one point-of-view character.

So keep a record of what's happened so far, to whom it happened, and where it happened in the story time line. I've found it helpful to create a table in Word or Excel with column headings such as *Chapter*, *POV Character*, *Action*, and *Other Characters*. After you write a chapter, record who, what, when, and where. The *POV Character* column will clue you if you've neglected a character for too long. The *Action* column will be a handy reference for what motivates action in the future—and for where you need to go back and change things in order to set up an unexpected twist later in the story.

DO WHAT WORKS FOR YOU

There is no right way to write a novel. A writer who outlines the plot of his narrative first may actually be the envy of a pantser who knows she faces a serious editing task because of the potential side trips that might pop up during her wander. As a pantser, I hope that plotters also feel a sense of discovery when they build the storyline.

When I read a novel, I can't usually tell if the author was a plotter or a pantser, and, frankly, I don't give a damn. Just give me a good read!

PLOT IT, OR PANTS IT?

Some Who Wander-Write Are Most Definitely Lost

ANNE GREENWOOD BROWN

I am a fast writer. I have to be. With a full-time job, three teenage children, and multiple editors' deadlines, crunch time is all the time. Therefore, I make use of every available minute, sometimes even pulling out my laptop during the intermission at a choir concert. But for me, that precious time would be wasted if I merely dabbled in experimental fits and starts without any real plan as to where my story was going. I have all the respect in the world for pantsers, but I simply can't afford to be one.

A few years ago, I wrote an article for Writer Unboxed called "Paying It Forward." I think it's important for writers to share their personal tricks of the trade. Some will work for you, and some will not. If you're time-crunched like I am, you may appreciate the tricks I use for preparing myself well enough *in advance of writing* so that I can work efficiently through a first draft and get more quickly to the hard work of revision.

DECIDE WHAT THE GOAL IS AND WHO WANTS TO ACHIEVE IT

Central to every good story is a character with a goal and something that stands in his or her way. Charlotte wants to save Wilbur's life, but her own short lifespan is working against her. A boy named Harry wants to save his friends from the powers of dark magic, but he'll have to give up his own life to triumph over evil. This is not to say that every good story has to be a matter of life and death. In *Fried Green Tomatoes at the Whistle Stop Cafe*, Evelyn Couch wants to improve the richness of her life, but her lack of self-confidence stands in her way.

The point is that both the character and the goal have to be compelling (which is not necessarily synonymous with *likable* and *relatable*). Making this who/what decision is the first step in my outline process.

CREATE YOUR OUTLINE

Next, I use a six-part outline, which I define in these broad terms: *Introduction, Rising Action, Progress, Raising the Stakes, Final Push,* and *Dénouement*. For each of these six sections, I outline the action in a fair amount of detail, essentially asking myself what needs to happen to get from Point A to Point B and *why* the main character would make those choices.

In this outline, I also make notes about character development, foreshadowing, symbols, mood, and so on. The outline for a young adult (YA) novel might look something like this (very abbreviated) example:

A. **Introduction**, *wherein the protagonist and his or her current situation are introduced.*
   1. Meet Angelina, a country girl whose family operates a small organic farm.
      a. She has long dark hair, gray eyes, and is taller than most kids her age (including most of the boys), which makes her self-conscious.
      b. Her father tends the dairy cows; she is assigned to the chicken coop.
   2. Angelina has a paralyzing fear of the spotlight, public speaking, and pretty much everything that puts her on display.
      a. **Backstory:** Her mother entered her in a 4-H speech contest when she was twelve years old, and she passed out, chipping her tooth on the podium and cutting her lip, which has left a scar (something more to worry about).
      b. The irony that she tends the chickens is not lost on her.
   3. **Goal:** Angelina wants to buy a new car so she can get to the city more often. She can't wait to graduate, attend college in Minneapolis, leave farm life behind, and pursue a career in the arts. **Obstacle:** She's too busy with her farm responsibilities to get a job; she has no money.
      a. **Backstory:** She has been self-conscious about farm life since middle school, when someone commented that she smelled like a barn—and not in the warm, soft hayloft kind of way.

B. **Rising Action**, *wherein the protagonist faces a change of plans.*

1. Angelina is given an opportunity to earn a large cash prize when a calf of unusual size is born on the farm; her father suggests she raise him and enter him in the county fair. If she wins, she'll have enough to afford a car—not a new car but *a* car. *Her* car.

   a. Still, Angelina is unsure about entering the competition because it would require her to lead the calf into a large arena in front of not only a panel of judges but also the entire farming community.

2. She creates a plan to get over her anxiety by slowly acclimating herself to the spotlight.

   a. First, she volunteers to read the school announcements over the loudspeaker.

      1. While she makes herself sick in the process, she also inadvertently makes a few nervous jokes that get the attention of Josiah, who lives in Center City.

      2. [At this point I'd add more examples to my outline, pulling in her future plans to pursue a career in the arts.]

      3. She raises the calf: caring for him, feeding him from a bottle, brushing him, etc.

      4. Josiah asks to do homework with her after school. She agrees, but she doesn't want him to come to the farm—she thinks he'll look down on her country lifestyle.

C. **Progress**, *wherein the protagonist works toward her goal and things go well.*

1. Angelina volunteers for an onstage demonstration at the school assembly; her body shakes through the whole thing, but she doesn't pass out.

2. She goes on a date with Josiah in a public place.

   a. She catches some negative attention from other kids who think she and Josiah are poorly matched. (Do they really think that, or is she merely transferring her own anxiety onto them?)

3. First. Kiss. Ever. Woo-hoo!

D. **Raising Stakes**, *wherein things go awry, conflict sets in, and all seems lost.*

1. The calf gets sick while Angelina's on a date with Josiah.

2. Tortured by guilt, she stays up all night nursing the calf back to health.

3. Some boys start calling her "cow girl" and generally making fun.

   a. She sees Josiah at the back of the pack and thinks he's in on it, too.

4. Heartbroken and betrayed, she won't answer Josiah's calls.

E. **Final Push**, *wherein the protagonist puts it all on the line, faces the climax, and reaches the goal.*

1. She shows the calf at the county fair and wins the cash pot.

F. **Dénouement**, *wherein the protagonist lives "happily ever after" or at least something close.*

    1. Angelina buys herself a car and reunites with Josiah.

My actual outline would be even more detailed, but this is a fair approximation. The beauty of a detailed outline is that I rarely suffer from the dreaded writer's block. Because I know where the story is going, I can jump around within the outline, writing whatever part I'm in the mood to write on that particular day.

However, as important as this detailed outline is for me, it naturally comes with one significant hazard. Once I'm done with the outline and I have imagined the story in such intricate detail, it often feels redundant and overly burdensome to write the whole story out! This is when I envy the pantsers' daily surprise and the euphoria of "discovering" where the story has led them.

But then I get over it and get back to business.

ESTABLISH YOUR PACING

Every genre has an average or typical word count, which is generally dictated by book publishers and literary agents. For the sake of this essay, let's assume that middle-grade novels average 45,000 words, young adult runs about 75,000 words, commercial fiction clocks in at about 90,000 words, and fantasy can sometimes exceed 120,000 words.

Because I write YA, I use the 75,000-word guideline and apply these percentages to the sections I previously outlined:[1]

A. Introduction: 10 percent of the total word count (7,500 words)

B. Rising Action: 15 percent (11,250 words)

C. Progress: 25 percent (18,750 words)

D. Raising the Stakes: 25 percent (18,750 words)

E. Final Push: 20 percent (15,000 words)

F. Dénouement: 5 percent (3,750 words)

Does this seem rigid? It is. I don't stick to these exact numbers, but I try to get as close as I can. I do this because paying attention to this formula provides excellent pacing, and poor pacing is one of the biggest reasons an agent or editor will reject a manuscript. Even if the final draft of my story is longer than the average YA novel, the story will have grown within this well-paced framework.

Scrivener has been a helpful tool in this regard. If you've never heard of it, it's a word processing and project management software created specifically

---

1 I base these word count guidelines on my modified version of script consultant Michael Hauge's pacing recommendations for screenwriters. (See more at bit.ly/1DTzVoO.)

for writers of longer texts such as novels, screenplays, and research papers. One of the tabs on Scrivener's toolbar allows you to set a target word count for the whole manuscript, as well as for each plot section. Using this tool allows me to keep my pacing on track.

So that's my method for outlining a first draft. Some of you will love it. Others will hate it. Both reactions are fine by me. One thing I've learned from hanging out with other writers is that there is no one right way for everybody. What we all must do, however, is find those tools that allow our words to shine. So shine on!

 ## A CONVERSATION BETWEEN A PLOTTER AND A PANTSER

ANNE: Obviously pantsing works for you, Ray. Did you come to that through trial and error, or was it a natural fit?

RAY: It's a natural approach for me, perhaps because of my many years in advertising prior to tackling novels. A print ad concept or a television commercial script is so short that coming up with an idea from scratch is natural and easy. You just go with the flow. Because they're so brief, discarding a lot of notions is no big deal. What about outlining for you?

ANNE: I definitely came to it through trial and error. I'd always outlined academic papers and legal briefs for work, but when I was starting out in fiction, it weirdly never occurred to me to outline a creative project. As a result, I'd always get these fantastically beautiful opening scenes and then sit back and go, *Uh … now what?* Lots of false starts. It wasn't until I worked out the story in advance that I ever got anywhere toward finishing something.

RAY: I admire all writers who can finish a novel; it's such a giant task. I've gotten to a point where I can complete a first draft in fewer than six months. I pantsed my novel, *The Vampire Kitty-cat Chronicles*, by writing just one morning a week. It took fifty-three weeks, but that was only fifty-three days of actual writing, so more like two months total.

ANNE: Wow, to me, it's amazing that you can do that without an outline. The quickest first draft—and I'm truly talking first draft—I did was for *Girl Last Seen*, and that was because I had a co-author. We wrote the first draft in five weeks. On my own it's about two months of daily writing to get to a first draft. And then, of course, several more months for editing and revision. Do your first drafts typically include false starts?

RAY: I do encounter false starts, but they are never frustrating, just part of the process. For my novel *Hiding Magic*, I started it three times with a male protagonist, but it just wouldn't come alive. Then I realized that it was the female protagonist's story, and it immediately took off when I slipped into her point of view. Have you ever found that a character has led you away from your original plan, plot-wise? I would think that once you've committed so much time to your outline, you'd resist change.

ANNE: I haven't had a character lead me away from my plot outline, per se, but as I get to know the characters better, sometimes their motivations change. So while they may end up doing the same thing, my explanation for why they choose to do it sometimes changes.

RAY: Right. So much of that comes from the character's backstory. Do you work out a complete backstory for your main character prior to writing a novel?

ANNE: Not a complete backstory. I have an idea as to what kind of family he comes from, as well as his biggest fear and where it comes from. Then, as I get to know my character better through the writing process—his dialogue in particular—I go back and fill in some of the finer details. For example, I may start out knowing that a character is desperate to belong because she was abandoned as a child, but it may not be until further down the road that I realize why that abandonment happened. How about you? What kind of backstory work do you do?

RAY: Most of my backstory evolves as I go, although in the run-up to starting a novel, I will write pages of notes that may include bits of backstory—but those early notes often go by the wayside when I discover what *really* happened. I start with a character's *nowstory*—what she does, what her situation is. As I need it, her history seems ready for me to tap into when I think about what is motivating her. The one thing I try to have up front is a character's "ghost," an event in his past that haunts him, affects what he does, and can lead to inner conflict.

In one of my novels, Jewel, a woman who was a disposable character used as a prop to set up the protagonist's abilities, decided to take a much bigger role in the story and eventually became second only to the protagonist in determining what happened. I started with her buying a drug for her addicted brother. That was all I knew at the time. Then, in a bit of internal monologue where she thinks of what her mother said about being tough, I immediately knew that her mother was dead. I then discovered the character had raised her little brother after their mother had been killed in a mugging eleven years before. That backstory just bubbled up when I thought about the character as she took part in the story.

At the 2014 Writer Unboxed UnConference (writerunboxed.com/ un-conference), author Meg Rosoff talked about writers having a more direct connection between the conscious and unconscious minds. I believe that's what works for me and other pantsers—my conscious pantsing taps the unconscious part of my mind and finds backstory elements somehow ready and waiting.

ANNE: That gets us back to your earlier question about whether, as a plotter, I resist changing my original plans. I think that question raises a valid point. While I hope that I've thought my story through enough at the beginning to make changes unnecessary, I would never resist a change that will clearly make the story better.

RAY: What's an example of your plan not working out?

ANNE: Well … my first published book (*Lies Beneath*) was sold with one ending, but when a film agent got on board, he suggested that I rewrite the ending because it would never work onscreen. Specifically, he said I had to have my hero and villain in the pivotal scene together—rather than miles apart as I had written it. Even though the likelihood of a movie is very slim, I changed course because I could see that his suggestion boosted the conflict. I took that lesson to heart and have applied it to my subsequent novels.

RAY: I think that whether you're a plotter or a pantser, a professional is willing to develop and improve on the things that work and is willing to try new techniques before discarding them outright.

 **PRO TIP**

I worked on *Blackbirds* for about five years but never really finished it. I never could—the story wandered like a person lost at the mall. When the time came that I finally learned outlining—a skill taught through a screenwriting mentorship—I knew I had to scrap everything and start over. Outlining was the governing principle. I had to learn how to think about the story from start to finish, not just wander through it. I am a pantser by heart but a plotter by necessity.

—CHUCK WENDIG, AUTHOR OF *BLACKBIRDS*

WRITE LIKE YOU MEAN IT

How to Maximize Your Minutes

BARBARA O'NEAL

I am a prolific writer. Over my twenty-plus-year career, I've written nearly sixty novels, many novellas, and hundreds of blog posts, articles, and short pieces. I continue to write at least one novel per year, sometimes more. The longest it takes me to draft a novel is six months, and I've done it in six weeks.

Some of you might be thinking, *Ah, you churn 'em out, don't you?*

Do you wonder where that thinking comes from? Before I share my tips on how to write faster, let's get a couple of things out of the way.

BEAT BACK THE BELIEF IN THE "WRITER AS TORTURED ARTIST"

Regarding fast writing, two mythologies are in play here.

The first is that good writing must take years and years of suffering, despair, and all manner of angst and struggle to produce something worth reading. As George Orwell put it, "Writing a book is a horrible, exhausting struggle, like a long bout of some painful illness. One would never undertake such a thing if one were not driven on by some demon whom one can neither resist nor understand."

The second is that writing fast is "churning it out," without regard for quality, as if writers can work only at one speed—slowly.

If writing is as torturous as Orwell claimed, why in the world would you do it? Find something that suits you better. Yes, writing is demanding. It requires intense focus. It is challenging. It is also heady. Exciting. Rewarding—maybe one of the most rewarding undertakings any of us will engage in.

If I don't buy into the "tortured soul" mythology, I'm free to love writing with the passion such an artistic pursuit deserves. I'm free to follow the words where they lead. I can write as fast as the wind.

The idea of the long-suffering artist is part of our cultural heritage. We hold a vision in our minds of the writer or painter or composer engaged in the process late at night, hands in hair, sweating (and probably drinking) to give birth to some Great Work of Art.

While some writers take years to craft a novel, that's hardly true of all of them. One of the most literary living American writers, Joyce Carol Oates, has written more than fifty novels and a vast number of essays and short stories during her career. One of my favorite writers, the celebrated M.F.K. Fisher, wrote hundreds of thousands of words over her lifetime. She was often desperate for money and wrote to get it. This does not appear to have ruined her voice, as she is one of the most revered food writers of all time.

Professional writers write. Some write faster than others, but the pace of the writing does *not* determine quality.

How can you learn to write faster or build on whatever speed you now have to produce more work? Time, preparation, practice, and record keeping provide the cornerstones of writing more quickly.

CARVE OUT TIME

If you wanted to train for a marathon, you would not just run whenever you were struck by the mood to do so. You would set up a training schedule and stick to it religiously. You would arrange your life to support that training.

The first step toward writing faster is to find the time for it. That may sound like an obvious idea, but you'd be surprised how often writers fail to plan their writing hours. Just as a runner must have regular hours on the trail, a writer needs regular time at the keyboard. Where will you find your time?

The best time is, of course, during your freshest hours. If you can commit even a half hour a day during your most creative period, you'll reap ample rewards. Often, however, those hours are claimed by a day job or family demands. In that case, find whatever hour you can and commit to it. If you are going to write, you're going to have to, well, write. Claim the hour after dinner before you have a beer or your lunch hour twice a week, or plan to get up an hour earlier to write undisturbed. You might have to give up something, at which point you will have to decide what is most important.

Once you make the time commitment, make it consistent. Nothing piles up pages faster than sitting down at regular times.

PREPARE BEFORE YOU WRITE

Luckily I learned to write before anyone told me it should take a long time or that I should suffer for it. From the age of twelve, I gleefully wrote novels in spiral notebooks whenever I could, lying in the sun or scribbling covertly during class. It was a joy. Why wouldn't I spend all my time on it?

But when I went to college, the anxiety of knowing my work would be read in the campus newspaper gave me pause. For several months, I wrote like that tortured artist, tearing out my hair, locked in fear. Thankfully I was a journalism student who was forced by deadlines and finals to sometimes write a big story in as little as a half hour. Or in the middle of the night. Or as we were preparing to send the paper to the printer.

Quite to my astonishment, I learned that if I had my facts—the interviews, the information—a story I wrote in twenty minutes at 3:00 A.M. carried almost exactly the same cadence and voice as something I carefully crafted over several days. It was a mind-blowing revelation, but after four years, I learned to trust it.

Planning and plotting are the plain, unsexy sisters of the writing process, the prim-mouthed women who clean up after the drunken artist. But these two sisters make the actual process of writing pages much easier and faster.

Virtually all writing requires some research. To write fast, get your research done ahead of time and keep your materials at hand as you work.

The next step is plotting. Writers who fly by the seat of their pants—pantsers—and writers who like to plan ahead—plotters—have long been at odds about the best way to write (as you've seen from the duo of essays from Ray Rhamey and Anne Greenwood Brown). Pantsers claim their process is wrecked if they have to tell the story before they write it, and I will address that problem in a moment. For now, let's assume everyone is a plotter.

Take the time to plot your story before you begin to write. Many, many books have been written to help you find a plotting style. Sample them until you find one you like. Personally, I need to have four or five things in place: the characters, the situation and problem, about five to ten scenes that reveal something important ("Tallulah finds out her mother has been lying all her life"), a general idea of the book's ending, and a solid opening, even if I end up changing it.

Does such a spare style really count as plotting? Yes. While it may not reveal every plot point or every scene, it offers enough at the beginning of the drafting process. This is very like the pencil sketch an artist makes before starting to paint—it's a guideline, a method to understand the space and balance in a piece.

An outline helps prevent time-consuming mistakes, like discovering your plot has no conflict or that your book is only a series of episodes, not a cohesive story with a beginning, a middle, and an end.

Don't plan *too* much, however. I have learned that I can plan as much as I like, but the story happens when I am actually writing, when I've let go of all the mannerisms, plots, and tricks, and played the final round of solitaire and turned off the Internet to allow the story to emerge.

This method often allows me to spend less time revising after I have finished my rough draft. Employing an outline and then spending time each day to edit and rewrite the previous day's work stabilizes the structure and aligns the characters, allowing me to focus on smoothing clunky language and finding places to add beauty or underline metaphor. You may find the same to be true, but perhaps you will need to revise a lot. That's fine. By creating a finished draft, you have something to work with. As the famous Nora Roberts is fond of saying, "I can't fix a blank page."

Pantsers, this is where the process will work for you. Write your first draft as if it is the outline, and then go through the revision process by imposing the structure on the material. Go for it, and be willing to rewrite and restructure as much as you like.

KEEP TRACK

If you don't know when you write your best work, take a page from Rachel Aaron, a young science fiction writer who landed a contract for a series of books when she was pregnant. Facing deadlines and the responsibilities of caring for an infant made her a master of her own patterns. For months, she kept track of when she started writing, when she stopped, how many words she wrote during that time, and anything else that might have influenced her, such as writing at a coffee shop while a babysitter took care of her child.

A few years ago, I realized I'd grown lax. I wanted to see if I could speed up my writing, so I used Aaron's method to record my writing times. I discovered that I was right about my best hours: They are first thing in the morning, before anyone else gets up. But I had also thought that writing was a loss after lunch. Not so, my friends. In fact, I'd often produce more words in the early afternoon than I did in the first session of the day.

Only you can know your patterns and make adjustments accordingly. Try keeping track over a couple of months, and see if you can improve anything. There are many apps for doing this, but you can also create a simple spreadsheet and monitor yourself that way. Be sure whatever method you use allows you to note times and patterns.

SET THE MOOD TO FIND YOUR WAY IN

Give yourself permission to find a way into the story each time you sit down. The beginnings are usually the slowest—I give myself several weeks to write at a pace that's less than a quarter of the speed I'll write at for the rest of the book, say, 500 words a day. As I discover the world I'm creating, I try to remember what Hemingway said: "Find one true sentence, and write that."

Later, as the story gathers momentum, you still must reenter the story world each day. I start by reading the work from the day before, making tweaks and aligning ideas, finding better words—lightly editing, not diving into big changes. Usually by the time I finish the exercise, I'm aware of what I want to do that day.

Here is where another of Rachel Aaron's suggestions comes into play: Before writing the new scenes, write down a few things you want to happen during this particular writing session. She writes down beats for the whole scene, whereas I simply scrawl a few ideas about where I want to end up. Do whatever works.

LEAVE THE WORLD OUTSIDE

During this drafting process, it's absolutely crucial to make everyone and everything wait outside the office door (or wherever you write). Do not think about your teacher, your critique partners, your husband or family, your friends, or the desire to trounce everyone with your literary genius.

Your only goal is to open the window into the other world you've created and let yourself look through it, then step through and become a part of it. Allow your fingers to simply interpret what you see and hear. You want to create *flow*, that immersive, trancelike state where time passes quickly and you emerge at the other end with a sense of having been far away.

For that reason, once you begin drafting, *do not use the Internet*. Do not check e-mail. Do not search for a fact you think you need—just write "TK" (which stands for "to come"), and return to it later. Writers have argued with me over this—but the bottom line is, if you break, you end the trance. You hurtle back to the real world, the window slams shut, and the story world has to be entered, painstakingly, again.

Give your story respect by letting it enchant you. Leave *this* world alone. If, like me, you are weak about the Internet (as writers tend to be—was there ever a medium so thoroughly suited to our brains?), try using an app to lock yourself out. I use Freedom; there are many others.

EMBRACE YOUR OWN SPEED

Perhaps some of these ideas will help you write a little—or a lot—faster over time. In the long run, however, it isn't speed that matters. It is the pace at which you can write your best work that counts.

 PRO TIP

If you have a hard time working in a distraction-free zone, consider purchasing a pair of noise-cancelling headphones and listening to white noise or classical music. It works.

 HOW TO GET IN YOUR OWN WAY, METHOD 7: BEAT YOURSELF UP

Writing takes self-discipline, but self-discipline doesn't equal being a self-jerk. Calling yourself a lazy failure won't boost your word count, but it might inspire you to comfort-eat lots of cake.

—BILL FERRIS

FAT OR LEAN?

Consider Your Approach to Drafting, and Refine Your Process

ANNA ELLIOTT

We've all heard the children's nursery rhyme about Jack Sprat and his wife—how Jack could eat no fat, while his wife could eat no lean. This couple reminds me of my close friend and writing partner, Sarah, and me. She writes very lean first drafts of her novels. I, on the other hand, like to stuff my first drafts to nearly the point of bursting. Our approaches are as different as can be, but we've both produced multiple published novels—more than thirty between us. Each strategy has its unique benefits and challenges, and neither is better than the other. It's simply a matter of deciding which approach works best for you and your story.

WRITE IT SLENDER

I asked Sarah to tell me a bit more about her process and why it works for her. She shared the following insights:

> The way I write, my first goal is to get the plot down because that's the skeleton of the story. I write that first; it's usually between 40,000 and 50,000 words. I focus on getting the basics of my story down on paper rather than making every single sentence, line of dialogue, or description perfect. I don't edit as I go, so the first draft is rough—typos abound because I'm typing almost as fast as I can. And although all the story elements are present in terms of dialogue and plot twists and other major events, I keep the detail to a bare minimum. I set down just enough to let me get a true sense of the story I'm trying to tell. Then when the basic outline is in place, I go back to the beginning and work

all the way through the draft, doubling the story in size with all the other elements that make a novel: character details, emotion, description, and so on. Truthfully, every single sentence will be rewritten by the time I'm done with the final editing stage.

This method works for me because I don't do a detailed outline. For me, the best part of writing a novel is the process of discovery that a slender first draft entails.

Is the lean-draft method right for you? If you're currently refining your writing process (and most of us usually are; I definitely am, even after multiple books published), try it on for size. Choose a portion of your novel-in-progress, be it a chapter or a scene. Once you've started writing, don't backtrack or stop to edit. Weak sentences can always be strengthened, and flat dialogue can be polished to a brilliant sheen—later. For now, establish the basics: who says what to whom and the major action that takes place. If you're a fan of Anne Lamott's philosophy about "shitty first drafts," now may be the perfect time to bring that mentality to your own work. Just *write it down*.

Did you find that exercise helpful? Did you feel like a paleontologist, uncovering and assembling the bare bones of your book—bones that will later be covered with the muscle and skin of a living, breathing story?

WRITE IT FAT

If the lean-draft method is like paleontology, then I would compare the "write it fat" method to sculpting marble—except that first I have to *produce* the block of marble from which my novel will ultimately be chiseled. My first draft is that huge, unwieldy, solid-stone block. And my favorite part of novel writing is exactly the same as Sarah's: the process of discovery. But instead of writing a sparse draft, I've found I work best if I sink deeply into each scene and describe every detail, emotional response, and movement. I find that writing a fat (some might even say flabby) first draft helps me fully understand my characters and their emotional arcs.

I make a quick one- to four-sentence outline of what's going to happen in the scene before I start writing; this game plan helps me avoid getting bogged down in details. Then I try to fully immerse myself in the scene.

I cut and trim at the editing stage. That part of the process is like chiseling the sculpture from the stone block; your floor becomes covered with the chips of marble that you've hacked away. But I don't mind the mess. Trimming doesn't have to be painful; it can be like cutting your hair when it's driving you crazy.

I often save those chips in a separate file, and I sometimes find a use for them in another book.

Is the fat-draft method more your style? To find out, try imagining a whole scene or chapter as a movie playing on the screen of your mind. What do you see? What do you hear? What expressions move across your characters' faces as they speak and act? Write it all down! Don't worry about whether it's needed; you can make that call later. You may write down five descriptive details and later decide that the first four are irrelevant and that only one is story worthy. But in my experience, you'd never have uncovered that one golden detail without going through the process of discovery.

EXPERIMENT WITH YOUR UNION TO PROCESS

I firmly believe that there are as many ways to write a novel as there are novelists in the world. Indeed, I've often found that the "best" method varies depending on the story. What worked for your last book may have your current manuscript tied in knots. So if you've always been a lean-draft devotee but find yourself struggling to pin down the heart of your novel-in-progress, try a fat draft. Conversely, if your current manuscript feels bloated and unwieldy, try writing lean. And don't commit to one method and exclude the other if you think a change might help.

Jack Sprat and his wife were married, after all.

FIND THE MUSE WITHIN THE STORY

How to Recognize and Search Beyond Ordinary Inspirations

DAVE KING

Writing is hard. If you don't have something driving you to keep going, some dream that will get you through your fifth revision or past the writer's block that sets in after chapter eight, you won't make it. You need a muse.

But there's a danger in picking the wrong one. Some muses will lead you happily through your final draft, only to abandon you with a novel in a drawer that you never look at again. After being worked over by one of these false muses, you may get so discouraged that you take up another hobby. Which would be a shame because being a writer is a wonderfully fulfilling way to spend your life.

No, if your true calling is writing, you have to find your inspiration in the right place: your story.

RECOGNIZE THE FALSE MUSES

A number of muses will call to you with their siren song. Here's how to recognize and avoid them.

MONEY

I know clients who got into writing for the money. Some of them dream of making it big, with royalty checks and movie deals pouring in. Less delusional clients simply want to know if their novel will make enough money to be worth the investment of having it edited. I tell them all the same thing: It's possible to make a living as a writer, but there are a lot of easier and more reliable ways to do it.

The writing world once had plenty of room for hacks who cranked out formulaic novels with no real thought behind them just to turn a buck. But so many people are writing well now, and so much good writing is reaching the market, that even the most generic stories are well written, with heartfelt intent.

Even the medium where hacks used to thrive—novels based on movies or television—has transformed. For those of you unfamiliar with it, the ABC series *Castle* centers on Richard Castle, who writes police procedurals. In the show, Castle shadows NYPD detective Kate Beckett. He uses his experiences to write a series of novels whose main character, Nikki Heat, is based on Beckett. As an adjunct to the show, ABC produced an actual series of Nikki Heat novels, anonymously written under Richard Castle's name.

I've read a couple of them, and they are not hackwork. The writing is more than competent, the plots have some nice twists, the settings are authentic, and the action is fast paced and clear. More important, even though the anonymous author is using characters someone else created, you can tell she (I've seen good arguments that the writer is a woman) loves these characters. She's inspired by them and what happens to them. She's doing it for the story rather than the money.

PREACHING

Another muse that misleads a lot of writers is passion for an idea. I can understand the attraction. Ideas are important and often beautiful, and it's natural to fall in love with them. Novels have sometimes changed people's minds about important issues. But like the hackwork of yore, there is little room for sermonizing novels in today's market. The last bestseller of this variety that I can think of is *The Celestine Prophecy* by James Redfield, a ten-part New Age homily decked out in a wafer-thin story. I'm sure others have been written in the quarter-century since, but no one has heard of them.

So if you're trying to sell your ideas to the world by wrapping a novel around them, you'll likely wind up with something that is neither an effective sermon nor a good story. Novels can convey ideas, but only if you're focusing on your story first, with the ideas in second place.

It's not just that preaching interrupts your story in order to dump information on your readers—think of the endless lectures on fiscal policy that break up Ayn Rand's *Atlas Shrugged*—but it often forces your characters to act out of character for the sake of putting your point across. Real people's lives aren't perfect examples of abstract principles. So if your ideas are your main focus, you'll end up stretching your characters thin enough to wrap around them.

As soon as you start using your characters as mouthpieces, you undermine the suspension of disbelief. Your readers may still learn something, but if they no longer believe in your characters as people, they aren't going to care about what they learn. If they see through your attempt to sermonize, you'll probably generate a backlash. People don't like being preached to, and they like being preached *down* to even less. When you preach down to them without acknowledging what you're doing, you may as well give up any hope of changing minds. The only people who will keep reading already agree with you.

It's worth looking at what may be one of the most successful sermonizing novels ever written, *Uncle Tom's Cabin*. By humanizing the plight of slaves, this book inspired and spread the abolition movement and may have helped push the country into the Civil War. It literally changed the world.

But while the book does contain a fair amount of preaching—it was written in an age when sermons were much more tolerated in fiction—the *sermons* didn't change people's minds. Rather, it was the *emotional connection* readers made with Harriet Beecher Stowe's very human characters. It's clear that, like the author of the Nikki Heat books, Stowe loved her characters enough to bring them to life. Her readers' empathy for Eliza and George and the rest of the cast made it impossible for them to view slavery in the same way. Even Uncle Tom, who later became an archetype of a black person who passively submits to injustice, would have been seen as a noble character at the time. By sticking to his faith despite his suffering, he proved that he was a better Christian than his white owners, a notion that turned the world of Stowe's readers upside down.

STYLE

Style matters. I'm often surprised and delighted when I read an original description or a unique stylistic technique that brings a fresh approach to the reading experience. But style can become a false muse when it serves as an end in itself rather than a means of conveying your story.

This problem shows up most clearly when a writer has a personal voice so idiosyncratic that it overrides her characters' voices. It's hard for characters to become individuals when everyone sounds alike. So if you're deliberately adopting a distinctive voice, stop. Start listening to your characters instead.

You can test whether your personal style is vetoing your characters' voices by gathering all the dialogue of a given character in a separate file and then reading through it. Do the same for your other characters. Each file should contain a distinctive vocabulary and a unique worldview. If it doesn't, then you need to start listening to your characters more than yourself.

Unfortunately, a lot of readers—and reviewers and book awards—reward stylistic navel-gazing before genuine entertainment. They lionize originality and even hold some contempt for traditional storytelling with likable characters put in challenging situations. But the books that are written to please this market rarely reach a wider readership, and many of the stylistic techniques that are celebrated as original turn out to be fads. Jay McInerney was praised for his use of the second person when *Bright Lights, Big City* first came out. In retrospect, it seems like a gimmick.

It's really a matter of priorities. A fresh style is a gift, but only when your original ways of expressing yourself and looking at the world belong to your characters rather than to you, the author. Then you can bring those characters to life, and your readers will love them. When you make stylistic beauty your main goal, you shortchange both your characters and your readers.

In *Wolf Hall*, Hilary Mantel made some original choices with her speaker attributions, using ambiguous antecedents or leaving out attributions entirely. She may have intended to create a sense that her characters' daily speech was detached from their inner lives, which would have been appropriate for her setting in the court of an absolute monarch. But what she actually created was confusion over who was saying what. She must have realized that her stylistic originality was getting in the way of her story because her speaker attributions were much more conventional in the sequel.

On the other hand, Sue Grafton's Kinsey Millhone books often appeal to readers with descriptions that are both strikingly new and perfectly apt. In *"D" Is for Deadbeat*, for instance, Kinsey describes a character she's just met as having "a dimple in his chin that looked like a puncture wound." Since the books are written in the first person, these delightful original touches belong to Kinsey and show her self-confidence. She trusts herself enough that she can look at the world in a way no one else has and describe it the way she sees it. The style enhances the story without getting in its way.

Lauren Groff, author of *The New York Times* bestseller *Arcadia*, also uses language distinctively by creating rich metaphors and dwelling lovingly on details. Here's a description of the main house in the eponymous commune at the center of *Arcadia,* as seen by Bit, a young boy being raised there:

> ... far atop the hill, the heaped brick shadow of Arcadia House looms. In the wind, the tarps over the rotted roof suck against the beams and blow out, a beast's panting belly. The half-glassed windows are open mouths, the full-glassed are eyes fixed on Bit. He looks away.

Again, the descriptive gifts that capture the house's menace are rooted in Bit's history. He is a child of an iconoclastic community, raised by people who deliberately reject the conventional. Of course he'd see the world in original ways.

FIND YOUR MUSE

So once you've turned your back on false muses and prepared the way for the real one, how do you find her? How do you find inspiration in your story?

CRAFT

Even if you aren't misled by false muses in the course of telling your story, your progress might be slowed because you haven't yet mastered your craft. The best writers make writing look easy. It's only when you try it yourself that you realize just how tough it is. And it's hard to stay inspired by your story if your descriptions are too inept to bring your locations to life, or your dialogue mechanics are so cumbersome that they interfere with your characters' voices. To follow your muse, you need to write at a certain level of competence.

To learn your craft, you can join writers' groups—in person, online, or both. You can read books (like this one) on the writer's craft. You can hire a professional editor. Or you can also simply keep writing. As you do, you will learn to critique your own work and eventually develop the skills you need to get your vision on the page.

Of course, it's also possible to obsess about craft, to get lost in those writing books that reduce the art of creating a story to a series of rules. I've had clients quote some famous writer who said that a line of dialogue should never be more than ten words long or that you should never use a prologue. I've told them that they should use whatever techniques best let them tell the story they want to tell.

If you're thinking about whether you should use third-person objective or third-person limited point of view as you're writing a scene, your focus is not where it belongs. It should be trained on your characters and what happens to them. The trick is to know the details of your craft well enough to apply them unconsciously, freeing your mind to follow your story. Don't worry, when you go back and revise, you can refine the details.

YOUR TRUE MUSE

Inspiration is, at heart, a matter of love, and what you fall in love with about your book is as individual as you are. Ask yourself what excites you most about your story. Is it your carefully constructed plot, which springs unexpected twists on your reader? Is it a particular character you can't get out of your head, whose story you have to follow?

In his prologue to *A Maggot*, John Fowles wrote of how a single image inspired him to write the novel. "For some years before its writing, a small group of travelers, faceless, without apparent motive, went in my mind towards an event. Evidently in some past, since they rode horses, and in a deserted landscape; but beyond this very primitive image, nothing."

J.R.R. Tolkien was inspired by his setting—he spent more than a quarter-century refining the history, mythology, geography, and languages of Middle-earth as a sheer labor of love before his friends persuaded him to start publishing stories about it.

A writer I know dreamed about a particular character traveling through a landscape. When she wrote down the dream, she found that the story continued, even though she was awake. So she kept writing. Fully rounded characters showed up, and a plot developed before her eyes. She was writing a novel.

Are you guaranteed to find inspiration on this level? No. But if you're looking for your muse in the right place, she is not hard to find. After all, she's been hanging out with us for tens of thousands of years. The earliest cave drawings are stories made visible. Once we developed written language, it didn't take us long to go from making scratches on clay tablets to keep track of how many sheep we owned to creating *The Epic of Gilgamesh*—which is still a good read after more than four thousand years.

Storytelling is in our bones. When you create people on paper and follow their lives as they unfold, projecting yourself into someone else's head, you connect to humanity's deepest roots. Writing stories takes you out of yourself by forcing you to think about the motivations—and consequences—of human behavior. Putting a character you love into conflict or danger and watching him fight his way out reveals the courage and convictions that have shaped our species into what it is. This is why false muses are so unsatisfying—they do not make us more human.

Writing stories makes you more aware. As you learn to craft distinctive settings and plausible dialogue, you also start to pay more attention to the settings of your actual life. You listen to how people express themselves, spotting those moments when they turn complex thoughts or emotions into simple, heartfelt words that are unique to their personalities. As you craft plot twists, you notice how real-life stories play out in unexpected ways.

Writing stories makes you wiser. As you craft villains who remain plausible human beings, you learn that no one thinks of herself as evil but that flaws are part of the human condition. And when you start creating heroes who remain sympathetic despite their flaws, you come to see that the flaws we all carry don't have to be fatal ones. We may turn out okay after all.

So look to your story, and ask yourself what attracts you to it. What about it speaks to the deepest part of you? You're likely to find your muse sitting right in front of you, where she's been all along.

 **PRO TIP**

The passion you have for your story isn't useful only for bolstering you and keeping you connected to your work. It can be a contagion that passes to your future agent and editor or directly to your readers through your enthusiasm for the tale.

—THERESE WALSH

COMPOSING HUMANS ON THE PAGE

How to Mine, Visualize, and Empathize Your Way to Authentic Characters

JULIANNA BAGGOTT

Let's all agree that we're starting with the same premise: Fiction, though not factually true, aims at a deeper truth. If you disagree, then the rest of this essay will be of little use. Worse, it might cause deep agitation.

Now let's also separate authenticity from originality. W.H. Auden put it this way: "Some writers confuse authenticity, which they ought always aim at, with originality, which they should never bother about."

Originality is, to my ears, a tinny term. Authenticity is rich and resonant. Originality feels like something you pull off. Authenticity is something you dig for.

I'm interested in the digging.

MINE MEMORIES

Oliver Wendell Holmes once wrote, "Memory is a net." This net is a gift to writers. It means that your memories come pre-edited. What remains when you pull the net from the ocean floor has endured. Some memories are there for good reason (joy, trauma, shock), but others are surprising. They're bits and pieces that have remained. Details, gestures, a sudden jolt brought on by a smell—these memories, no matter how small, hold psychological resonance. They are uniquely your own. Even if someone else witnessed something you remember, his memory won't be the same as yours. In fact, your own memory will change over time, and it certainly changes in the telling. As Grace Paley boldly put it, "Any story told twice is fiction."

Memory offers authenticity.

As fiction writers, we face resistance from the outset. Our work is clearly labeled as false; readers know that the novel and the short story aren't true. We have to convince them. How? Well, often through details, which have a way of wedging past the reader's resistance and accumulating into a sense of the real, even if the world is otherworldly.

I write across genres, everything from historical fiction to literary realism to magical realism to science fiction and fantasy. It might surprise you that I believe deeply that literary realism—the rendering of a 1970s suburban kitchen—requires worldbuilding, a term often relegated to the confines of science fiction. It might surprise you that I believe that the wildest fantasy setting—the futuristic dystopian world of a girl with a doll head fused to her fist—is rooted in memory. (It's possible that nothing surprises you.) In both cases, I rely on details from my own memories, making them undeniably real. If I create that sense of undeniability in the springy cord of the avocado-colored wall-mounted telephone or the click of the doll's plastic eyelids, then I'm much more likely to draw you into something far harder to render: the character's deep interior world, full of fear and longing and her own flashing memories.

Valerie Martin put it this way: "The desire at the start is not to say anything, not to make meanings but to create for the unwary reader a sudden experience of reality." I have a more jaded view of readers and consider them always wary, but I agree wholeheartedly that this sudden experience of reality is essential. It's actually a moment that I immediately recognize as a reader. It's the moment I enter. I'm in. It's real. My own world exists less, sometimes not at all.

Memory isn't always just the detail work, the filigree. It's sometimes the soul of the story.

My memories can also become my character's memories. A writer must create and continually fill a bank of memories for their characters. Our greatest, most intimate currency is what we're willing to tell, the memories we're willing to share, the secrets we're willing to confess to another human being. Memories, even very small, fractured ones, are of great value to our characters as a way of giving context to the people they've become, who they once were, their worldview, what they fear and desire, what haunts them.

When I teach fiction classes, I always start my students off with memory exercises. I simply ask them to provide a memory of birds; teeth; water; a strange neighbor; an unusual pet; something stolen, lost, or found … the list goes on and on. And then we stitch the memories together into a story. The work is always textured in a way that seems to operate the way life does—with a good measure of chaos.

Memory is so tied to creativity that it's an enduring definition of creativity itself. Sarnoff Mednick famously stated, "Creativity is associative memory that works exceptionally well." Note that he didn't say that a *good* memory was what was needed. An associative memory is something else altogether. It's a leaping kind of memory, one that flits and alights, flits and alights, and sometimes crashes through the woods like a frightened deer.

Associative memory works best when you retract the walls of your rationality and allow it to wander.

VISUALIZE

I've been on the road a good bit this season. Recently I left a half-finished novel for more than a week before returning to it. Before I departed, I tried to push the pages—some were a little rough—to a place where I felt I could leave them. But still, in my absence, my novels tend to sink like an entire city into quicksand.

When I got back, I found the steeple of the story still poking out. It was the last remaining vestige. I tried to pull it up to the surface. My brain resisted. It required too much at once. I took two days to work on smaller, more manageable projects, pushing them along to other people's desks. And then on day three, I started over.

The morning was grim. I reread. I stared. I went back to the large pieces of paper taped to my wall, maps of sorts. Nothing was really working.

Let me be scientific for a moment. Writing is real work. Roy Baumeister, a psychologist at Florida State University, talks about it in his book *Willpower: Rediscovering the Greatest Human Strength*. He and his team of researchers tested the glucose levels in people's blood before and after mentally taxing work and found that they'd used glucose in ways previously associated with physically taxing work. If I've learned nothing else from Baumeister's research, it's that I now write with a chocolate bar on my desk.

On this day, chocolate failed me.

By late afternoon, I knew I had only one real choice: to lie down and hope a scene or two would rise up from my subconscious. As my Southern grandmother would have put it, I took to the bed.

I was exhausted. I closed my eyes. Within a few minutes, a small character named Ms. Mu appeared, packing a train bag. I hadn't seen her since the beginning of the novel, but I'd known she'd have to come back. And she had.

Then I saw a character who'd only been a blurry face under water. Now he was living in South Philly; he had more to say. Bits and pieces continued to emerge in this way. A question I'd never thought of before popped up. My mind wandered. I dozed off for a few minutes—a rare feat.

When I woke up, I quickly jotted all over one of my large pieces of wall-taped paper. And I found that I could pat in the dark from one scene to the next, filling things in. The logical mind had relaxed its grip and faded. My intuitive mind took over.

That intuitive mind is deeply authentic. It comes from the subconscious. It holds a certain purity. I'm not suggesting that it should be gripped tightly like some holy object. Not at all. It can fail to serve the greater story. I'm only saying that it often holds some strange truth.

I also have my students practice visualization. They close their eyes, and I say a few sentences about a person in a scene, with almost no other details—I allow them time to fill those in. The results are pretty amazing. What I hope they learn is that their minds are naturally generative.

As a point of practice, sometimes we need to surrender. Actually, I would say that surrender, in general, is an important concept for the fiction writer. We plot. We map. We try to tell the story artfully. But when we surrender and bow to the story itself, and to the characters, those moments can feel the most authentic. We get out of our own ego-driven way and write.

It's also not a bad way to live.

PRACTICE EMPATHY

I think of writing as the daily practice of empathy. It's my job as a writer, day in and day out, to step into the lives of my characters, in particular their fully realized interior worlds. As human beings, we rush around. It's a tall order to fully connect and acknowledge, even briefly, the fact that everyone you see and encounter and pass by on the street has as rich an interior life as you do. They're afraid and hopeful. They've been in love, and they've known sorrow. They dream at night. They imagine. They hold countless memories. They are full and rich and complex.

As people who need to make it through their busy day to day, it's time-consuming and exhausting to acknowledge the humanity of those around you. In fact, it's far easier to treat others as clichés, as mere representations of people.

And yet, I'd argue that if you practice empathy—practice seeing people not as clichés but as living, breathing souls—you're far less likely to create rote or inauthentic characters. If you see fictional people as fully as you see real ones, you're more likely to render them fully on the page. Practicing empathy helps you know others. It may even help you know yourself. This is how you gain authenticity—you have to practice and live it.

This is the hard way.

There is no easy way.

 **PRO TIP**

Create characters you'll want to spend time with, who have layers you're interested in excavating.

WRITE TRUE

Bring Authenticity to Your Work with Details from the Natural World

JULIET MARILLIER

authentic [au-then-tic]
–adjective
real, actual, genuine; original, first-hand

—Shorter Oxford English Dictionary

We owe our readers truth in our writing. Not literal truth, or we'd be limited to recording what we had for breakfast and how far we walked the dog, but a deeper and more profound kind of truth. It's a truth that can permeate our fiction whether we are writing a space opera or a Regency romance or a hard-boiled detective story. It's the same kind of truth that can be found in traditional stories from all cultures, and it has its roots in nature. Sometimes it's called *authenticity*.

The term *authenticity* appears in reviews of nature-based works such as James Rebanks's *The Shepherd's Life*, an evocative, plain-speaking memoir by a sheep farmer who lives and works in Britain's Lake District. *The Shepherd's Life* is indeed real, actual, and genuine. It is a firsthand account—three generations of the Rebanks family have farmed the same land. Reading this book puts you right there on the fells with the sheep and the hardworking dogs and the men and women whose lives are governed, like those of their animals, by the changing seasons and the vagaries of the weather. We are invited to share not only the daily work of a fell farmer but the moods of nature in the Lake District, the impact of historical events such as the Great War on the families who live there—many sons were lost—and, above all, the mind-set that comes from working so close to nature. Carol Midgley, writing in *The Times*, said of *The Shepherd's Life*, "What is most striking about this book is its authenticity; this is the real thing."

In his lovely book *Meadowland: The Private Life of an English Field*, John Lewis-Stempel records the passing of the seasons in a single field on a farm in rural England. Here the author lives, works, observes acutely, and records in beautiful, clear language the changes in this field over a full year: the behavior of plants, animals, birds, and insects; the stream and its inhabitants; the weather; the soil. Such a book could only have been written by a person who lived and breathed nature, a person who understood his own relationship with the natural world in a way far deeper than the purely intellectual. The writing possesses an innate truth that goes beyond any attempt to analyze, summarize, or commentate. Simply, it is living the story.

So, can a writer be truly authentic only when writing memoir, autobiography, or nonfiction? Not at all. We can carry that real, actual, and genuine quality into our fiction. To do so, we must believe in the characters and their setting; while we are writing them, they must become real to us. And in our preparation to tell their stories, we must know their environment as if it were our home ground. The best practice for that is to understand our own place in nature and to be mindful of what shapes us into the individuals we are. We experience the world around us through our five senses. As writers, we need to sharpen our awareness of the senses so we can carry those experiences into our fictional worlds and make those worlds real and authentic to the reader.

Some novelists have an exceptional skill in bringing natural settings alive on the page. Here are just a few examples, all very different: *Prodigal Summer* by Barbara Kingsolver, *The God of Small Things* by Arundhati Roy, *The Snow Child* by Eowyn Ivey, *Gingerbread* by Robert Dinsdale, *Traitor* by Stephen Daisley, and *Burial Rites* by Hannah Kent.

My prime example is a classic novel, *Precious Bane* by Mary Webb, first published in 1924. In *Precious Bane*, the bond between characters and nature is powerfully present on every page—almost in every sentence. The novel is set in the English county of Shropshire, where the author lived as a child, and it's told in first person by a young woman using the local dialect. Dialect can soon pall, but here it's done with such liveliness and sensitivity that it makes both narrator Prudence Sarn and her environment, including the other characters, utterly real for the reader. Prue is not a woman of learning; she's a hardworking farmhand. Her senses govern her perceptions. She lives closely with the natural world. Both she and the reader understand that she is an integral part of it. Here's a sample:

> It was a wonderful thing to see our meadows at Sarn when the cowslip was in blow. Gold-over they were, so that you would think not even an angel's feet were good enough to walk there. You could make a tossy-ball before a thrush had gone over his song twice, for you'd only got to sit down and gather with both hands. Every way you looked there was naught but gold, saving towards Sarn, where the woods began, and the great stretch of grey water, gleaming and wincing in the sun.

In Stanley Baldwin's 1928 introduction to *Precious Bane*, he wrote, "The strength of the book ... lies in the fusion of the elements of nature and man." And that, I believe, is key to authenticity in our writing, whether our setting is contemporary or historical, whether it is the real world or an invented one.

As a druid, I hold two beliefs that help make sense of this. First, humankind is not set above the rest of nature but is an equal part in the great web of living things. Not so very long ago, humankind lived and worked in a constant awareness of nature. We understood the seasonal cycles. Along with the weather, the seasons determined when and how we did our work. We respected and feared the power of storm, flood, and fire. But we've largely moved away from that life. In a world of fast technological change and an obsession with "progress," we are increasingly separated from nature. Indeed, we are so out of tune with it that we may exploit and degrade it. Or we are so tied up in our daily lives that we simply forget to see it.

That's a broad generalization, of course. But it is often true for many of us. And if we lose sight of nature and our place in it, how can we convincingly write about it? How can we make the natural world and the characters who live in it real and authentic on the page if we are out of touch with them ourselves? Don't most stories happen in the natural world—or a natural world of some kind?

The second druidic belief relevant to this discussion is that storytelling has great power to teach and heal. Since the days when stories were told around the fire after dark to keep monsters at bay and to make sense of life's challenges, traditional tales have been shared in communities around the world. (It is fascinating how versions of the same stories spring up in disparate, geographically separated cultures.) Those stories possess a kind of truth that is deeper than factual truth—I call them "truer than true." They hold in their heart the values that keep us alive, lead us along wise pathways, and give us the strength to meet challenges and make hard decisions. The tales may have the trappings of fantasy, of magic, of monsters and spirits, and things that go bump in the night. But those crowd-pleasing garments clothe inner wisdom. The stories tell us about loyalty, courage, and faith; comradeship, endurance, and patience. They show us when to be wary and when to take risks. They teach us how to love and how to let go. The oral storytelling tradition is no longer strong in our society. That makes it even more important for us to write with awareness of those inner truths, the values that help keep people strong, wise, and good.

I'm not suggesting we all write novels based on fairy tales, folklore, or mythology, though a traditional tale may well inspire a crime novel or thriller or historical romance. I do believe it's important for us, as writers, to remain aware of that oral tradition and how vital it was to society for so long, and to be mindful of our responsibility as storytellers. We are not only entertainers; we are also teachers, healers, and wise elders. As a reader, I like a novel to contain a note of hope or learning at the end. I don't mean all novels should have happy endings; that wouldn't be authentic. And a novel does not need a didactic message. But I like to see a character gain wisdom as a result of what's happened in the story or reach a light at the end of the tunnel. That way, a novel has the same power as one of those old traditional stories.

That leads us back to nature. In fairy tales and folklore, nature is a powerful force. Woodlands are dark and mysterious hiding places for the unknown and the unknowable. Rivers rise to drown the evildoer or the unwary. Caves, lakes, and mushroom circles are portals to different worlds. A single leaf or berry proves transformative; an act of kindness toward a creature in trouble leads to unexpected benefits. Thorns grow thickly around a castle, shutting out the world; a mountain of ice stands in the way of an ensorcelled prince's rescue. Nature is an integral part of almost every traditional story. This is as it should be, since those tales are our maps for living and we are ourselves part of nature.

How do we use this wisdom in our own storytelling? In simple ways that help us improve our craft, regardless of the genre.

USE YOUR FIVE SENSES TO EXPERIENCE THE WORLD AROUND YOU

Practice engaging all five senses daily in different environments. Have your characters do the same in their own world. Use their sensory perceptions to bring settings to life. Be sparing with this—a few deft touches are more effective than lengthy descriptive passages. Think about Prudence Sarn and her tossy-ball. The paragraph I quoted from *Precious Bane* includes the senses of touch, sight, and hearing.

WALK THE GROUND

If you can visit your characters' setting, do so. Employ your senses there. How does the environment shape your characters? How does it affect the way they think and feel, the way they act, their relationships with each other? Take photographs and video for reference. Eat local food. Read local newspapers. Listen to local music. Talk to local people.

If you're writing historical fiction, learn how the environment of your characters has changed over the years and why. Visit cultural museums. Read documents dating from your period. Join a historical reenactment society. Learn how it feels to wear period clothing, use the weapons, play the musical instruments, handle the tools, dance the dances. Write with a quill pen. Go camping in the wilderness. Wherever you can, be hands-on.

WALK IN OTHER WORLDS

What if you're writing a novel set in a secondary (invented) world? If that world is based, closely or loosely, on a historical period and/or culture in the real world, keep the details accurate—the inclusion of uncanny or fantastic elements is not a license to defy logic. For instance, if your characters travel mainly on horseback, make sure your horses don't perform impossible feats of endurance or agility. The vital rule for worldbuilding is to make your world internally consistent. The raw materials for your secondary world will come from the world you know—where else?—though, of course, you may mix, twist, and change them.

Your invented world should feel real, actual, and genuine to the reader. There should be no jarring notes—for instance, names that are a mismatch linguistically or historically but are used for characters or places within the same invented culture, or plants and animals plucked seemingly at random from different parts of the real world growing or living together in the secondary world. You want your reader to forget, while immersed in the story, that your world is not actually real. So be consistent. Use sensory detail subtly to bring the world to life. Avoid info dumps (blocks of explanatory information). Instead incorporate small, telling details of your world as the story progresses so the reader is led in gradually. As for conscious anachronism or culture mashing, those are for experienced writers—approach with caution.

KEEP DIALOGUE REAL

The topic of authenticity in dialogue could fill up a whole book of its own. Capturing the "real, actual, genuine" quality in dialogue does not mean replicating the way people talk in the real world. If we wrote like that, our novels would struggle under the weight of the verbiage. The pace would be funereal and the meaning often unclear. To write convincing dialogue, first know your characters and their setting from the inside out. How has your character's psychology been shaped by the circumstances of his birth, upbringing, or life experience? What regional factors come into play? How do the characters' ages or circumstances affect the way they talk? What vocabulary is appropriate to the time, location, and culture? In other words, how is dialogue in this particular instance shaped by the nature of things?

A writer of great dialogue takes all of those factors into consideration and then refines the dialogue to include only what is essential to build character, create a mood, or carry the plot forward. You might distill a real conversation down to a quarter of its actual length for the purpose of effective storytelling.

DON'T LOSE SIGHT OF THE NATURAL WORLD

The novel may be set in a hermetically sealed chamber, the interior of a spaceship on a long interplanetary journey, or a solitary-confinement cell. How can you anchor the story in the natural world if the characters never experience what lies outside the limited confines of their environment? Use your imagination, but build on your experience. There's the natural world the character dreams of—the one she remembers, longs for, hopes for, fears. The distant planet seen through the viewing screen. The flesh-and-blood life imagined by a golem, an android, a robot. The traces of nature still present even in the enclosed or clinical environment.

Whether your setting is contemporary, historical, fantastic, or just plain weird, write as if that world were your own. Let us touch, taste, hear, smell, and see it through your characters. Know those characters' inner truths. Do this, and the reader will believe in your story. It will feel real, actual, and genuine. More than that, the story will stay in your reader's thoughts long after he has finished the book.

WRITER'S BLOCK
How to Unclog the Well

KIM BULLOCK

I'd rather clean a toilet with a toothbrush than watch a cursor blink; its timing precisely matches the rhythm of a beeping alarm clock. "Time to get up," it says. "No more words for you. Do something productive like dishes or laundry."

Search online for the term *writer's block*, and you'll see almost two million hits, many of them suggestions for how to outsmart a wayward muse. *Don't write at your desk. Make a game of word count goals. Disable the Internet. Use brain wave apps.*

These methods, while variably effective, are like taking a long stroll around the base of a mountain rather than climbing it. Until you reach the top, you won't know if you're facing a single mountain or the Rockies.

Obstacles often serve as warnings. Maybe your characters bore you, a beta reader's criticism was too barbed, or you are resisting repeated advice to dig deeper. These are all signs that you should brave the mountain pass rather than stick to the valley floor.

Your true enemy is *fear*. It comes in many forms, all of which are detrimental to productivity.

ASK FOR HELP IF YOU NEED IT

Something's wrong with your manuscript. A subplot you love doesn't work, but you can't bring down the ax. You're unsure of your audience or which point of view to use. You suspect your story switched genres halfway through. Word count goals will only intensify the floundering.

If you can afford one, hire a developmental editor or a writing coach. Even a fifty-page critique, friendly to most budgets, can alert you to issues with pacing, POV, grammar, plot, and characterization.

Defining problem areas empowers you to solve them.

WRITE FIRST, WORRY LATER

I wrote the first draft of my work-in-progress with an audience looking over my shoulder, two of them my protagonists' ghosts. This book was not only my great-grandparents' love story but also a novelization of my great-grandfather's struggles in the art world. I realized a hundred pages in that I was composing a 250,000-word birth-to-death biography that would please my aunt but never sell. Later drafts included all the family stories (to please my relatives) and a plethora of details about the Toronto art world circa 1916 (to please my art historian contacts). Oh, and there was no sex. My father wouldn't want to imagine his grandparents getting it on.

Writing through filters is bound to cause clogs. It's not *your* voice if you let Aunt Hilda tell the story.

MUSTER YOUR COURAGE

One of my worst bouts of writer's block occurred when I had to write the death of a two-year-old. It took months to work up the fortitude to compose that scene.

"But I *have* a two-year-old," I whined to the beta reader who pointed out that the prose was flat and emotionally distant. "Writing this is like killing my own child."

"Exactly," she said.

I poured myself a bourbon and rewrote the scene, giving the dying child my daughter's thumb-sucking habit and well-loved blanket.

It was hell. It was also one of the best scenes I've written.

If a story will bring you to a dark place from which you can't escape, set it aside until you are strong enough to dig deep. When you shy away from the scenes that cause you the most fear and pain, readers will know you are holding back and will feel cheated.

BANISH SELF-DOUBT

I spent years crippled by the compulsion to perfect each chapter before moving on. Some days I'd waste hours agonizing over a single sentence. Twice I declared the whole manuscript a steaming pile of literary excrement before diving into month-long home-improvement projects. I'd drafted other novels with ease, but those stories only served to hone my craft before I tackled the book of my heart—the story that others needed me to get *right*.

Perfectionism is often rooted in self-doubt. If you can't turn off your inner editor, particularly in the drafting stage, this may be your personal demon. Now is the time to build up your confidence. Confide in your writer friends; chances are they have wrestled with the same fear. Take a writing class or inspiring workshop. Write something else—a poem, a short story, even a journal. If deadlines help you focus, set one for yourself and stay accountable to writing friends.

CONSIDER THAT REJECTION DOES NOT EQUAL FAILURE

It's easy for writers, especially those who are unagented and unpublished, to worry about having their work judged. Well-meaning friends and family compound the issue by questioning when the book will hit shelves. If it's never displayed prominently at Barnes & Noble, they might believe you're a talentless hack.

The possibility of failure can paralyze creativity and discourage writers from completing a manuscript. Unfinished books can't be submitted. If you don't send your novel into the world, you definitely won't be rejected and Uncle Joe won't whisper comments about your book at the next family gathering.

Don't let this fear silence your voice.

Rejection sucks, but it's also a reality at every stage of the publishing game. Remember that little book called *The Help*? Kathryn Stockett's bestseller was turned down sixty times before acceptance. Twenty-six publishers said no to Madeleine L'Engle's *A Wrinkle in Time*. Even the one who accepted it thought it was too complicated for children and would never sell.

No one considers these authors failures.

PREPARE FOR SUCCESS

I'm in awe of successful writers. How do they write a new book every year, market their backlist, remain active on social media, blog, and raise multiple smiling children? Between errands, chores, and chauffeuring my daughters to dance class, I'm lucky if I can squeeze in two hours of writing time a day. If I cared that my house looks like a tornado zone, I'd never open my laptop.

For the unpublished writer who can barely see past the current paragraph, let alone imagine starting another novel, the amount of work it takes to sustain a career might terrify. Fear leads to doubt, and doubt poisons the muse.

To combat a fear of success, assume it will come and prepare accordingly. Befriend authors who willingly share their survival strategies. Set boundaries at home to allow for "off-duty" time dedicated solely to getting work done. Write down story ideas as they come, no matter how vague, so you have kernels to work with later.

Fear can become the proverbial elephant in the room. If you cover her with a soft blanket and use her as a chaise lounge, then she'll never leave. Instead, strip her bare. Write down all of your fears, no matter how ridiculous they sound. Cross off all easily dismissed worries. (Most are.) For the rest, stare down the elephant by setting goals that directly challenge those fears. Write that scene that will infuriate your mother-in-law. Compose a query letter, even if the novel isn't complete. Write a fan letter to an author you admire. Someday soon you'll have an unobscured view, and the cursor will be too busy moving to blink.

 PRO TIP

There are at least a dozen reasons why you should consider keeping a writer's journal—one per novel—but here's one of the biggest: Journaling can help you identify why you're blocked and can help you write your way out of that block, too.

—THERESE WALSH

 HOW TO GET IN YOUR OWN WAY, METHOD 8: OVERTHINK IT

When writing, it's easy to psych yourself out with thoughts like, *One day, people will put a velvet rope around this coffee shop table because of what I've written here today, so I have to get this right!*

—BILL FERRIS

LIGHT IT UP—
DON'T BURN IT DOWN

What to Do When You Think You Can't Write Another Word

GWEN HERNANDEZ

Have you reached the point where you think your manuscript would be better off in a bonfire than on a bookshelf? That point where you're beyond blocked: You hate your characters, you're bored by your plot, and you wonder why you started writing this story in the first place? If so, you're not alone. Most writers I know have been through the "just burn it" phase at some point in their career, often more than once. It's happened to me with nearly every manuscript.

Over the course of a full novel, it can be difficult to maintain love for your work. Fatigue sets in as new ideas compete for your attention, your characters refuse to cooperate, and scenes don't play out on the page the way you imagined they would. After months—or even years—of working on the same story, it's natural to feel discouraged. In fact, most writers are great at starting books, but they're not so good at finishing them.

Before you torch your manuscript, see if one of the following tips can help you push through to "The End."

REKINDLE THE SPARK

"The hard part about writing a novel is finishing it."
—ERNEST HEMINGWAY

When your work no longer seems appealing, think back to the beginning, before you typed a single word, when you were so excited you couldn't wait to sit down and write.

What lit that spark? What premise, conflict, character, setting, situation, or issue inspired you? Why did you feel compelled to tackle *this* story and not another?

Try writing for several minutes about the moment the story called to you. Recapture every detail you can remember. Does the original idea still excite you? If so, think about why it's making you unhappy now. Did you veer too far from your original vision? Is the story not unfolding the way you expected? Maybe you need to return to an earlier point in the manuscript and forge a new path. Or maybe you just need to get the rest of the idea out and reshape it later during revisions.

Whatever tack you take, remind yourself daily why this story matters to you. Rekindling that spark can provide the dose of extra motivation you need to keep writing and maybe even fall in love with your manuscript again.

WRITE DIRTY

"Don't look at your feet to see if you are doing it right. Just dance." —ANNE LAMOTT

Still struggling? Send your pesky internal editor to Fiji, and just write—even if the words feel like junk—until you reach the end. Remind yourself that you can fix all the "bad" parts later. When you look at your work with fresh eyes, even the next day, you might be surprised by how good it is.

Or not. No problem. You can fix it. That's the beauty of revision.

Don't let your worries about craft, marketability, or what your mother might think get in the way of telling the story. You started writing for a reason. Remember your spark? Put it on a sticky note on your computer monitor, and read it every day before you write. Then focus on the writing. Worry about the rest later.

Develop the book-finishing habit now. The confidence boost you'll get from writing to the end will help power you through your future books.

CUE THE WORDS

"I only write when I am inspired. Fortunately I am inspired at nine o'clock every morning." —**WILLIAM FAULKNER**

Having trouble getting in the mood to write? Come up with a cue. Every habit is triggered by a cue, a preceding event that tells your brain to perform the action. To foster a regular writing habit, try starting each session the same way.

Not sure what will work? Experiment a little. Recordings of ocean waves, rain, a babbling brook, or mood-setting music are great for helping you transition to writing mode (and, as a bonus, they block out distractions if you wear headphones). Other cues that can help you train yourself to write on command include lighting a candle, sitting in a specific chair, wearing a particular hat, or going through a short routine of stretches or breathing exercises before you begin.

You might also start by reading a quote about writing that inspires you (along with that spark you wrote down). Every writer has been where you are. A good quote can remind you that you're not alone in this solitary pursuit. I've included a few of my favorites throughout this essay to get you started.

Find a ritual that works for you, and you'll soon have a writing habit—and a finished book.

COMMIT TO YOURSELF

"Start writing, no matter what. The water does not flow until the faucet is turned on." —**LOUIS L'AMOUR**

If you write, you're a writer. That's all it takes. But sticking with it takes commitment.

When I write regularly, the ideas flow more easily and inspiration strikes with greater frequency. If I stop writing—whether because of story fatigue, writer's block, or outside commitments—the well of creativity dries up. Setting aside even a small amount of time each day to pound out some words will keep your subconscious immersed in the world of your story, secretly working in the background to solve your plot puzzles and character conundrums.

The muse shows up for work only when you do, so make a commitment to write a certain number of days per week for a specified amount of time or number of words. Then use the cue you created to help you follow through.

Momentum is the key. The more you write, the more you'll want to write. Writing is your gift to yourself. Your story is your gift to the world.

Steer clear of the funeral pyre, and find a way to love your story again so you can finish the book.

 HOW TO GET IN YOUR OWN WAY, METHOD 9: BEMOAN THE FACT THAT YOUR WRITING SUCKS

You can always fix it in the second draft. Give yourself permission to suck. In fact, expect it. This way, you'll be pleasantly surprised when you see that it's only mildly execrable.

—BILL FERRIS

SAY MY NAME

How to Empower Yourself with One Simple Word: *Writer*

JO EBERHARDT

I am a writer.

The first time I said those words to a stranger, I was standing in the emergency department of a children's hospital while my five-year-old son struggled to breathe.

I'd thought those words many times in the privacy of my own head. Once or twice, I'd even suggested to friends that I could, sort of, possibly, maybe, one day be something like a writer. I had three completed manuscripts on my computer, but not only were they not published, they were probably not publishable. I wasn't a writer.

And yet every article I read online told me the only prerequisite for calling yourself a writer was to, well, write. I made up my mind to tell someone.

But I didn't.

The idea of saying those words filled me with dread. What if someone called me out? Who was I to claim the mantle of *writer*, when all I'd done was write hundreds of thousands of unpublished words? Anyone could do that. Right?

On the day my five-year-old son was rushed to the ER with severe pneumonia, I was terrified. There was nothing I could do to help my child. I watched helplessly as ER staff stuck him with needles and positioned an oxygen mask over his face. In an effort to calm my nerves, a nurse tried to make small talk. "So what do you do?" he asked.

In that moment, I was so scared for my son that the fear of saying those words faded to nothing.

"I'm a writer," I said.

SHOUT IT OUT

From a purely grammatical perspective, a writer is someone who writes. But we imbue this word with nuances of meaning that give it power over us. We make the word *writer* into a status symbol—something to be earned.

"I'll call myself a writer when I'm published."

"I'll call myself a writer when I make enough money with my writing that I can quit my day job."

"I'll call myself a writer when Stephen King, J.K. Rowling, and Neil Gaiman show up on my doorstep in the middle of the night and present me with the Golden Pen of Writerdom."

Sure, a writing career is marked by many milestones (although I've yet to meet someone who's achieved that last one I mentioned), but that's exactly what they are: milestones. In a writing career. So when does that writing career start? When can you legitimately call yourself a writer?

The answer contains one simple word: *now*.

When we name something, we make it real. We name our children, our cars, our boats, our pets, and our indoor plants. We agonize over the names of our characters and debate the benefits of publishing under a pseudonym.

We know that names have power. When you call yourself a writer, you define yourself and transform your dream into reality.

You are a writer from the moment you make a conscious decision that writing is your career path. Maybe you're still working a day job. Maybe you don't know exactly what your career path will look like beyond eventually writing a story someone else will read. But if you're writing consistently, actively honing your craft, and keeping the end goal of writing for publication in mind, you are a writer.

When you tell yourself you're a writer, you give yourself permission to write. When you tell other people you're a writer, you apply positive pressure to yourself to keep writing. If you've just told your best friend's roommate that you're writing the next great American novel, you had better believe she's going to check on your progress every time she sees you. That external accountability will keep you on the straight and narrow.

BE PREPARED

After I had told the ER nurse that I was a writer, I took a deep breath and returned to worrying about my son. But the conversation didn't end there. "Wow!"

he said. "That's amazing. What do you write? Would I have read any of your books? Where can I buy them?"

I was not at all prepared for that part of the conversation. I stammered and stuttered and admitted that I hadn't actually been published yet, all the while waiting for him to decry me as a fraud or, at the very least, a liar.

Every time you tell someone you're a writer, you'll be hit with follow-up questions, so you need to be prepared with simple answers. Rather than react defensively, be honest. "I'm not published yet, but I'm currently working on a historical fantasy novel set during the Crusades."

These conversations can feel awkward and uncomfortable, especially when you're not prepared for them. And there's this nagging voice in the back of your head reminding you that you don't need any special qualifications to call yourself a writer. You haven't graduated from writer school. You don't have an advanced degree in writerology. And, sadly, there is no secret society of authors who wander the streets at night and bestow golden pens on worthy writers-to-be. Anyone can call herself a writer.

So what makes you so special?

FIGHT IMPOSTER SYNDROME

Imposter syndrome is, simply put, a fear of being found out. It's the belief that you actually have no idea what you're doing and that, at any moment, someone is going to realize you're making it up as you go along.

Imposter syndrome is incredibly common, and not just among writers. You'll find it among teachers, scientists, politicians, business owners, and just about everyone else in the world. Do you know who doesn't suffer from imposter syndrome? Narcissists and low achievers.

Narcissists never doubt their own self-worth, and low achievers don't seek out hard work. So if the idea of telling someone you're a writer fills you with fear and makes you question whether you can claim such a lofty title, congratulations! You have a realistic understanding of your own abilities and the hard work involved in a writing career.

Overcoming imposter syndrome is as simple—or as complicated—as remembering the following three things:

1. Don't compare yourself to others to validate your role as a writer. Deep down, they may be just as doubtful about their abilities as you are about yours. Even if they're published. Even if they've had multiple books published.

2. Concentrate on your achievements. I guarantee that if you read something you wrote five years ago—or even one year ago—you'll think it's terrible. You've already come a long way on your writing journey, and that's something to be proud of.

3. See yourself through the eyes of others. Those uncomfortable questions people ask about what you write and where they can buy your books? They're not attacks. They're exclamations of excitement and support. The average person is in awe of writers. We create stories from squiggles of ink on sheets of dead tree. That's a kind of magic.

I'm not saying you can wave a pen and banish imposter syndrome. What I *am* saying is that it's normal, it has a name, and it can be overcome with a little bit of courage.

OWN IT

You've got this. Go out, and tell people you're a writer. The worst that can happen is that you feel a little awkward during the ensuing conversation. That's a small price to pay for the validation, confidence, and accountability that come with claiming the title of writer for yourself. Oh, and if you're visited in the middle of the night by three cloaked figures brandishing a golden pen, please give them my name.

 HOW TO GET IN YOUR OWN WAY, METHOD 10: WONDER IF YOU'RE A "REAL WRITER"

Writing is a verb, so if you verb it, you're a noun. Or something. Have the self-confidence to say you're a writer without explaining a perceived lack of publications, agents, or McMansions. Any time you spend fretting about this nonissue is a waste, including time spent reading this very paragraph.

—BILL FERRIS

 PRO TIP

Every new writer struggles with the "writer" label, including writers who've gone on to become multipublished, award-winning novelists. They didn't let their label worries hold them back. Why should you?

PART THREE

INVITE

You might be able to write a first draft in a closet, but you can't appraise it in one. In an effort to serve the work, we need to seek other perspectives—and not from friends and family who may tell us what we want to hear at the expense of what we need to hear. The hidden value of unbiased critique is in gaining more certain knowledge of your work—that insight holds such power. Don't bypass this stage and short-change your work-in-progress or yourself.

THE PSYCHOLOGY OF CRITIQUE

Resist the Natural Impulse to Shut Down

THERESE WALSH

You've spent months, even years, working on your book. You give it to a candid beta reader with all the wide-eyed enthusiasm of a child showing a parent a piece of macaroni art. You hope to receive a treasure trove of golden praise, but what you get—more often than not—is advice that encourages you to try a new tact; to work harder on that character, arc, or another element of the story; to try, try again.

Listen: There's no shame in wanting the gold. We all desire approval of our work on some level, even if we tell ourselves we know a story isn't entirely ready. But even when you know you might not get gold, some part of you still hopes for silver or at least bronze. When you're given no treasure at all, you may think the fault lies with your beta reader. Thus you shortchange yourself out of the real reward: a better story. Or, put another way, what you receive from your beta readers is a map to where the golden treasure may indeed be found.

You want that map, and for more than one reason.

RECOGNIZE THE FAR-REACHING BENEFITS OF CRITIQUE

The first step in readying yourself for criticism is to consider all that it can offer. Yes, criticism can unmask specific weaknesses in your story, but it can also reveal weaknesses in your storytelling toolbox or even an assumption that is working against you—that everyone would unquestionably connect the story dots in just such a way or feel a specific emotion based on a set of given circumstances. What if your story twist isn't so surprising after all? What if the protagonist you love so much has mannerisms that grate on everyone?

Don't be ashamed of weak spots in your manuscript. Rather, be glad to have identified them, because once you're able to name them, you can study how to remedy them, improve upon your education with a directed approach, rectify your blind spots, and see the world from a clearer—and often more comprehensive—perspective.

We often don't think of criticism as a good thing. But it can be the best thing, because it can be *the* thing that evolves your work and maximizes the *progress* for an author in progress.

Don't doubt its potential importance in your evolution. It's very, very important.

If you remain hungry for others' honest perspectives of your work, it'll be easier to hear anything and everything they convey. Do you have to make changes based on those critiques? Of course not. In your search for gold, you'll unearth a lot of plain old rocks.

But don't think about filtering and appraisals right away. First, set your mind to receive.

WELCOME DIFFERENT PERSPECTIVES

I won't go so far as to say that no one likes to convey bad news; some people love conflict and even thrive on it. But I'd wager that most people are uncomfortable in conflict situations, including discussions about what doesn't work in someone's story. All of the same dance moves apply here as they do for other such moments among humans: The person who brings it up may tread carefully at first—providing hints rather than brutal honesty—and may retreat at the first sign of stepping on toes.

You don't want her to retreat, because all that good stuff she was about to tell you could be lost. That map you crave? Flung out to sea.

Take steps to welcome feedback from the people delivering it:

- Tell them you value their honest opinions and are grateful for their help and time.
- If you hear tentative feedback or sense that a reader is holding back, remind him that lessons learned through critique will not only benefit your work-in-progress but will also help you learn what works and doesn't work for

readers—and how you can improve. You need this knowledge in order to be successful in the marketplace.

- Ask questions to prompt them and define the territory (e.g., "Did anything in the story make you feel impatient, bored, or confused?"), but avoid asking leading questions (e.g., "You found the protagonist's actions plausible, right?").

It may be difficult to hide disappointment when you hear feedback you don't expect. Unfortunately even microexpressions of frustration—with the exchange, the work, or yourself—can shut down a sensitive critiquer. Do your best to keep an encouraging expression and tone in a face-to-face discussion. If you have a hard time with this, ask to receive feedback through e-mail or an online forum, where you can process it before responding.

The constancy of your gratitude and acceptance of others' perspectives will keep the door between you and your critiquers open, which will naturally advance the conversation. And advancing is what you want, because what a reader says last is often the hardest for her to share—and the most valuable for you to hear.

RESIST THE URGE TO EXPLAIN OR DEFEND

The best way to receive feedback is with wide ears, a supportive nod, and lots of silence. This may seem easy, but often it is not, because you may feel the compulsion—the very human response—to explain yourself: what you meant, where you were going with that point, or what the reader was *supposed* to think. Again, tread carefully or risk shutting down your reader before he's said all he wants to share. This isn't the time to explain or defend but rather to listen deeply. Taking notes while your reader speaks is a great way to keep yourself in the moment. It also prevents you from formulating justifications, deciding on the spot whether you're going to reject or accept a criticism, or analyzing ways to fix a potential problem. Try to resist these impulses. You'll analyze later. You'll fix things later. You can ask follow-up questions later.

And if a story means a lot to you—because it's personal, or because you've been working on it for a decade (or what feels like a decade)—keep those details to yourself or you might get a watered-down version of the truth you seek.

Know that as the amount of perceived work seems to pile up throughout your feedback, you may feel overwhelmed or want to throw your hands up and cry, "I quit!" This, too, is a defense mechanism—a response to a challenge you're not sure you want to, or even can, face. In these moments, take a deep breath.

Don't judge your ability to scale a mountain before you know that mountain's size. Resist, too, the urge to shut down before the critique is finished. Remember that map to the gold? You want the whole map, not half of it.

 **PRO TIP**

Learn to control your knee-jerk response to criticism now. Instead, develop a level of awareness that allows you to home in on signals from a different body part: your gut. This ability to put your work before your ego can be important now and also down the road, when you work with editors and receive feedback from your readership.

All of the urges described above are *personal* responses that pull you away from your *professional* goal: to serve the work. Try to call them out when you feel yourself tuning out, making excuses, or rejecting someone else's opinion without full consideration for what she's trying to express. Sometimes the idea that seems most repellant when you first hear it stays with you, later awakening your gut sense, which tells you, *That hard concept that requires a lot of back-breaking digging to access? That was true. You need to do the work.*

We are human, and our very human way of processing and protecting against criticism, rejection, and resistance can't be denied—but it *can* be understood and managed. You are not your work, but you are *like* it in that you can both change and grow and improve. You can both evolve.

 FAQ

Should I get feedback on my work while it's in progress?

As tempting as it is to get feedback from friends, other authors, and even my agent while I'm at work on a novel, I've learned (the hard way) to wait. My sense of the characters and the story (and my ego) are not sure enough while I'm navigating my way through a first draft. While I'm writing, I do share my work with a total of three people: the three other published novelists in my critique group. That's it. Once I've finished the rewrite, though, I share it with a larger circle. I send it to three or four passionate readers. I send it to a couple of people who are only vague acquaintances, who will be more objective than people who know me. I send it to my agent. I ask them to keep some questions in mind as they read: Does the story make sense? Do the characters feel real? Are the characters' motivations clear, and do those motivations make sense? Is there any part of the book that drags or feels repetitive? Once I get that feedback, I ignore any comments that I hear from only one reader, figuring that's just personal preference. But if two, three, or more people say they found a plot twist completely unbelievable, or that a character felt wooden, or that they *hated* the final scene, then I sit up and pay attention. I comb over those spots in the book with a fresh eye. And then, even if it's painful, I do my best to fix them.

—KATHLEEN MCCLEARY

HOW TO GET IN YOUR OWN WAY, METHOD 11: BELIEVE THE GOAL IS FOR EVERYONE TO LIKE IT

You can't "win" your novel critique. If your goal is for everyone to love it, it may be a sign that your book didn't take enough risks.

—BILL FERRIS

THE ART OF THE INVITATION

How Asking the Right Questions Can Shape Your Critique Experience

ANNIE NEUGEBAUER

During the seven years in which I ran a weekly critique group—as well as the numerous times I've traded manuscripts with more than a dozen critique partners—I've learned that communication is by far the most important skill writers can hone. Most writers know the importance of clarity and honesty when it comes to giving critique, but what about when it comes to *asking* for it? Communication must come from both sides to be effective.

It's a fascinating experience to hand a manuscript to someone, give no guidance, and ask for her feedback, but it's not usually the best way to get the most useful critique—especially if the critiquer is new to the experience or to you. If someone has offered her time and effort to help you improve your work, honor that gift by leveraging her feedback in the way that's most useful to you. This means telling her up front what you're looking for, what you're not looking for, and how you'd like to receive it.

ASK FOR WHAT YOU NEED

The first thing I always tell my critiquers is the stage of the process my book is in. For long-time partners or particularly experienced critiquers, this alone might be enough information. For newer partners or critiquers, you might want to elaborate. Here are some examples of the information I might share:

This is a partial draft, the first 20,000 words of a 70,000-word novel. I'm afraid the direction I'm taking has derailed my manuscript. I'd love for you to give it a quick read and share where you'd expect it to go, where you'd like it to go, and any problems you see. I'd also love to hear how interested you are in what happens next. Have I set up a book the reader wants to finish?

This is my rough draft. I'm sure it's full of typos and sloppy writing, so please don't focus energy on grammar, style, or polish. Right now I'm looking for broad impressions. Does the story work as a whole? Where do you gain and lose interest? What characters and plotlines appeal to you? Is the concept intriguing? Is the ending satisfying?

This is my third draft. I'm looking for broad impressions and reader response as well as more specific things. Do certain scenes strike you as slow or out of place? Do certain themes need to be expanded? How does the style of the prose work for you overall? Does it seem like anything is missing?

This is a late draft. I'd love for you to read it as if it were the final version. I'm looking for any and every issue you find, from large to tiny. Please mark typos or weak sentences. If you think the draft still needs an overhaul, please tell me that, too.

Aside from draft-related feedback, if you have specific needs, you can't go wrong with stating them. I like to ask readers to mark their reactions—where they laughed, shed tears, shuddered, put the book down, and so on—because those responses are valuable in assessing engagement. If you struggle with grammar and know you'll need as much help as you can get, tell your critiquers. The surefire way to get what you need is to literally, plainly, and bluntly *ask for what you need*.

Occasionally reader feedback is best gleaned if the specific concerns aren't pointed out until *after* the critiquer has finished. I like to get the most authentic read possible from critiquers, which means that I avoid projecting my concerns up front. This way, if they pinpoint something, I know it's a real problem rather than one I've suggested to them beforehand. Try using a follow-up questionnaire: Before you hand over your manuscript, instead of saying, "I'm really struggling with Character X. Other readers have told me he's passive. Does he seem weak to you?" wait until your reader gives you his feedback. If he points out weaknesses in Character X, you know it's a noticeable problem. If not, follow up; ask, "How did Character X strike you?" That way, his opinion guides you rather than the other way around. Here's the caveat: If you plan to ask follow-up questions, let your reader know ahead of time so that he doesn't feel like you're dumping extra work on him after he gives you feedback.

On the other hand, if you've already identified a problem but aren't sure why or how to fix it, explaining the issue and asking a critiquer to "solve for X" can be very helpful.

HOW TO GET IN YOUR OWN WAY, METHOD 12: DON'T TELL PEOPLE WHAT YOU'RE LOOKING FOR

The five or six typos and grammatical errors people find won't help you when you ax that whole chapter.

—BILL FERRIS

SET BOUNDARIES

Clarifying what you want is just as important as asking for what you need. There are two reasons to set boundaries with a critiquer: (1) You know something is a problem and you want to save her time because you're not ready to address it yet (or you've already decided on the solution but haven't implemented it), or (2) you need to protect your momentum on the project by avoiding certain types of feedback before you're ready for them.

Many people write sloppy first drafts. If you know large sections of the book will be cut or rewritten, there's no need to polish yet. As mentioned in the rough-draft example, if you know your draft is a mess and you plan on cleaning up the prose later, it's courteous to let your critiquer know this—and to instead guide her focus to large-scale problems. Likewise, if you're on a deadline and know your structure and characters are finalized and you're only looking for final edits, tell her. It saves time and effort for both of you.

Sometimes hearing critique at the wrong time can derail a writer. Some will argue that all writers should be open to all forms of criticism at all times. That's an admirable goal, but many writers haven't reached a place of absolute critique acceptance. The next best thing is to be aware of our defensiveness and frailties and honor our process by giving the critiquer a heads up.

I was in a bad place when I wrote my fifth novel. I fought for every word, and I was consumed by self-doubt. I felt raw and insecure and ready to trash the whole thing, so I knew I needed craft critique before I was ready to handle reader response critique. Here's how I requested it:

Since this project is new and these characters are so personal to me, I'm not quite ready to hear character critique and emotional reactions just yet. If you could hold off on that and focus instead on structure, theme, clarity, and pacing, it'd be the most helpful to me right now.

This worked beautifully and helped me find my footing again. However, I do want to caution against overusing critique restrictions. Writers should strive toward being open to all criticism, and the best way to build up that strength is to practice—which you can't do if you always ask your critiquers to avoid pushing your buttons. Only you can know the right balance on this, but when in doubt, I encourage you to include fewer restrictions so you can build your tolerance and grow in your receptiveness and, ultimately, your craft.

GUIDE THE TONE

Finally, to get the most out of the process, learn to guide the tone of your feedback. The preferred degrees of positive and negative feedback vary from writer to writer and from critiquer to critiquer, but all critiques should contain a mix of both.

New critiquers, especially, may feel hesitant to give harsh critique, but often that's the most useful feedback. If I'm at the stage where I'm looking for brutal honesty, I like to assuage my critiquer's fears. For example, I might reassure her with the following:

I know you won't want to be the bearer of bad news, but your honesty is so important to me! If there's a problem in my book, I'd much rather hear it from you now than from agents (or readers and reviewers) after it's too late to change it. So please don't hold back.

Likewise, often in an effort to be helpful, some critiquers focus so much on what needs improvement that they forget to point out what's working. Seasoned writers, who are often less sensitive to critique, are especially prone to "cutting to the chase" at the expense of praise. Here's an example of a reminder to highlight the positives:

Of course I want to hear all the things that need work, but I'd also appreciate if you could point out the things that are successful. This helps me pinpoint my strengths so I can work on making them even stronger. It also helps me know what to avoid cutting, and/or what to expand on if I end up doing overhauls.

In fact, I often purposely invite the same critiquer to give both criticism and praise. It's a great way to remind seasoned and newbie critiquers alike to balance their feedback, because ultimately both are vital.

Putting your work in front of someone and asking her to analyze it takes courage. Likewise, offering to dissect someone's work and tell him everything that is and isn't working takes time and effort (and also a bit of courage). The best way to respect your critiquers' generosity is to guide it in the most useful directions possible. Their feedback is meant to help you, after all. If you cut out the guesswork and tell them exactly how they can best do that, you'll both be happier for it.

 HOW TO GET IN YOUR OWN WAY, METHOD 13: TAKE EVERYBODY'S ADVICE

If you're in a writer's group, you'll realize you can safely ignore some folks' advice altogether. If that sounds elitist, console yourself in knowing that some folks feel that way about *your* advice.

—BILL FERRIS

READING THE TEA LEAVES OF CRITIQUE

How to Draw Meaning from Murky Feedback

JAEL MCHENRY

Critique is one of the best and worst parts of the writing process. Best because the right feedback from the right person at the right time can improve your book in ways you never would have figured out yourself. Worst because hearing criticism—right or wrong—can be painful and unpleasant, not to mention demoralizing.

But whether it's good or bad, critique is *necessary*. A story produced completely in isolation is unlikely to be as strong as one that benefits from feedback.

Still, critique can be confusing. What are your readers really saying? What are you supposed to do about it? What if your four readers have four different opinions about the best way to fix an issue? These questions and more bubble in your brain during and after critique sessions. So let's start at the beginning and lay down some helpful tips for digesting someone else's words and deciding what that means for the words you've written.

STOP. BREATHE. WAIT.

No matter how brilliant an insight might seem, jumping in to revise your draft immediately isn't the best idea. Even advice that seems like a stroke of genius at first needs to be thought through. This goes double if the criticism is more intense or wide-ranging than you expected, as in these cases:

- "This first-person past-tense book would be way better if it were in third-person present tense."
- "The best friend is more interesting to me than your narrator. Have you thought about writing this with him as the main character instead?"
- "Your ending is unclear. Just stop the story on page 300—that's a much better ending."

Any time you receive critique like this, the first thing you should do is … nothing. Don't jump into changes like these without careful consideration. Sleep on it, at a minimum. After that, you can open up your thinking and make some decisions about where to go from there.

 **PRO TIP**

If a criticism stays with you for a while or begins to gnaw, your gut could be recognizing an idea worth taking.

WORK FROM YOUR CORE

Critiques aren't commandments. Just because a reader weighs in with an opinion on something, that doesn't mean he's right or that you need to change the story to address his criticism. The story is yours. No matter what you do or don't do, it's your name on the book, and that's absolutely the way it should be.

Frankly, I struggle with this part of critique. Even after years and years of sifting through and reacting to reader advice, it isn't always immediately clear to me whether incorporating someone's concerns will make my book better or just different. You can hone the skill of discernment with practice, but each critique is different. Give the comments you receive a gut check every single time, whether large or small.

Comments from other writers have a tendency to come in a little off-center from what you truly need: More often than not, these writers offer criticism based on *the book that they would have written*. More action? Fewer characters? Shorter sentences? These aren't necessarily universal principles of "better" writing. But if you have a beta reader who loves action and you'd rather keep your scenes realistic and character driven, make sure you're not changing things just to accommodate her tastes.

The story is yours. Keep it that way.

CHOOSE YOUR SOLUTIONS

Often critique takes the form of problem identification. Agents, editors, beta readers, and others might make observations like these:

- "I felt like this section moved too slowly."
- "Too many characters?"
- "I couldn't tell what actually happened at the end of this scene—is she dead or not?"

Other types of comments focus on solutions:

- "This chapter is boring—delete it."
- "I was confused by this scene. Add a few lines of narration to explain it."
- "I didn't buy that she would punch him, so maybe she should slap him."

If your readers offer solutions, walk it back to the problem they're trying to help you solve. There are a dozen different ways to fix a "boring" chapter. You might delete whole paragraphs. You might move some action from a later chapter to an earlier one. You might delete subplots, consolidate characters, sharpen dialogue, or add more vivid description. But you don't ever have to take a specific action suggested in critique in order to make your work better, even if the issue is totally valid. Problems have many solutions. Find the one that works best for you.

INTERROGATE YOUR DEFENSE

I've cautioned several times against blindly making changes to accommodate critiques. But make sure, also, that you're looking at the other side of it: Give every comment a fair shake. Don't dismiss things too quickly.

The point of critique, after all, is to help make your work better—not to be mean, not to castigate you, and not to make the critiquer feel superior. Most readers offer critique in the spirit of goodwill. Producing a quality critique is time-consuming, so don't assume that your readers are listing all sorts of issues with your story for their own amusement. They want to help you. If you're tempted to dismiss a comment immediately, take a step back and ask yourself whether there's some merit to what they're staying.

Some bad defenses include:

- "But that's how it really happened!"
- "But it would take too much time to make that change!"
- "But you're reading it wrong!"

While each person's opinion is theirs alone, you can learn a lot from critique, so listen to what your early readers are saying—because if they're saying it, then there's a good chance your final readers will think the same thing.

You have a chance to make the book better and better until the point when it's published. Why not take advantage of it?

 HOW TO GET IN YOUR OWN WAY, METHOD 14: TAKE CRITIQUE PERSONALLY

Even if your beta readers hate your book (which they don't ... probably), they still like *you*. A thoughtful critique is hard work, and they wouldn't give you one at all if they thought you were a no-talent jerk.

—BILL FERRIS

CREATING CONVERSATIONS WITH STORY EVOLUTIONISTS

How Beta Readers of All Kinds Can Help Your Story Evolve

BRUNONIA BARRY

EDITOR'S NOTE: Brunonia Barry is the international best-selling author of *The Lace Reader*, a novel that sold for seven figures in a major book deal. The following is a description of the process Brunonia went through to ready her book for publication—a process that may very well have helped foster Brunonia's tremendous success with her novel, and one that you, too, can attempt.

• • •

For the last six years, I've been part of a critique group. I find great benefit in having an accessible place to workshop my works-in-progress (WIPs), and I urge you to find or create one that fits your needs. Advice on craft is invaluable, especially when it comes from a group you're comfortable with. But these groups have some limitations. For one thing, it's difficult to read a story more than once; at least it is for me. First impressions are indelible, and, even in the best critique groups, repeated readings tend to numb the reader to what's on the page. It's difficult to pick up subtle changes in the narrative.

The very quality that makes the critique group great can also be its biggest drawback: Its members are writers. And at some point in the evolution of our stories, we need to find *readers*. Early readers we trust can be the key to a story's success.

FIND FRESH EYES NEARBY

Family can be a good place to start seeking critique, providing they are good readers and really want to participate, but they do come with baggage. I hail from a family of good readers, but we don't all like the same kinds of stories. And sometimes our manuscripts are too personal or familiar. My relatives delight in finding the characters they believe most resemble themselves and trying to add extraneous details. It can be quite entertaining, but it's not necessarily helpful. Also, reading a manuscript as a favor is a big commitment. On occasion, and under duress, I've asked family members to read a manuscript more than once, and with the exception of my saintly husband, it's difficult for them to do and almost impossible for them to remain motivated. I wonder if you ever get an objective opinion from people who know you so well.

As with any trusted readers, the law of diminishing returns eventually kicks in. Everyone you know has already read and commented. So where do you look for additional fresh eyes? Personally, I've found great success with the focus group.

RECRUIT A FOCUS GROUP

When the second draft of my first novel was finished, I needed to find out how readers would respond. Having come from another industry where we regularly used focus groups, I began to long for the kind of feedback these groups provide. In the same way that other industries test products, I needed to test my WIP. I wanted to know what worked, what was clear, what remained murky. I had so many unanswered questions: Would readers like the book? Would they even want to read it? Would they root for my protagonist? Did my characters have complete arcs? It was important to answer these questions before I put my book out there because I knew I'd only have one chance. The same "single reading" rule applies in the marketplace—agents and editors are not likely to reread a manuscript. I needed to find out if my book was ready.

Who are your customers? This was always one of the first details we tried to clarify before conducting any focus group. There's no point to asking a group of stamp collectors what they think of a new fly-fishing rod; it simply doesn't apply to them. Similarly, with your manuscript, it's important to identify likely readers. Who are you writing for? What is your story really about?

Though my novel was contemporary, it was heavily influenced by history, which played as large a role as any character in the story. It was also a family saga: Three generations of women from the same family share a gift that has become a curse. Add to that a dark undercurrent of mental illness, religious fanaticism, and abuse, and it became clear that I would have to choose my focus group carefully. I needed seasoned readers who wouldn't mind crossing genres. And contrary to what you'd find in a business focus group, where members tend to be strangers, I needed a group who knew each other well enough to express their opinions without fear of reprisal. In other words, I needed a book club.

FIND THE RIGHT BOOK CLUB

Book clubs are the most serious groups of readers I've met. Over the years, I've held discussions in person or through Skype with more than a hundred of them. Each club is different, and each has its own dynamic and particular reading preferences, but, almost without exception, they are the most dedicated and sophisticated readers outside of graduate classes in comparative lit. Many clubs I've met with have been reading together for a long time, so they are quite comfortable expressing varied opinions, and that is where the group dynamic begins to pay off. They are not afraid to disagree. This is good news for writers: Disagreements act as prompts for discussions that can teach you much more about your stories than you ever knew.

I found my first book club through my local independent bookstore. Prior to writing my stand-alone novel, I'd been writing for a tween series and had done a few signings at the store. The manager asked what else I was working on. She seemed interested in the subject matter and told me to keep her posted on my progress. I knew that the store recommended and ordered books for a number of book clubs, so when my book was finished, I thought the store would be a good place to start. I asked the manager if any of the clubs they worked with might be willing to help out a fledgling author. I pitched the book, detailing character, plot, and thematic issues. "Let me think about it," she said. "I'll get back to you." I wondered if she really would get back to me or if this was too much to ask. Two weeks later, I received a call. She had found me the perfect book club, one that had been together for almost ten years and read all genres of fiction and nonfiction.

During that month, all of my insecurities surfaced. I thought about cancelling. Was I doing the right thing, trusting a book I knew needed rewriting to a club that was accustomed to more polished works? But I assured myself this was the point. The only way to test the novel was to put myself out there. Pushing my fears of humiliation aside, I forged ahead.

> ## PRO TIP
>
> When looking for a critique partner, I look for someone whose talent exceeds mine, in the hopes that his or her insights will take my work to heights higher than I can reach on my own. I've been floored by how many times my partner felt the same way about my work. The truth is, we all bring our unique talents to the pages. What one writer lacks, another excels in and vice versa.
>
> —MM FINCK, AUTHOR OF *#LOVEIN140*

ENCOURAGE HONESTY

I hosted the meeting. Though I'd been nervous about it, the group's easy familiarity erased my fears. But I realized early on that, like me, they also had some trepidation. They were accustomed to very frank discussions of the books they read, but they had never had an author present. How did this thing work? I told them I had a list of questions, but first they should discuss the book as they usually would, as if I weren't there.

This proved to be more difficult than I'd imagined. It started well enough. They took turns describing the book. Each said she liked both character and plot, and complimented my writing style. It was quickly apparent that my biggest challenge would be getting honest feedback. These were nice people. I could tell they didn't want to hurt my feelings.

If this was going to be successful, I needed them to be both honest and opinionated.

Normally, focus groups do not have the product creators present in the room when questions are asked. Few people want to be critical in front of the inventor. Often creators are relegated to a back room hidden by a two-way mirror, listening to comments remotely. Sometimes opinions are even received at a later time, after the group leaders compile and process them.

Realizing I'd made a mistake that must quickly be corrected, I changed tactics.

"Thank you so much for taking the time to do this for me and for letting me know what works for you. Of course I want to hear that you enjoyed the book and the characters, but what would help me most would be to hear what doesn't work. So I'm going to ask you some questions, and I need you to be brutally honest. Nothing short of that will help me to get this book published."

A book club that has been reading together for years possesses a great dynamic, and usually there is at least one member who is outgoing and daring enough to jump in. It helps if you can identify her early on. In this case, it was the club's founder, the one who had persuaded them to read my novel in the first place.

"Tell me what you didn't like about the book," I prompted.

Taking a breath, she spoke. "I thought Cal was too much like my ex-husband," she said. "He's such a creep."

The room erupted into giggles and nods of agreement. The ice had finally broken.

They all agreed that Cal was a creepy guy, which led to discussions about other characters in the novel. I was amazed by the diversity of opinions. A character reminded one reader of someone she knew, but the next group member didn't see him or her that way at all. There were universal opinions, of course. However, where their thoughts differed, I began to wonder if I had drawn the characters sharply enough. Or was this a case of the collaborative process between writer and reader? We may write the words, but our readers bring their own life experiences to the reading, often creating something we haven't foreseen.

CREATE A LIST OF SPECIFIC QUESTIONS

As my questions became more detailed, the club's responses grew more helpful, and I could tell which characters were well depicted and which needed work. They answered every one of my queries in great detail. When I ran out of questions, we moved back to the roundtable discussion they usually had, but it was more honest this time as they circled the room and voiced their real opinions. I listened without comment; I think they almost forgot I was there.

This was gold! I was being told everything that was wrong with the novel. Where they agreed, I knew I had a problem and took copious notes. Where they disagreed, the issue in question became even more interesting. They argued each point of my story. The surprise ending confounded some, while others found it made perfect sense. Two had even reread to make sure I had planted clues throughout the novel that they should have seen. I learned which characters my readers empathized with and which ones were not yet fully developed on the page. I realized that I had to simplify my time line and draw a clearer contrast between past and present because the story jumped back and forth too often for many readers to follow. I also learned that the real work was at the beginning of the novel: I had to find a way to get into the story quicker.

ASK THE PERFECT QUESTION

There may be one question, that, if answered, would help you more than any other. For me it was: "Where did you stop reading and put the manuscript down?"

Every story has points that lag. You have to know where those places are because they may not be as obvious to you as they are to a reader. I had always joked that one of my goals with the book was to keep my readers from sleeping. At what point did these women decide they needed some well-deserved rest?

You might assume that rest would come at different times for different readers, depending on their schedules and how long they'd been reading. This wasn't the case. Almost every reader stopped reading at the same points throughout the story. For the most part, these were not my intended story breaks; they were places that needed rewriting.

The final question I asked was one that is asked in almost every focus group: "Would you recommend this to a friend?"

Without hesitation, the club said they would. In fact, they said they were already doing so. If I let them know when the book was coming out, they would make sure other clubs knew about it.

I tested the book with three different book club focus groups before I felt it was ready for the world. Each one taught me something important, and I am grateful to all of them for their generous help. I think we enjoyed our collaboration, and when the book was finally published, true to their promise, they spread the word.

Whether you decide to use the focus group approach or not, I urge you to test your work with many readers before you set it free. As writers, we often fall in love with our creations and see our characters only as we intend them to be. Whether our intentions are realized on the page is something we need to find out. Getting a glimpse into the reader's viewpoint is a valuable and necessary insight. A good reality check in service of our work is one of the best things we can obtain.

 FAQ

....

Should you shy away from asking fellow writers to beta-read your work?

Not at all. In fact, I seek them out. I've found almost all of my quality beta readers in my critique group. We meet once a week in person, and over the years I've gotten to know everyone's critique styles and writing levels. Once I trust someone and feel like he'd be a good fit, I approach him outside of group and ask him to swap manuscripts. I've found half a dozen stellar, can't-do-without-them betas this way! Some people may fear that writers can't critique without forcing their aesthetic on your work, but a good beta reader (or critique partner) is like any good editor: She tries to make it your best book possible, not *her* book. Maybe I've been lucky, but I feel like any good critique partner keeps that in mind, as should the writer when he's sifting through feedback. Of course, reader-only betas are valuable, too, but only writers or editors are going to have the advanced knowledge of craft necessary to point out deeper or subtler problems, which I find invaluable.

—ANNIE NEUGEBAUER, AUTHOR OF "HIDE"

My best beta readers came from a network of fellow writers. Some I met at conferences and writing courses, and a few were gathered through word of mouth. The key, for me, was finding beta readers who write and read in different genres, not just my own. This provided me with a more rounded opinion pool, as well as outside-the-genre-box thinking.

—DEE WILLSON, AUTHOR OF *A KEEPER'S TRUTH*

Where can I find beta readers who are not writers?

I actually found my best, most honest beta readers through my local library. I simply went in, asked the librarian if any local reading groups met there, and asked if she would pass along my information, as I was looking for people to critique my book. She worked her magic, and voilà—a reading and discussion group was critiquing my book the next week!

—LAURA SEEBER, AUTHOR OF *THE REVELATION OF JACK*

I openly stalk people I find with a book. One day, I had to go to physical therapy, and the receptionist always had a book open. When I asked her about it, she confessed to reading a book a day. I started chatting and asked about which genres she preferred, and she said she liked the one I was writing. I told her about beta readers and what they do, and she's now one of my beta readers.

—KRISTEN LAMB, AUTHOR OF *RISE OF THE MACHINES:*
HUMAN AUTHORS IN A DIGITAL WORLD

I was writing a young adult novel when my son and his friends were the age of my intended audience and when most of my friends had kids around the same age, so I offered to pay them an honorarium of ten dollars each if they'd read the manuscript and answer ten questions (on a piece of paper, not in person). Their input was so much more valuable to me than the hundred dollars it cost me.

—NATALIE HART, AUTHOR OF *AS REAL AS IT GETS*

What about friends and family? Can they make good beta readers?

In an early draft of my first novel, I made a glaring error involving POV. A beta reader who shall remain my mother failed to point it out to me. She claimed she didn't know how much I could handle. Honestly, I think she simply missed it. That is the exact reason we should never use family members unless we can be sure they are willing and able to give us a swift kick in the fanny if such a thing is necessary.

—MIKE SOVA, AUTHOR OF *PARLOR CITY PARADISE*

In my early days, my beta readers were friends who read a lot of the type of stories I write. Friends aren't a bad source if they are honest. Eventually my friendship circle expanded. All of my critique partners were or became friends—workshop colleagues, writers represented by my agent or agency, fellow members of writers' associations, and so on.

—MM FINCK, AUTHOR OF *#LOVEIN140*

 PRO TIP

I found a local bookstore with an espresso book machine, which could produce a bound book in a few minutes using PDF input files. So I produced several galley copies of my work-in-progress. That way, my willing crew of beta readers received a physical book to read. I didn't want to simply hand out a stack of papers or send a Word document file. The espresso machine was one of my best tools while revising the book, not only for my beta readers but also for me. Something about holding my WIP in book form allowed me to see things differently. It was easier to see what wasn't working.

—JOHN KELLEY

(Look for an espresso book machine near you at ondemandbooks.com.)

 HOW TO GET IN YOUR OWN WAY, METHOD 15: SHRINK YOUR CIRCLE

It's easy to rely on your regular group of readers. Getting outside perspectives can make a real difference, though. It's hard to break new ground when everyone knows exactly the same stuff.

—BILL FERRIS

Community Conversation

ILLUMINATIONS OF THEME

How Critique Can Teach Us What Our Work Is Trying to Say

JEANNE KISACKY

My background is in design, not writing, and that has given me an unusual relationship with critique. Design education relies on group critiques, not tests or papers. Students pin their drawings in front of the whole group, and then the teachers and students critique it, pointing out strengths and also weaknesses.

When this process worked, it was fabulous. A good critique could literally turn the light on in the artist, giving her a clear understanding of how to improve the piece. When it didn't work, it was horrendous. The artist, unable to translate the critique into a clear strategy, would grow confused and defeated. Living through years of these pin-ups taught me how to take criticism but also how to identify what made for a good critique.

A good critique can identify the nascent larger significance of a creative work. The artist, whether designer or writer, can then harness that theme as a guide in discerning what to excise and what to insert, honing the artistic details into stronger form. The end result is a work that rings powerful and true. In this essay, I offer guidelines for why you need such a critique, what you should expect from it, and how to use it to turn on the lightbulb within your work.

FIND YOUR THEME

What is your story about? If your answer to that question merely involves a detailed list of characters, settings, and events, then you might benefit from an outside critique.

The characters, settings, and events are your story; the larger meaning that all those story details evoke is what your story is *about.* Think about it as the *theme* or the *point* or the *message.* It is a meta-story: a larger, perhaps universal narrative or conflict that transcends cultures, classes, races, and ages. It is an exploration of the human condition.

Just like a powerful piece of music can transport the listener beyond the experience of the individual notes and inspire visceral emotions, a strong piece of writing can pull readers out of the specific story and draw them into a higher level of awareness. This experience takes the focus away from what is happening and inspires readers to consider why it is happening. Not just *why,* as in the simple cause and effect that lead from one story point to another, but *Why?* with a capital *W.*

Many very successful, highly popular stories include strong themes. Here are a few examples:

- *The Hunger Games* by Suzanne Collins is a story of a girl trying to survive a brutal, structured political event that generates a steady stream of life-threatening situations. It is also about rising above oppression by choosing to take individual action in a political system designed to prevent it.
- Gillian Flynn's *Gone Girl* is a story that details the spectacular dissolution of a marriage. It is also a story about the absurdity of traditional marital relationships in the social dysfunction bred by this modern world.
- In the movie *Up,* produced by Pixar Studios/Disney and written by Pete Docter, Bob Peterson, and Tom McCarthy, a man flies his house to a remote location as a means of fulfilling a promise. The story is about mourning and letting go of the past.

These are not the only themes that can be drawn from these works. Different readers and reviewers of the same book will discover various points and nuances. That variety spawns conversations, reader recommendations, social media attention, watercooler chitchat, and professional reviews.

Clearly, a strong theme is something a writer wants to generate.

UNDERSTAND HOW THEMES MANIFEST IN STORIES

When a story has a strong theme that gives purpose to the actions and characters, readers think about and remember the work for days, months, or even years after they've read it. Without a strong theme giving purpose to your characters' quirks, readers may recall a story's memorable cast without remembering the story they inhabited.

If this kind of harmony between story and theme were easy to create, then all works would have it. In truth, a majority of books include passages where the story and theme work together (usually identifiable as the "good" parts that readers savor) and passages where the story and theme are out of sync (usually identifiable as the boring parts that readers skim or skip altogether).

How, then, do themes work?

From a reader's perspective, themes work like literary magic; they imbue thrilling sequences of events and memorable characters with a sense of larger significance. Readers become aware of not just the story events but also the value of coherence in a crazy world, or meaning in a senseless system, or bravery despite oppression. You get the idea.

From a writer's perspective, how does this effortless magic happen? Through honesty and hard work.

The theme develops when you do the following:

- Become aware of where your work has a larger resonance.
- Clarify exactly what that resonance is.
- Revise until the themes and the story are integrally connected and mutually reinforcing.

This is not easy. It requires seeing the proverbial forest and the trees at the same time.

DISCERN THE THEMES IN YOUR WORK THROUGH CRITIQUE

Developing a theme requires the writer to hold in mind a clear vision of the larger meaning of the story while developing its individual details. This dual mind-set allows the writer to tailor each sentence, each passage, in a way that serves the theme. It also requires a writer to be aware of the themes manifesting in his work, and a writer's daily experience can derail that awareness.

On a daily basis, a writer's focus is necessarily on story movement. What happens next? What is said next? How does the character respond to developments? The theme grows out of the sum total of each of these decisions but often only becomes perceptible after a full draft is done.

Even with a complete draft in hand, it is nearly impossible for a writer to see her own work objectively enough to discover what themes it manifests. Critical self-assessment is almost always filtered through extraneous concerns (and the thoughts that signal them). For example, productive self-editing is often derailed by these emotions:

- exhaustion ("I'm too tired to fix that now.")
- self-congratulation ("That was a minor gaffe, but the rest is so good that I can let this one go.")
- fear of big changes ("Why is this passage not working? Oh, never mind; I'll fix the typos and grammar for now and worry about the big problems later.")
- complacency bred by familiarity ("I've read this so often that I can recite it from memory, so of course it's the way it should be or I would've changed it earlier.")

Those filters keep a writer from clearly seeing the themes in her own work, and that is a tragedy.

Every writer I know whose work needs revision but who is clear on what needs changing is focused and happy (even euphoric). It is when a writer feels lost and doesn't know what needs to be done to fix the work that the process bogs down. Knowledge of a story's larger themes provides a writer with an editorial road map—a means of identifying what needs fixing and how to fix it. This is where outside critique can become illuminating. It offers the writer insight into the larger themes evoked by the story. That insight can enable purposeful, powerful, directed revisions.

Several years ago, I read the work-in-progress of a writer who was struggling with revision following some abstract suggestions from her editor. I told her that she wasn't writing a story about sisters, a recent suicide, and an unfinished life's work; she was writing a story about the meaning of life and death and the struggle everyone goes through in coming to terms with it. She needed to see the strong theme that was already in her work—the road map that gave her the ability to know which scenes were off the path and which were on target.

Several days after I shared these insights with my friend, I heard back from her. She was out of the bog, seeing all the instances of how the theme played through her book and the ways she could make the whole work harmonize with that theme. They were big changes, tough to make after a series of many other big changes in the book's life. She could make them because they made the work better. The task would not be easy, but it was no longer a black hole of uncertainty.

The goal of critique is to give a writer a deeper awareness of the strengths and weaknesses of the story and the themes it evokes.

USE THE THEME TO FOCUS REVISIONS

A critique, in the most basic sense, is an outside opinion that indicates what needs improvement and what is already strong. Thematic critiques that focus on the work as a whole rather than on story details can reveal to a writer two crucially important things:

1. what themes are resonating in the work
2. how and where the story does or does not stay true to those themes

Knowledge of those two things provides the writer with a focus for revision. That sounds simple enough, but in practice, getting and heeding a good thematic critique is challenging.

The same work, particularly in an early stage, can have a number of competing or incomplete themes. Deciding which theme to develop is a critical decision, difficult to make until the writer has done some hard thinking about the story and how it should resonate.

Additionally themes can be shifty: hard to get a good read on, hard to discuss in terms of pragmatic nitty-gritty editing, and easy to misinterpret or misjudge. Discussing themes is often abstract, almost philosophical, rather than a conversation about what happens in specific scenes to specific characters. Trying to rewrite a scene to draw out a theme can be like trying to pin the tail on a cloud.

Writing is a lonely, frustrating, at times bewildering task. Facing down critique, trying to understand it, and then digesting it into a new clarity is one of the most rewarding experiences in rewriting. Without that self-discovery, that internalizing and then refocusing of the work by the writer, a crucial step in creativity is lost.

FACE THE CRITIQUE, DEVELOP IT, AND IMPROVE YOUR WRITING ALONG WITH YOUR SKILL SET

Synthesizing a thematic critique improves the writer as well as the story. Thinking through the repercussions of rewriting a scene to draw out a theme makes the writer far more aware of how the details of writing influence the thoughts and feelings evoked in the reader. That skill gets easier and better with practice. It can bring the writing to a new level, where theme and details can work in harmony even in the earlier drafts.

You will know you are on the right track when the lightbulb goes on and the thought of all the revisions needed to strengthen the theme doesn't make you tired but instead excited.

You will know you are on the right track when your path to make the work better is as bright as day, shining before you. Illuminated.

 COMMUNITY CONVERSATION

The Writer Unboxed community weighs in online. Please consider adding your voice by visiting Writer Unboxed via this QR code or link to the site. Join the conversation at writerunboxed.com/illuminations, and use the password "aip" (all lowercase).

Writer Unboxed is a moderated community, but comments that evolve a conversation in a positive manner are always welcome.

SUSAN SETTEDUCATO: "Facing down critique, trying to understand it, and then digesting it into a new clarity is one of the most rewarding experiences in rewriting." Yes! This is so beautifully said. As a fine arts major, I sat through many critiques, both useful and horribly destructive. What I learned was that finding someone who really sees what you are trying to do engenders an extraordinary kind of trust. Trust is big. Trust in one's teacher, one's editor, one's beta readers. I guess this came up for me as I was reading your essay because there's a kind of alchemy that happens with a good editor and a receptive writer. The first time someone pointed out the larger themes in my story, I did feel that light go on. I felt it in my body like a buoyancy or a giant inner *yes*. The Japanese have a word for this that translates loosely to "belly art." In working with my present editor, who has helped me pin down the point(s) of my story, I've gotten to feel that amazing entrainment. Not all

---

the time, but enough to know that it's real. And I've certainly experienced it in other books, and as you say, those are the stories that stick. Thanks for this.

JEANNE KISACKY: Susan, as a fellow fine arts survivor, you clearly know of what you speak! Trusting your critique partner is a crucial aspect of being able to get past the criticism and to the inspiration. Trust defuses defensiveness, and no matter how scary it is to make yourself vulnerable to a critique, the joy of that moment when you see the potential in your own work is worth it. May you continue to find those moments where you feel it in your body "like a buoyancy or a giant inner *yes!*" What a fabulous way to describe it.

TOM POPE: Jeanne, I love how you have verbalized the ineffable. And to reply, I must grope through a dark realm.

Theme may become apparent only late in the process, but doesn't it arise fused with the character and her objective? Shouldn't it be so? After all, art comes from the author, who breathes theme every day. And if that's true, theme has the same force and perhaps point of conception as do backstory and character challenges.

Peering into that first inspiration of story, I sense all the elements of the finished work present, though at best only in molten form or as vibration. That's what's so exciting. When I start writing, it seems that theme is part of what charges the expressive drive and shapes the work unseen. Later, if my first draft is going well, somewhere in the second half, I start to relax, and away from the text I conjure ideas about what lies deep. (Note to self: Trying to label things hinders the muse.)

Looking forward, my standard for a great work is one in which the thought, speech, character decisions, and narration on the page are rooted in theme but never declare it, throwing its discovery into the readers' lap. Critique partners, beta readers, and editors are invaluable because they feel theme and note points of a draft's disconnect from it. Their feedback clears this author's plaque. With their help and with time, I'm better able to go back and revise the words, staying true to the template the theme has laid.

JEANNE KISACKY: Tom, trying to come at theme head-on never does seem to work, does it? Your description of process is beautiful, and I agree with you that in a great work "the thought, speech, character decisions, and narration on the page" will inevitably carry theme ... and yet still only hint at words, "throwing its discovery into the readers' lap."

A story is a ground-level view—a walk with a character through a sequence of landscapes and events where the present details loom large and immediate, and the horizon and obscuring elements limit awareness and vision. A theme is the sum total of what all of those experiences evoke, a sense that there is something larger underlying the immediate details. Joy to the writer who can sense and evoke elements of theme as the first draft is written, but joy doesn't come to all of us easily. There are times when the walk with the character gets confused—when the story gets lost and the writer struggles to discern the false trails and dead ends. In that case, an awareness of theme offers a sense of the through-path. A thematic critique does not release the writer from focusing on story nor give him carte blanche to succumb to the direct and overbearing statement of the *point* of the work. Rather, it provides an awareness of what needs sharpening. A thematic critique should lead the writer to fix the story, and in doing so, the theme shines through.

Theme does indeed "arise fused with the character and her objective." A thematic critique is an affirmation that the character and her objective are in sync and meaningful.

NATALIE HART: SOLD! As a writer who also edits, I've always known the value of an outside eye and always been glad for the feedback—although that pin-up process sounds super-brutal. Brooding in private or ostentatiously refusing to open the critique e-mail for two days is sometimes part of my process. But I've never had a thematic critique, and now I have to have one for every manuscript. I know the theme I'm going for, but whether I've maintained a good, rich focus on it is so difficult to grasp. Since I know what I'm trying to say, I can (and do) fill it in, even when it isn't on the page. Your essay really made me excited, which isn't usually the attitude one associates with critique, but I can't wait for my current manuscript to be ready for a thematic critique—I'm excited enough that I may resume truly regular work on it. Thank you, Jeanne!

JEANNE KISACKY: There is such a joy in feeling on target with writing and inhabiting that place where the doubts fade away and there is no such thing as writer's block. The best word I've ever found to describe it is *flow*, where the words just come onto the page as if by magic. I'm so glad that this piece may have helped put you back on that path.

The best advice I've ever been given regarding critiques for the critique-averse is to read the comments all the way through when you get them and then put them away and do other things for a day or two—go for long walks, clean the house. While you do this, a part of your brain is chewing on the comments. Then when you get back to the comments, they'll spark inspiration rather than doubt.

DONALD MAASS: Jeanne, thinking about theme tends to lead authors to abstractions. While that is not wrong, I suspect that it doesn't help develop story. To opine, "What my novel is really about is ..." doesn't by itself make a novel more meaningful.

What does help is turning that abstraction into story events. To put it differently, an identified theme can be a prompt, a spur, an imperative. *How can I make my novel fulfill its theme more deeply?*

Theme isn't an end or a summation; it is a beginning and a prod. It can generate more story and enrich the journey of a novel's characters.

The more that theme is embedded and hidden in what happens, the more we readers will recognize it. That in turn starts with the author recognizing it and then building in enough clues for us to get the point.

We can't talk enough about theme, so thanks!

JEANNE KISACKY: Donald, I agree we can't talk enough about theme and that the best strategy is to use the theme, which is "embedded and hidden in what happens," to strengthen the story rather than the reverse. Abstraction is definitely both an opportunity and a danger. I think that talking abstractly about a story's theme can pull a writer to the next level because the theme acts as a prompt, but it also presupposes that the writer, the writing, and the story have reached a stage of formation that allow for turning abstraction into solid story details. You are right: The danger is that after an abstract critique, writers may turn to abstract writing. And while a story with a theme about ending poverty could potentially be incredibly rewarding, a story that talks directly about ending poverty could be misery. Trying to tackle theme directly inevitably ends up sounding like preaching; maybe that's why it works so much better when embedded in a story.

VALERIE P. CHANDLER: Thanks for such a thought-provoking article. I needed it. (Isn't it funny how we have to be reminded of things at different points in our writing?)

I have a theme throughout my book, but it's been tricky not to hit the reader over the head with it.

Whack! Whack! This is the theme! See?

It's been a balancing act in making it apparent yet subtle enough that it doesn't pull the reader out of the story. So I've used allusions and literary references to add some depth.

I'm currently in revisions, so I have some cloud-pulling to do, too.

JEANNE KISACKY: That direct approach sometimes seems so simple, so much easier than figuring out how to get the reader to pick up on theme based only on story details. But it never works (except for maybe Robert M. Pirsig's *Zen and the Art of Motorcycle Maintenance*). So you have the reverse problem of most writers: You have a good sense of the forest, and now it's up to you to lead the reader, tree by tree, through it in a way that gives them a sense of the larger shape and importance of what they are walking through.

LJ COHEN: In my own writing, I'm rarely conscious of theme at the first-draft stage—at least not at the start of the story. I think theme is the thing that emerges when the conscious and the subconscious minds are working in concert. While the conscious mind chases after story—plot and character and setting—the subconscious mind is quietly mining perceptions and experiences, and layering the evolving story with elements that link all the disparate parts into a greater whole.

That is, when it works smoothly.

When I hit a wall in the drafting, or if something isn't working in the revision process, it almost always needs to be fixed on the theme level first. Otherwise I end up making blind, random changes that don't touch the core issues.

Of course that means, at some point in the process, I have to understand and clearly see the themes, which can be hard to do. I've never formally received a theme critique, but a good beta reader—and I have been fortunate to have a bunch of them—can lead you right to the heart of the problem.

JEANNE KISACKY: LJ, what a perfect way to say it: "... theme is the thing that emerges when the conscious and the subconscious minds are working in concert." You hit the nail on the head.

 PRO TIP

Does critique evolve the story or further illuminate a character's motivations or a theme? Making a change might also develop your instincts and skills as a storyteller.

 FAQ

Should agents and editors replace other beta readers after publication?

No, no, no! More voices mean more story, more depth, more sales. Many full-time authors I know continue to work with their critique partners. I know best-selling authors with teams of beta readers. Every reader misses things, so cast a wide net to make sure story opportunities don't get away.

—DONALD MAASS

Eye on the Prize

SKIN LIKE AN ELEPHANT

How Critiques Affect the Stories of Professional Writers

SARAH MCCOY

I confess that I am a story pleaser. It's an odd paradox, given that I'm not particularly a people pleaser. My parents advocated individuality and independence, so growing up, I carried a confident perspective that if a certain group of popular people didn't take to me, obviously they weren't *my* brand of popular. And that's okay! Human favor is a fickle wind, not something to set one's compass by. The point is never the opinion—it's what you *do* with that opinion.

Flash forward a few decades to when I walked into my MFA creative writing program. This was the big league, or at least it was to me. I didn't get my undergraduate degree in English; journalism and public relations were my bailiwicks. I had writing tools for an entirely different narrative form. Yet there I was—committed to being an in-residence *fiction* writer. A storyteller. Only I wasn't entirely sure how to do that. I felt the calling, however, to weave narrative yarns out of thin air, to entertain, to please.

GATHER AROUND: WORKSHOP 101

Into the workshop sanctuary I brought my first short story: lovingly crafted, double-spaced, one-inch-margined, collated, evenly stapled copies. The rules were simple: I handed out my work, and my fellow writers read, analyzed, and returned the following class period ready for discussion. As the author, I was to take the role of mute fly on the wall. I'd noted that the second- and third-year

MFA-ers wouldn't so much as lift their eyes from their journals during these critical evaluations, and I followed professional suit. The manners of *pro* writers! I was determined to join their ranks.

A week later, I entered my designated workshop. Oh, to even have a workshop focused on *my* work—it made me giddy … and *terrified*. I had a belly full of hopeful nerves that I'd done the job well. That my story had engrossed, enlightened, and amused as a pleasing offering to the story saints. With naïve confidence, I set out my journal to jot down all the encouragement and ideas for plot expansion that I knew would come from my esteemed tribe. Then, with my face down and ears up, I waited for them to begin.

"Let's start with the title," said my professor, a sage woman of words whom, to this day, I bow before reverently. "*The Awakening* by Sarah McCoy." She waited with eyebrows peaked.

A hand shot up across the table, one of my fellow first-years. (Old student habits die hard—we'd been instructed to speak candidly in conversation without being called on.) "You can't title a work by the same name as another book, particularly a book of literary canon. *The Awakening* was already used by Kate Chopin."

I flushed. I. Was. A. Rube. I hadn't read any Chopin and cursed my non-English bachelor's degree, insufficient in a room full of literary scholars. I jotted down the name. First thing in the morning, I'd go to the library and get that book. I'd read all night so that by the next class meeting, I'd be much wiser.

My professor smiled. "Correct. You cannot. Now, what else is wrong with the title?"

What *else*? We were still on the title! I looked up and met the eyes of my colleagues—a knee-jerk reaction, a cardinal sin of workshop. My professor's brows lifted higher. I broke out in a visible sweat and mumbled an apology. Cardinal sin number two broken: The author was never to speak. They graciously ignored my muttering and went on to probe, dissect, and review every character sigh, action, prose cadence, and semicolon. I was numb through it all, too busy silently berating myself for failing my readers from the beginning— from *hello, this is my name*—to think clearly. I spent the next couple of weeks obsessively revising in an attempt to include every critique in our three-hour workshop—to please every single reader.

Have you ever chewed a piece of gum for so long that it turns into a wad of mealy mush? That was my work-in-progress, *The Awakening*. I tried to console myself: It was my first exercise in professional creative writing; it didn't have to be perfect; it didn't have to work; I ought to learn from it and move on. But

I couldn't. What bothered me went far deeper. All of my life, I'd been a person who respected other people's opinions but would never have based my entire self-worth on them. Yet here I was, allowing these subjective judgments to entirely transform my story worlds—extensions of my imagination, of myself. I was miserably *un*happy about not having made other people happy with my storytelling.

I wish I could tell you that I worked through that. I wish this was a missive on how to overcome that compulsion and say, "Fie to you! Like it or not, I shall be what I shall be!" But the truth is that I spent the next three years in my MFA program feeling each negative critique like a burn until I'd formed calluses over every inch of my authorial skin.

"You've got to have skin like an elephant," that same sage professor told us. "Anything less and you'll bleed out at your first scratch. The pro-writer world is a safari."

LISTEN TO THE PROS(E)

I asked some pro-writer friends about their experiences with critical feedback. Their stories are insightful glimpses into how critique—from readers, editors, friends, and others—colors their work and writing process.

> When I first started writing, I was very eager for opinions. I hadn't yet learned to trust my own instincts, and I think that's something that comes with time. When I finished my very first novel (long ago chalked up to a "learning experience"), I eagerly printed it out and sent it to two trusted, well-read friends. After a few days, they both got back to me: "Oh, wonderful, Melanie!" "I'd certainly read this! Well done!" I was so happy—until I realized that somehow, when printing it off, I hadn't included the final two chapters; what they'd read and "honestly" critiqued wasn't even the entire manuscript. When I gently pressed my friends about this, they both did then hesitantly reveal that they'd thought it'd ended a little abruptly. "But it was still good!" That was the last time I ever asked a friend for a critique. It's just not possible for someone who likes you and wants you to succeed—and someone who has to see you in real life, at the school pickup line or the supermarket—to give you an honest, kick-in-the-pants critique. And that's the kind of critique you need in order to succeed, until you are in the place where you can do that to yourself … . And as embarrassing as that experience was, I am thankful for it, because it really did force me to rely on my own instincts rather than someone else's.
>
> —Melanie Benjamin, *New York Times* best-selling author of
> *The Swans of Fifth Avenue*

I will never understand the writers who say they don't read their reviews. Reviews are written by readers, and readers are an author's customers. Ignoring your customers is never a good idea. Writers cannot afford to be delicate flowers. They must be mighty oaks. Online reviews on sites like Amazon and the like have been helpful to me. If you look at the reviews for my first two novels (*Something Missing* and *Unexpectedly, Milo*), you'll see very positive reviews and ratings, but you'll also find a consistent criticism: My novels start out slow. Reviewers advise potential readers to give the books a chance. Stick with them. Don't give up. They say that the stories are worth the slow start. I paid attention to these reviews. I accepted the fact that I may have a tendency to ease into a story, exploring character before really launching into the plot. And while that may be the way I prefer to tell a story, most readers prefer a little plot to get the story moving early on. As a result, I write a little differently today. I find a way to get my plot rolling a little earlier. I look for ways to hook my readers in the early pages. And I think my books are better because of it. Writers don't need to adhere to the criticism of their reviewers, but to ignore the reviews completely is a ridiculous waste of potentially valuable data.

—Matthew Dicks, international best-selling author of
The Perfect Comeback of Caroline Jacobs

For one of my earlier books, I noticed that I had more than one hundred five-star reviews on Amazon and was feeling quite proud because that means my book's wonderful, right? And then one night on tour, needing a little feel-good moment before going to bed, I looked at the reviews again and saw that the most recent review was a one-star [review]. He'd read less than a chapter before dismissing it as a "chick book." Being the thin-skinned writer that I am, I ignored the one hundred good reviews and obsessed on that one bad review as if that were the only one that held any truth. I turned my obsession into a mini-Internet stalking episode until, three hours later, I realized what I was doing. That's when I had my epiphany: It will never be in a writer's best interest to allow an anonymous review to affect her writing or self-worth.

—Karen White, *New York Times* best-selling author of *Flight Patterns*

I had an editor once who said I had to ask the same three questions of all my female protagonists, and those questions had to inform the story throughout the book: *What does she want? Why can't she have it? How is she going to get it?* The books I wrote with her had far more drama and suspense than my previous books, and although I have softened my stories and gone back to my character-driven roots, I am always aware of those questions in the back of my mind.

—Jane Green, *New York Times* and international
best-selling author of *Summer Secrets*

We had written two manuscripts that hadn't sold. Hell, we couldn't even get an agent! Everyone said the same thing: Your writing shows promise, but something is missing. The only problem? We didn't know what that "something" was. Then, while writing our third novel, a published writer friend generously offered to take a look and gave us some amazing feedback: Show; don't tell. It was simple, but in just a few spots, she had put her finger on exactly what we were doing wrong. That weekend we added ten thousand words based on her critique. And before we knew it, we had a finished manuscript that sold very quickly to Atria Books—and a ton of gratitude for our wonderful writerly friend.

—Liz Fenton and Lisa Steinke, co-authors of *The Year We Turned Forty*

Some people love to revise. I'm not one of them. The pleasure of writing, for me, comes from that initial imaginative thrust, when I'm filling up white space. And yet, revision—prescribed by my editors, as stressful and frustrating as their advice can be—has saved all of my published novels. It's not that I don't polish on my own. I do. Mercilessly and constantly. That's how I begin every morning, fine-tuning what I worked on yesterday. But after I've taken the draft as far as it can go, there's always more work to be done. Work I can't recognize on my own. I need that outside set of eyes to tell me this subplot is distracting, this character's motivations are muddled, the point of view ought to switch from first to third, the final act is a train wreck, etc. Maybe this will change, but it's been true for my four novels: I will cut hundreds of pages from every manuscript and write hundreds more to take their place. And by the time I'm done, I recognize how essential the changes are, how much prouder of the story I am, how my editor is a coach who helps me realize my potential.

—Benjamin Percy, award-winning author of *The Dead Lands*

I spent two years working on a historical novel [while] under contract to Algonquin Books. I didn't show my editor any pages after she'd approved the proposal, figuring it would be best to give her a finished—meaning revised many times—draft. When she finally read it, she had serious issues, one of which was that she thought there should be a modern-day story threaded through the historical one: not a simple frame, a nearly equivalent storyline. This was not at all what I had in mind, but I respected her opinion and decided to give it a try. This necessitated pulling the entire book apart, eliminating characters, changing plot points and character roles, throwing out well over a hundred pages and adding in about 120. It took another two years. But now we have a book we're both proud of, *The Muralist*, which was a number one Indie Next List [selection], so clearly she was right. And so was I for listening to her.

—B.A. Shapiro, *New York Times* best-selling author of *The Muralist*

LEARN FROM THE WRITER SAFARI

For my part, I've officially been on safari since 2009 with the release of my debut novel. Since then, I've published a novella in an anthology and two more novels (including my latest, *The Mapmaker's Children*). I thought it was tough having a dozen writers sit around a table critiquing my work—until I received thousands of readers' reviews.

Everyone has an opinion, and I respect those opinions. I listen earnestly to reviewers, honored that they've taken the time to read my work when there's a plethora of good writing out there. But I've since learned to use critiques constructively—as kindle for my writing goals. They refine and sharpen my narrative tools so I can be even more efficient in crafting future novels. I've also learned that not every criticism need be branded on my bibliographical body. The challenge for authors is to objectively decide which subjective opinions are seasoned timber and which are soggy greenwood. Leave the wet sentiments to smoke up someone else's campfire, and use the critical lumber to blaze your trail.

When we look back on our respective writing legacies, what we're all seeking is a "The End" that's well done—a life story that satisfies. I try to remember that, so long as I feel my heart beating in my chest, I'm only in the midst of a chapter, and that it's important that our journeys please the pleasers, too.

GIVING BACK

How Helping Someone Else Write a Better Book Turns into a Win-Win-Win

KEITH CRONIN

Writing can be a very solitary pursuit. It's not a team sport (unless you're collaborating), and all the responsibility—and the associated insecurity—falls solely on your shoulders. When working on a single project for months or years at a time, it's easy for a writer to feel isolated. But through the wonder of the Internet, writers can now meet, interact, and form entire communities—all without ever leaving the house.

At its best, this ability to connect with other literary kindred spirits can be truly life-changing. At the very least, it's incredibly empowering for writers of all skill levels to have the ability to communicate with—and learn from—other writers across the globe. But as Spider-Man taught us, with great power comes great responsibility. (Okay, depending on your background, you might have been taught this by Winston Churchill or perhaps the apostle Luke. Me, I get my philosophical insights from comic books. Don't judge.)

My point is this: Writers have access to this incredibly powerful resource, and I believe we each have the responsibility to not only take advantage of the Internet's endless flow of information but to *contribute* to that flow. Possibly the worst aspect of the Internet is that it has generated a culture of "takers" who have grown to expect—and feel entitled to—an infinite stream of content, typically provided at no cost. So I'm on a mission to combat that sense of entitlement and to promote the Internet as a platform that enables us not only to take but also to participate and contribute. In other words, to give something back.

HOW TO GET IN YOUR OWN WAY, METHOD 17: BELIEVE YOU'RE ENTITLED TO YOUR READERS' TIME

Do you know what a hassle it is to critique a manuscript? By definition, early drafts have loads of problems. Your critique partners have better things to do than reread your 160,000-word epic fantasy for the third time. Like write their own manuscript, which, by the way, could use a fresh set of eyes.

—BILL FERRIS

Obviously, the Internet is not the only vehicle via which writers can connect. Many writers meet regularly in critique groups or in larger, more formal organizations that focus on a particular literary genre. But not everybody lives near a local chapter of the Mystery Writers of America, nor can everybody afford to fly across the country to one of the giant annual conferences held by the Romance Writers of America. However, nearly all writers have access to the Internet, which in turn gives them access to each other.

The reason I'm harping on the Internet is that it has allowed me to form connections—and in some cases, deep friendships—with writers whom I never would have met face-to-face. But by interacting and communicating with them online, I've had some amazing "you show me yours and I'll show you mine" moments. (Hey, I'm talking about *manuscripts*. Get your mind out of the gutter.)

HELP SOMEBODY WRITE A BETTER BOOK

One of the biggest challenges writers face is maintaining some objectivity about their work. Most writers—myself included—feel it's essential to have other people read and comment on their work at the near-final stage, to help them decide whether a manuscript is ready for prime time. Over the years I've gained invaluable insights from beta readers whose comments identified plot holes and weak spots as well as components of the story they liked and wanted to see amped up. In short, they helped me write a better book.

In turn, I try to help other people write better books. Not just because it's a nice thing to do. Not just for good karma (more on that later). But because analyzing and critiquing the work of others helps me do a better job of writing and editing my own work.

Oddly, as much as we may love to get feedback on our work, a surprising majority of writers I've encountered are reluctant to give feedback in return. I've heard a variety of excuses, usually along the following lines:

I'm always hungry for critiques on my work. But I don't feel justified in critiquing anybody else. After all, I've never been published. I've never secured an agent. So what qualifies me to critique someone else's writing?

I'm so new at this. I think I'm probably the last person who should be offering any reciprocating comments. I figure I should just stay quiet until I have more experience.

I don't feel I have the language or grammar skills to make comments and suggestions on other people's writing, other than "I liked that part," or "That ending didn't really work for me," or things like that.

You could sum up all of these reasons in the immortal words of Wayne and Garth from *Wayne's World*: "We're not worthy!"

I have two responses to these excuses. One is admittedly a dose of "tough love," while the other is perhaps more encouraging. So let's get the tough love over with first.

1. **SORRY, BUT THAT'S BULLSHIT.** If you're at a point where you're serious enough about your writing that you're trying to get it published, you're also ready to start developing and exercising some editorial skills. The reality is that writing and editing go hand in hand. You won't magically become "good enough" to critique other people's work—or to write publishable prose, for that matter—without first developing those skills. Bottom line, if you're ready for the decision-making involved in trying to write something publishable, you're ready to form an opinion about whether a piece of writing works. Okay, now that I've gotten that out of my system, let's move on to warmer, fuzzier waters. (Wait—how can water be fuzzy? Ewww. Anyway, moving on ...)

2. **YES, YOU *ARE* WORTHY.** Even if you're a newbie. Even if it's been years—or decades—since you last cracked a grammar textbook. Even if you don't know a dangling participle from a flux capacitor. You are worthy because you already have the one tool every writer needs: your gut.

GET IN TOUCH WITH YOUR GUT

Critiquing calls on you to do two things: *react* and *analyze*. When you read something with the goal of providing a critique, you need to pay attention to your own reactions. That's where your gut comes in. Don't overthink this part. You don't need to go into grammar-Nazi mode or diagram any sentences. Just keep asking yourself at a gut level: Do you like it, or does it not quite work for you? Were you cruising along nicely until you hit that word or that plot twist? Keep your radar up as you read, and pay attention to any speed bumps you hit.

Bear in mind that this is something *everybody* is qualified to do, regardless of her level of experience or education. We're just looking at whether or not you liked something. Liking is an innate human behavior. I mean, you know whether you like chocolate. You know whether you like back rubs. Guess what? You also know whether you like what you're reading.

After you read and react, it's time to analyze. Why didn't that scene work? Why did that word jar you, or why did that grammatical construct pull you out of the story? The extra step of figuring out why you didn't like something forces you to develop your critical thinking, leading to some aha moments that you can apply when critiquing other writing, including your own.

But give yourself a break. A sentence may sound wrong to you, but you might not know the precise grammatical reason. So how would you rewrite that sentence to sound better? Again, trying to improve a piece of writing is something anybody can do. And who knows? Maybe this will prompt you to do a little research and discover the grammatical rule that you had intuitively sensed was being violated. In my experience, the lessons you learn this way—when you're actually trying to solve a problem rather than simply memorizing some arbitrary rule—are far more likely to ingrain themselves in your brain, and they will inform your own writing from that point on.

RINSE AND REPEAT ... AND IMPROVE

Learning to critique is a cumulative skill. Through repetition, you'll actually feel yourself getting better at it. Repetition is key for two reasons. First is the whole "practice makes perfect" aspect. But the even more powerful skill that repetition provides is the ability to see patterns—both bad and good—in other people's writing.

Although we're all unique, the reality is that most writers make a lot of the same mistakes, particularly during the early phases of their development. It could be related to simple mechanics, like mixing up *less* and *fewer*, or incorrectly punctuating dialogue. It could be a stylistic weakness, like not varying the length and structure of the sentences in a paragraph, or maybe it's the tendency to spew a page or two of literary throat clearing before getting to where the story should actually start.

Whenever you figure out what was bugging you about a piece of writing, that cognitive process will create a new arrow in your quiver of literary critique projectiles (how's that for a strained metaphor?). Seriously, it's amazing how the process of thinking critically and identifying a specific problem will sensitize you to other instances of that same problem. The more you critique, the easier it becomes to spot these flaws, because they begin to appear as readily identifiable patterns.

And here's the coolest part: With this increased sensitivity, it will be easier to find and eliminate these flaws in your own writing. This is important because let's face it: We generally have to function as our own editors most of the time. And with the growing emphasis on self-publishing, the ability to edit—whether it's somebody else's work or your own—has become an absolutely crucial skill.

GET READY TO MAKE YOUR MARK

One of the great things about this rapidly evolving technological era is that you can read and mark up a manuscript in whatever way best suits your lifestyle and/or work flow. I used to print everything out and mark up the physical manuscript with a pen. Later I shifted to reading manuscripts on my computer, marking them up using the Track Changes feature in Microsoft Word. These days, I e-mail Word documents to my Kindle—a simple trick surprisingly few writers are aware of—and mark it up using Kindle's commenting function. This frees me from needing to be near my computer or lugging around a thick stack of paper. It also gives me the most realistic simulation of reading a published novel, which makes the experience feel more natural and organic—and less like grading somebody's homework. Whatever method you choose, just make sure you have the ability to visually tag the specific parts of the manuscript you want to comment on.

Okay, now that you're set up and ready to start critiquing, let's do this thing.

I've talked about dividing the act of critiquing into reacting and analyzing. When I'm in reacting mode, I try to keep my momentum going so that I don't get bogged down in analyzing things too much. I record any reactions or comments as quickly as I can.

In fact, you don't need to write anything; you can just underline a word, make an X next to a paragraph that rubbed you the wrong way, or write a question mark next to a passage you didn't understand. Later you can study the places you marked to identify what made you stumble. My memory is not great, so I'll leave myself notes like "Why would he do that?" or "This is implausible."

I recommend that you try not to fall into total copyeditor mode during this phase, but do flag any glaring typos you encounter. Just remember to read first with your gut (or your heart or whatever metaphor you prefer) because that's how most people will read *your* stuff.

During this part of the process, don't just focus on the negative. Make a point to mark the good stuff, too. Draw a smiley face when something delights or amuses you, or an exclamation point when you're surprised or dazzled. Then go back and analyze it to see why it impressed you. And, of course, consider whether it's something you can adopt in your own writing.

While these simple marks help you capture your reactions without interrupting the reading experience, I've found they can have other benefits as well. One friend I've read for is a highly sophisticated British author who has been quite vocal in his dislike—okay, more like scorching hatred—of all emoticons. Yet he wrote back to me after I critiqued one of his manuscripts, admitting that he had become addicted to finding each new smiley face in the marked-up manuscript I'd sent him. In a surprisingly revelatory confession, he described how he became increasingly frustrated and disappointed if too many pages went by without any smiley faces. This experience taught me that even when we critique writers known for their stiff upper lips, we still need to show them a little love.

Once you've marked up the manuscript, it's time to go into analyzing mode. While this is the hard part, I also think it's the good part because here's where I really start to feel my brain growing. At this point, I'll create a new document to capture my observations. Later on, I'll harvest from that document to draft a summary of my critique. My end deliverable to most authors I've read for is a marked-up manuscript and a page or two that summarizes both my overall reaction and any observations about specific parts of the manuscript.

BREAK IT TO THEM GENTLY

Occasionally you may encounter a manuscript that simply doesn't work. Here's where it's important to acknowledge how subjective tastes are. There are plenty of best-selling novels that I find unreadable, and I suspect you can say the same. So just because you hate what you're reading doesn't mean somebody else won't love it.

When I encounter this issue in a manuscript I've been asked to read, I'll spend some time carefully drafting a note to the writer, explaining that I've concluded I'm simply the wrong person to review this piece. Here's my rationale: Completing a manuscript is a huge achievement, and I don't want to crap all over somebody's labor of love just because it's not my kind of book. So I essentially "recuse myself from the jury" in situations like these. While the writer is inevitably disappointed, I think this is a far more merciful approach than tearing apart something that I never would have chosen to read in the first place.

Even with a manuscript you enjoy, it's inevitable that you will have some negative reactions to share with the writer. That's okay; they want and expect some constructive criticism. But I think it's important to put the time and effort into being diplomatic, "caveating" your criticism (I'll repeatedly emphasize that this is "just my opinion"), and making sure to highlight both the good and the bad. Writing can lay a person bare emotionally, and it's a major gesture of trust that another writer asked you to review his work. Make sure you treat that trust with the respect it deserves.

GIVE THE GIFT THAT KEEPS ON GIVING

Obviously I'm a big proponent of critiquing, both as a powerful skill builder and as a way to give back. I've had some pretty incredible experiences as a result of corresponding with other writers and critiquing their work. For example, in 2004 an author who'd previously published a couple of romances sent me a manuscript to critique that had her publishers scratching their heads because it was such a departure from her first two novels. In her e-mail, she blithely added, "I know my current title sucks, so let me know if you have any ideas." The book completely blew me away, so I sent her some editorial comments and a list of possible titles. At the top of the list was the phrase "Water for Elephants," which Sara Gruen ended up using as her title. It's been an unbelievable thrill to see how successful that manuscript has become, and deservedly so. And at the time, Sara and I hadn't even met face-to-face. Thank you, Internet.

At this point I hope I've made a convincing case for the many benefits you can derive from reading and critiquing the work of other writers. If that's not incentive enough, consider this: *I got my first book deal because I critiqued somebody.*

Years ago a writer whom I'd only encountered at Backspace, a popular online forum for writers, reached out to me privately to ask for help on a query she was drafting for her latest manuscript. I did my best to help her and promptly forgot about it. Two or three years later, when I lamented in a Backspace post that I was about ready to give up on trying to sell my novel, she reached out to me again, asking if I'd be interested in a referral to a publishing house she'd worked with. I was, she referred me, they liked me … and all of a sudden I'd sold a freaking book. All because I, an unpublished writer, once gave a critique to an already published author who found my input helpful.

I'm not saying the same will happen to you. But who's to say it won't? I can tell you this: Historically, when I've given back *without expecting anything in return*, I have reaped the greatest rewards. Pretty cool, this karma stuff.

So please consider reading and critiquing the work of other writers. Or don't. It's your choice, and it's your opportunity. But don't wait to magically become qualified to do it. If you take writing seriously, you already are.

 HOW TO GET IN YOUR OWN WAY, METHOD 18: SAY YOU'RE TOO BUSY TO READ OTHER WRITERS' WORK

You can't read everything, of course, but you can learn a lot from your peers' work. For example, you can learn you're insanely jealous of their talent, thus inspiring you to up your game so you can one day crush them.

—BILL FERRIS

PART FOUR

IMPROVE

One of the primary gifts of critique is learning where our stories are the weakest and using that knowledge to examine our storytelling toolboxes for global shortcomings. Are our settings often flat? Are our plots predictable? Do our character arcs fail to satisfy? Being able to home in on specifics means that we can search for a remedying education—books or workshops that teach us exactly what we need to learn. In this way, critique helps us not only improve our work-in-progress but our overall storytelling chops.

HOW MUCH CRAFT DO YOU NEED?

When to Learn and When to Just Write

DONALD MAASS

We live in a simplified, reductive, white screen, checklist age.

I blame Apple. And the women's magazine *Cosmopolitan*. *Real Simple*, too. You can probably envision the headlines now: "Six Steps to Perfect Happiness!" "It's Easy!" "You're Almost There!"

Yeah, well, certain things are not that simple. Composing a symphony, for instance. Designing a space shuttle. Getting a bill through Congress. Emigrating to the U.S.A. Treating PTSD. Network administration. Closing a home purchase. Finding shoes for a wedding. Writing a publishable novel.

Publishable novel? There's a helluva lot to get right if you want to get your upmarket crossover mash-up on the list of one of the Big Five in a preempt. (If you don't know what I'm talking about, hoo boy, you're just at the beginning of complexity.) Simple it's not. We're talking fifty to a hundred story elements that need development; twenty methods for each; divine inspiration; buckets of perspiration; a multidraft, multiyear process; and the sickening suspicion that none of that really matters because, well, you know, fiction is an *art*.

And yet the reductive mind-set persists, even among literary giants and the authors of best-selling commercial blockbusters. Take ThrillerFest, the annual convocation of thriller writers. Each year the conference offers a teaching track in which thirty or more top thriller writers reveal the tricks of the craft—three each. To hear them explain it, keeping readers on the edge of their seats for four hundred pages is as easy as downloading iTunes. *One, two, three—terror!* Then there are Elmore Leonard's ten rules, the thirteen points in *The Hero's Journey*, and so on. Easy peasy.

Sure.

On the other end of the spectrum are those who eschew methodology in favor of intuition, experience, seat-of-your-pants story assembly, and the honing of steel-edged, luminous writing in the refining fire of critique and revision. It's another kind of reductive thinking akin to leaving the management of the world economy to the "magic" of supply and demand. Good luck with that.

But wait—isn't it true that at a certain point you need to stop thinking about your writing and just let it flow? Isn't it equally true that the stream sometimes needs to be diverted, shored up with levees and dams, regulated and tested for purity? Don't you need a certain amount of craft to start with, and if you do, how much?

STRIVE FOR A STRIVER'S MIND-SET

The question of how much craft you need comes down to the difference between wingspan and flying, outlining and intuition, faith in technique and trust in instincts. It's a tricky balance, and it's different for each writer. That said, here are a few considerations:

1. If you believe that too much craft will keep you revising until you die, you may have a point. But think about this: The most important piece of craft is the one you don't know.
2. If you believe that leaning solely on process is inefficient and that methodology (particularly outlining) will speed things up, that's somewhat valid. But think about this: The more you plan, the less you improve.

What you need is both craft *and* process—but again, how much? Enough to compensate for your writing weaknesses, push you out of your comfort zone, and challenge you to aim higher, because without reading a word of your work-in-progress, I can tell you this: However crafty you are, no matter your level of native genius, your manuscript is full of unused potential. Whether by craft or critique, you can still master more. And the more you master, the deeper and richer—and easier—each new project gets.

Isn't it sad when good authors fall back on familiar tricks and become boring? The best writers I know never stop learning. The best give themselves challenges. They stretch. They stay fresh. They read craft books, attend conferences, study fiction analytically, and participate in writers' communities.

ATTEND DELIBERATELY TO THE ESSENTIALS

Okay, though, what are the craft fundamentals? What is essential to know? Certainly a grasp of novel structure is helpful. There are a hundred ways to conceptualize it, so take your pick, but do remember that the type of story you are writing requires—and the audience you are writing for demands—certain things. Don't let down your readers. Solve the mystery. Build the world. Girl gets boy. Redemption is real. Even when it's ugly, life is beautiful.

Having an approach to scene structure is also helpful, as is knowing when to use a scene and when to use summary. Authors who write gripping novels, what we sometimes call "page-turners," have also mastered the methods of microtension: the line-by-line tension that makes everything on every page necessary to read. Character development, arc of change, story world detailing, thematic intention … it's a good idea to come at those things deliberately. You know how it is: If it isn't on your to-do list, then chances are it won't get done.

And then there are the techniques you don't know or thought you knew but forgot. Only further study or review will give you those. Remember: Major corporations spend a lot on research and development. You may not have billions for those tasks, but you definitely have time. Ask yourself: Can you afford *not* to invest in getting better?

How much more process do you need? If you're not in a critique group or working with critique partners who are at your level or better, well, you're losing out. Beta drafts nowadays are also an essential step. Film and television writing is collaborative and not automatically analogous to fiction, but singly authored stage plays are extensively workshopped. Why? You can't gauge audience reaction until you have an audience. Remember that revising for yourself is okay, but if you do that, your revision will probably please only you.

Whether you're considering craft as such or seeking more from process, have a plan. The best plan is one that makes you a better writer every day. The worst plan is one that sends you wandering alone in the wilderness of book publishing. Your chances of survival aren't very good.

UPDATE AND CUSTOMIZE YOUR UNIQUE TOOLBOX

One more thing: You might need to unlearn some craft. "Tried and true" techniques like cliff-hangers can be clunky. Description using the five senses is passé. The more modern method is building a story world, conveying that world not objectively but through the subjective experiences of your characters.

Why not outfit your own customized toolbox? Put into it everything you know, and then add to it some new tools you borrow or even invent. Do the same for process: Add what you're missing, but regardless of your approach, include time for feedback, honing, and play.

Finally, here's the most important piece of craft advice I can offer: Be human. Fiction comes from life, and your unique fiction can only come from yours. From what inspires a story to the interior life of your people to the truths that we urgently need to see, the most essential technique underlying the art is nothing more than your own passion.

 HOW TO GET IN YOUR OWN WAY, METHOD 19: PRIORITIZE IMPROVEMENT OVER ACTUALLY WRITING

Like Abe Lincoln said, "If you give me six hours to chop down a tree, I'll spend the first four sharpening the ax. Of course, by then it'll be getting pretty late, so ..." Inspiring words, right there.

—BILL FERRIS

A DROP OF IMITATION

How to Learn from the Masters

KATHRYN CRAFT

That byline you just read is a bit of a lie. This essay is collaboration because even as I type, I'm not alone. My teachers look on from the bookshelves along one wall of my office. Except for those who insist on sitting on my shoulder. And those who have moved right into my head.

I am talking about the authors whose works have taught me how to write.

Our devotion to including acknowledgments in books pays homage to a venerable arts tradition of fostering relationships between mentors and those who seek them. If you too would like to learn from the masters, the following explores ways to seek their guidance, on the cheap and on the sly.

ANALYZE WRITING YOU LOVE

I want to write novels that seduce the reader on the very first page; how about you? In pursuit of this desire, I began my study with first paragraphs. At the time I was a chauffeur mom with the odd half hour between my sons' various sports obligations, so I did this the old-fashioned way: in a library. Right down the shelf I went—King, Kingsolver, Kinsella—opening books to see what techniques drew me in. This simple exercise, which can also be done at home with Amazon's "Look Inside" feature, is fun and invaluable. You'll learn as much about yourself as you will the craft.

When you have more time on your hands, try breaking down an entire novel. I did this with Kristin Hannah's *On Mystic Lake*, which seemed similar in style to the stories I was interested in writing. (I'm hoping it bodes well that Hannah went on to become a prolific and best-selling author.) How did she hook the reader with her first paragraph? What did she reveal about her protagonist on her first page? When did she end her first chapter? When did the protagonist set her story goal? What were her major emotional turning points? If a scene really grabbed me—why? What did the best passages of dialogue achieve, especially by what was *not* said? I filled a spiral-bound notebook with my observations.

Author Michael Chabon took such studies a step further. In his *Maps and Legends: Reading and Writing Along the Borderlands*, Chabon says he wrote entire novels that imitated the styles of authors he admired. Such meticulous care to his writing education may be why he won a Pulitzer.

READ AS A WRITER

Reading supplemental materials such as author interviews can provide useful insight into the reasoning behind an author's decisions. I paired the reading of John Steinbeck's *East of Eden* with his *Journal of a Novel: The East of Eden Letters*. Louise DeSalvo, in her book *The Art of Slow Writing*, says she studied early drafts of novels by Virginia Woolf (available at woolfonline.com) to see how Woolf's revisions evolved the work. Internships are rare in creative writing—what author would let you watch over her shoulder as she writes?—but these companion materials can serve the same purpose, laying down a path to success that will help you adjust expectations for the hard work ahead.

The library can also offer a great education on the business side of the industry. Publishers agonize over details such as the cover design, title, and back-cover copy. These attributes must work together so that a book with no other advocate, sitting on a shelf, can attract the right kind of reader. Ask yourself: If a book "calls" to you, why? How does this book's packaging suggest the type of story it holds? Note which recent releases seem most like yours, and then read them to build a cache of comparable titles. A publisher loves nothing more than a business-savvy author who has appreciated this attention to genre detail in the writing and pitching of her novel.

Compulsive readers are rewarded with additional insights from all sorts of writing. An uncredited brochure essay I read when visiting Utah's Arches National Park wowed me with an emotional arc that spanned millennia. While waiting in a doctor's office, I was swept away by sensuous descriptions of body movement in a *Smithsonian* magazine piece on searching the underground clubs of Argentina for a true tango master. Although that master's name now escapes me, I'll never forget his definition of tango: "one heart, four feet." Always be on the lookout for great writing, and when you find it, ask yourself: *How did they do that?*

CONSULT WRITING GURUS

Writers have conflicting opinions on the use of craft books. I adore them. Rule shirkers hate them. Rather than think of the authors of these guides as rule setters, I think of them as gurus that can lead me deeper into my process. This works best if I arrive at the cover of their book with story-related questions already in hand.

With his book *The Key: How to Write Damn Good Fiction Using the Power of Myth*, James N. Frey helped turn my questions about why I found *Star Wars* so affecting into my first attempt at women's fiction. When I want to ensure I've properly tuned and fueled the engine of a new story, I turn to the down-and-dirty charts in Debra Dixon's *GMC: Goal, Motivation and Conflict*. Peter Rubie and Gary Provost's *How to Tell a Story: The Secrets of Writing Captivating Tales*, is worth the $3.99 Kindle price for one cogent paragraph on plot alone—it's that good at keeping my efforts focused. I've read Nancy Kress's *Dynamic Characters* three times anew, since different character sets consumed my thoughts with each reading. When I'm floundering, Lisa Cron's *Wired for Story* explains the importance of my storytelling mission and the science behind how I can best engage my reader. These authors, my fellow students of story, offer a lifeline when my own wisdom is crushed by 90,000 first-draft words.

One of my favorite guides is Donald Maass's *Writing the Breakout Novel Workbook*. This one will even pass muster with the rule shirkers. Maass provides the questions you should be asking to get to the heart of your novel. Warning: If you try to use this guide to create a first draft, your head might explode. This deeper-level thinking is better applied in the revision stage, once your cast of characters has been placed in a setting and their desires and motivations are becoming clear. If you complete the workbook, the result can't help but be a more richly textured, cohesive story.

For an extra boost, consider reading a novel at the same time as a related craft book. Barbara Kingsolver's *Flight Behavior* and Monica Wood's Elements of Fiction Writing guide, *Setting*, are a good pairing. To further my understanding of story structure, I read Jack Bickham's *Scene and Structure* at the same time as Dan Brown's *The Da Vinci Code*. Criticism of Brown's literary chops abound, but the man clearly did something right—he sold eighty million copies worldwide. With Beckham's tutelage in assessing Brown's scene structure, I learned how to raise questions and sustain tension that I could use in my women's fiction.

BROADEN YOUR SCOPE

Because our training consumes so much time with reading and trial and error on the page, writers often don't give enough credence to the way the term *literary arts* places us within a greater tradition. As a former dancer and newsletter designer who comes from a family with proficiencies in music, handicrafts, visual arts, acting, and even martial arts, I have learned from masters in all of our sister art forms. If you're not convinced, start with screenwriting, which isn't too much of a stretch. Bill Johnson's *A Story Is a Promise* is one of the best meditations on premise I've encountered. Anyone seeking a deeper understanding of storytelling structure will be rewarded by analyzing *Story* by Robert McKee.

Dancers communicate stories all the time without speaking a single word, and the effect can be stunning. Study how they do that—try searching for Paul Taylor's *Speaking in Tongues* on vimeo.com for a great example. Read choreographer Twyla Tharp's *The Creative Habit: Learn It and Use It for Life* to benefit from wisdom gleaned from those who practice a variety of arts. If classic storytelling structure leaves you cold, perhaps her discussion of a work's "spine" might appeal to you more. I dare you to read this book and ever complain of writer's block again.

Rather than stare at a blinking cursor, what might we learn from someone who creates characters in 3-D? Constantin Stanislavski's book on method acting, *Building a Character,* might revolutionize the way you think about populating your story. One of my favorite editing metaphors, about carving away what doesn't belong in order to reveal a story, comes from reading about the way sixteenth-century sculptor Michelangelo "found" his rendering of David within a slab of Carrara marble.

Architecture can offer a different take on building a story within a specific setting—read about Frank Lloyd Wright's Fallingwater, or better yet, visit it outside Pittsburgh, Pennsylvania. It's a house that doesn't appear to stand on solid ground but instead stretches over a thirty-foot waterfall. Frank Lloyd Wright told his clients he wanted them to live with the waterfalls, to make them part of their everyday lives rather than simply look at them now and then. How could you so fully incorporate your own setting into your story?

Cinematography offers us much about the importance of perspective. Watch the annotated version of films on DVD or documentaries such as *The Making of American Beauty*, a three-parter you can watch for free on YouTube, which explores the way one character finds beauty in trash rolling about in the wind. English Professor Rob Frank's analysis of the film *American Beauty*, also on YouTube, demonstrates how every scene in the protagonist's POV is designed with stripes or bars to show how Lester (played by Kevin Spacey) is imprisoned by his chosen life. After watching this you'll want to think about how best to use motifs in your work.

Late-night channel surfing recently led me to a television special about Stephen Schwartz, who composed one of my favorite musicals, *Wicked*. The show tracks the early life of Elphaba, the girl with the unfortunate green skin who is destined to become the Wicked Witch of the West, and her school chum Galinda, who will one day become Glinda, the Good Witch of the North. In introducing the musical number "The Wizard and I," about Elphaba's hopes that meeting the Wizard will change her life in a magical way, Schwartz called it the "want song." I leaned in because I'd always found this song so stirring. Schwartz explained that the want song, which is usually the second or third song in a show, and in this case Elphaba's first, shares the protagonist's deep desire so that we'll bond with her for the rest of the show. I'd never heard of this term, so I checked some other musicals. In *Pippin*, the title character's first song is "(Gotta Find My) Corner of the Sky." In his first solo in Jonathan Larson's *Rent*, AIDS sufferer Roger sings about wanting to write one last meaningful song before he dies in "One Song Glory." In the opening of your novel, do you give your character a chance to sing her "want song"?

SNAP UP A TRIED-AND-TRUE RECIPE

In her book *SNAP: Seizing Your Aha! Moments*, Katherine Ramsland examines the way innovators in a variety of fields came up with groundbreaking ideas. She describes a process of learning deeply about subjects that interest you and then adding this knowledge to a brain stew that will allow both halves of your brain—the right side that seeks metaphor, nuance, and emotion and the left side that analyzes and seeks patterns—to contribute to the creative process.

If you aim to learn from the masters, you may fear that the recipe of your stew looks the same as everyone else's:

- Let your curiosity lead you to your teachers.
- Sample widely, and analyze the work that interests you most.
- Add the lessons that resonate with your brain stew, and discard the rest.
- Simmer.

But curiosity, interest, what resonates with you personally, and the mysterious alchemy of simmering offer enough variables to your ingredients list that your stew will not taste the same as anyone else's. Learning from the masters will just cut down your preparation time. When your story is fully cooked and ready to serve, all that you have learned will have been seasoned by your own perspective to create a new expression, in the same way that artists have been creating for time immemorial.

I guess we literary artists earn our bylines after all.

 COMMUNITY CONVERSATION: LEARNING FROM THE MASTERS

The Writer Unboxed community weighs in online. Please consider adding your voice by visiting Writer Unboxed via this QR code or link to the site. Join the conversation at writerunboxed.com/masters, and use the password "aip" (all lowercase).

Writer Unboxed is a moderated community, but comments that evolve a conversation in a positive manner are always welcome.

SUSAN SETTEDUCATO: When I was in art school, one of my professors made us pick a Master to copy at the Philadelphia Art Museum. I chose a Millet landscape and spent a week standing in front of it, trying to emulate, stroke for stroke, what the Master had done to create his beautiful work. I grumbled the whole first day, but by day three I realized, as my hand traced Millet's movements, that something was rewiring inside my brain. I didn't end up with anything you could sell on the black market, but this exercise changed my work forever. I love what you say here about reading for specifics: the place where the story engine turns on, the place where you fall in and entrain with the main character, etc. ...

I'm making a list of the books you mentioned that I haven't already read. I'm especially anxious to read Twyla Tharp. My sister is a dancer, and we talk a lot about the similarities in what we do. Movement, arc, setting (love the bars in *American Beauty*!) all conspire to make something breathe. I've gotten into the habit of watching the extras on DVDs to listen to the writers talk about their processes. And, yes, sometimes my head feels like it's going to explode, but it's like eating too much at Thanksgiving; eventually, things get digested, and the nutrients remain within!

KATHRYN CRAFT: Thanks for sharing your painting experience, Susan. I've seen people engaged in such imitation at art museums, but because I have no particular talent for the visual arts, I couldn't conjure a first-person testimonial. It certainly takes an up-close-and-personal observation to achieve, doesn't it? This type of learning couldn't possibly be realized with a photograph of the painting, just as one can't learn to write literature by reading CliffsNotes. For writers, it is studying the word-by-word accumulation that becomes story that can serve as our mentorship.

VAUGHN ROYCROFT: I love the concept of an ongoing "brain stew," Kathryn, and I know of at least a dozen books that contributed lasting flavors to my work as a writer. But in pondering masters and their example, I thought of fantasy writer Robin Hobb. It's a bit odd that I think of her in that way since I didn't start to read her until I was well into my writing journey. And even though I have studied her openings and her technique and thought a lot about why I'm compelled by her stories, those things are not quite why she sprang to mind. It's more in the example of her career.

I'm inspired by Hobb's entire catalog, the breadth of her storytelling world, and the depth of each character. Not to mention the consistent quality from book to book. She's prolific, but there are no throwaways. When I start a new Hobb book, I'm immediately reminded that I'm in the hands of a masterful storyteller. I so admire the space she allows herself, the trust she has in her readers. There is action, but it's always grounded in layered and nuanced motivations. There is introspection but never at the expense of momentum. Her worldbuilding is rich, but it's a richness that's always in the service of story.

When I appraise this master's brilliant shelf of books and see how her constancy breeds dedication, I'm led to think beyond simply being published. Through Hobb, I'm brought to aspire to a bookshelf of my own. Thanks for stirring my brain stew, Kathryn!

KATHRYN CRAFT: Wow, Vaughn. To have anyone speak of a career with such love and devotion is a standard to which I can only hope authors might hold themselves, for the sake of literature in our country. In addition to inspiring us all, you have given those of us who don't write fantasy a worthy master from outside our own genre to learn from. Thank you.

VALERIE P. CHANDLER: Two things struck a chord with me. I enjoy studying book covers and first lines. It doesn't matter the genre; a good line is a good line. I've browsed the bookstore shelves and pulled book after book, reading them. I think the words should set the tone for the book, grab the narrator's or character's voice, and place the reader immediately in the story. One of my favorite first lines is: "It was a bright cold day in April, and the clocks were striking thirteen," from George Orwell's *1984*.

The other idea that caught my attention was about Michelangelo finding David in the marble. I think all of us can relate to that. We end up with that first draft that's full of extra "stuff" that we think is relevant and full of genius. Then we pare away the extra to get to the art inside. It's a balancing act to have the right amount of detail to add depth, but not so much that it bogs down the reader. Like I said, it's an art. Thank goodness the computer is more forgiving than a block of marble!

KATHRYN CRAFT: Thanks for the laugh, Valerie! And, yes, thank goodness the computer is more forgiving than marble; I'd be lost without the *delete* key, should we have to revert to typewriters. Although we do have to contend with those accidental crash-type deletions that wipe out entire stories; short of a David Copperfield-like spectacle, that wouldn't happen with marble!

GRACE WYNTER: As a newbie writer, an essay that includes actionable advice that takes me away from the routine of typing on my computer is a godsend for my tired brain and aching fingers. I hadn't even finished reading the essay before I ran to the little library in my house and began rereading first paragraphs of the books I love. An hour later, I returned and continued to read the essay, only to stop again to watch videos of Alvin Ailey dancers on YouTube. This was the break my brain needed and the shot of inspiration my heart was looking for. I'm now going to dedicate more time in my weekly writing schedule to broadening my scope.

KATHRYN CRAFT: Thank you for pointing out one of the greatest stressors for the modern-day novelist, Grace: sitting all day at the computer. Is it any wonder that craft books chastise us for opening our novels with a sedentary character having a good long think about her life, when that is what we writers do all the livelong day?

I realize that some writers are more sensitive to this than others, but I believe there is magic in walking away from the computer and involving all of our senses. In the mornings I write at my computer in my loft office, but in the afternoons I move down two flights to edit for clients in my living room. I sit in a more comfortable chair by a window with natural light. It makes me so happy to do this! Even those couple of flights of stairs help get the blood moving.

I live in a small town that allows me to do errands on foot in the late afternoons—I can walk to get fresh vegetables for dinner, to Staples for more paper, or to the bookstore or library. Even small activities like these are so helpful. Glad you picked up some ways to enliven your routine while still learning your craft.

 ## HOW TO GET IN YOUR OWN WAY, METHOD 20: GORGE YOURSELF ON ADVICE

Tips and tricks are fun because they make you feel like you're working, except without the boring parts (the actual work). At some point you've got to put down the how-tos and start writing. But not until you've finished *this* book, of course.

—BILL FERRIS

 ## PRO TIP

Improving doesn't happen by accident. If you write a million words or invest ten thousand hours without the express intention of improving your craft and skill—and a plan for making that happen—you can easily end up no closer to your goal.

—ROBIN LAFEVERS

WHERE WRITERS GATHER

How to Promote Your Interests at Conferences and Workshops Without Wasting Your Time or Money

TRACY HAHN-BURKETT

Writers, for the most part, work alone. I enjoy carrying on lively conversations with the characters in my head as much as the next writer, but at a certain point, I need to interact with people whose thoughts are not actually mine. Conferences and workshops provide excellent opportunities to meet other writers and business contacts, and to learn both the craft and business aspects of the writing industry. But figuring out which conferences and workshops were right for me took some effort when I began writing, and it still does.

Our writing skills, interests, and abilities are always developing, so no matter where you are in your career, you'll need to research and prepare in order to get the most out of your time and avoid wasting money. I recommend taking an annual approach to conferences and, to a certain degree, workshops. At the beginning of each year, sit down with a pad and pen and ask: *What do I need to accomplish in my writing life this year?* Define your goals, determine your budget, and select conferences and major workshops, leaving yourself some room for flexibility as the year progresses. Then you can begin preparation for each event as it approaches.

CONSIDER WHAT YOU WANT TO LEARN

Where are you in your career? Are you a beginner seeking to soak up any wisdom you can find about the craft of writing? Have you just completed a first draft and don't know how to go about revising the beast? Are you experienced and want some guidance on, say, how to make subtext more effective in your next manuscript? Look through conference and workshop listings to find those that offer sessions that address your needs. You can explore possibilities by consulting your local writers' organization, visiting the searchable directory at the Association of Writers & Writing Programs website, or simply by searching "writing conferences" or "writing workshops" and the current year online.

If you want to learn how to market your book or sell your stories, a conference focused solely on the craft of writing isn't going to help you. But a conference such as Grub Street's annual three-day Muse and the Marketplace in Boston, which addresses both craft and business, may be the perfect fit. If you want immediate feedback on your work, seek out a workshop, although some conference sessions offer a live-critique feature, too. If you're brave enough, find a Literary Idol session where volunteers read their work in front of an audience until authors, agents, and/or editors serving on a judging panel tell them to stop. Has one particular aspect of craft been giving you a headache for months, like point of view? Look to a local or state writing organization or online for a workshop specifically focused on that point.

CONSIDER WHO YOU WANT TO MEET

Are you seeking a community of like-minded writers—people who understand what this life is like in a way well-meaning friends and family never could? Try a local or state writers conference, or Writer Unboxed's own UnConference[1] in Salem, Massachusetts, which focuses on craft and community. Need a critique partner? Again, a local or state conference is a great opportunity to find someone you can work with, as is any workshop you can drive to and, sometimes, an online workshop. What if you write in a specific genre and wish to meet other writers who share your particular trials and triumphs? The Romance Writers of America holds a renowned conference every year, and they have local chapters you can join as well. For writers in other genres, look into Killer Nashville, ThrillerFest, the Society of Children's Book Writers and Illustrators (SCBWI), and more. If you write young adult fiction, a single workshop offered by an or-

---

1 writerunboxed.com/un-conference

Author In Progress

ganization like The Writer's Center in Bethesda, Maryland, can improve your craft, help you with your queries, and introduce you to potential critique partners and fellow travelers in the YA world.

What if you want to market your work? Are you looking to shop a completed manuscript? Then find a conference that includes pitch sessions. Make sure you follow the instructions, and don't accost agents and editors in the bathrooms. (Yes, people do this—but you shouldn't if you want to be viewed as a pro.) Are you trying to make business connections now that will help you in the future? Are you hoping for career advice or industry insight from experts? Look for conferences that offer lunch tables with professionals (often for an extra fee), happy hours, or other mingling opportunities. Swap business cards when you can; you'll use them later.

Conferences aren't just great for meeting people; they're also perfect for reconnecting with all manner of literary folk you don't have the opportunity to see very often. Whether you want to grab a beer and reminisce with that person you clicked with at the Pacific Northwest Writers Association conference last year, or you hope to reconnect with the agent you met when, darn it, your manuscript wasn't quite ready, there's always a good reason to get together again with contacts from conferences past. Industry professionals travel from all over the country for the largest literary conference in North America, the Association of Writers & Writing Programs (AWP) Conference, held in a different U.S. location every year. Contact people you want to meet up with ahead of time, because it's tough to find a specific person in a crowd of twelve thousand.

CONSIDER YOUR BUDGET

Most conferences aren't cheap, and if you have to travel for them, the expense can more than double. Some events offer scholarships, so apply for those if you're eligible. See if you can volunteer in exchange for a break in fees. And look at how your travel schedule syncs up with other parts of your life. Do you have to go to Florida for your day job? Can you attach the Sanibel Island Writers Conference to one side of that business trip? Is your family vacationing in Cape Cod? How about the Cape Cod Writers Center Conference? Obviously these types of combinations won't always work out, but it's worth seeing if you can combine travel expenses where possible. Finally, look for conferences or workshops you can attend without traveling. The annual New Hampshire Writers' Day, hosted by the New Hampshire Writers' Project, is just a short trip from my house. If you attend an online event, you might not even have to change out of your pajamas.

CONSIDER YOUR ENJOYMENT

Don't forget to factor in your own potential comfort and gratification—they're so important. If you are an introvert who shuts down in crowds, don't start out by going to a megaconference. Take a small workshop, or attend a local or regional conference or a conference that limits the number of attendees and includes lots of breakout sessions. Skip a session at a larger conference, and retreat to your hotel room. Maybe sit in an unattached café, and read or write a couple of pages. This will allow you the space to recuperate so you can return to the rest of the conference recharged and ready to engage again.

Conversely, if you view conferences as your chance to break out of isolation and party, you'll find plenty of companions at the bigger events. Go to all the happy hours and after-parties you want, but always be professional and respectful of those who are quieter and have come primarily to learn. Remember: Everyone is paying for this opportunity.

GET THE MOST OUT OF YOUR MONEY

As I said before, conferences and some multi-session workshops often come with a hefty price tag. Here's how to stretch every dollar—before, during, and after the event.

BEFORE

If you're given an assignment before a workshop or session such as completing the first fifty pages of your manuscript or drafting a query letter, complete it. Never attend anything without a notebook—either paper or electronic. At conferences, draw up a list of contacts you'd like to make. If there are people you want to meet or reconnect with, consider e-mailing them ahead of time or asking a common friend to introduce you. Make or order business cards. If you're nervous about attending a big conference for the first time, see if the conference provides any special means of preparation. Grub Street, for example, often offers a class each year before Muse and the Marketplace to coach new conferees about how to get the most out of the experience. If you're anxious about sharing your writing in a workshop, don't worry: You're not the only one. Every writer has been there, and we'll all be there again.

DURING

Don't sit in the last row unless those are the only seats left; it can be hard to hear back there, and your attention is more likely to wander. Exception: Some conference sessions encourage dropping in and out to see what you find interesting. In this case, if you're not sure a session is right for you, sit toward the back and come and go as quietly as possible.

Whenever you're in the lecture or workshop setting, put your phone away (and set it to vibrate so you don't interrupt the presenters). Swap business cards with people you connect with.

AFTER

If it's a conference or a lecture-heavy workshop, rewrite your notes as soon as possible. Every time I have failed to do this, I have regretted it. Also, as soon as possible, send thank-you or glad-to-meet-you notes or e-mails to new contacts to reinforce their impressions of you and to mark the beginning of auspicious relationships. If you promised to send work to anyone, don't delay. If you've just completed a multi-session workshop, take steps to stay in touch with anyone from the class with whom you'd like to maintain a relationship.

Consider your experience: Did you get what you expected? What was lacking? How will your writing practice change because of what you learned or whom you met? Would you go to this conference again? Would you take another workshop taught by this instructor? How about one offered by the organization? How would your approach be different? If something didn't work for you, what would you look for instead?

REEVALUATE AS YOUR GOALS CHANGE

The conferences and workshops you find suitable will likely evolve as you progress as an author, as will your role in them. Your requirements will become more exacting; you will look for specific authors, agents, or editors. Where once you only took notes at conferences, you may find yourself presenting at some of them. But you are never too advanced to learn; you are never too good to improve. Even if you're presenting at a panel at the Writer's Digest conference in New York, there's a good chance that you can learn something that will help you improve an aspect of your craft or marketing by attending another panel or two while you're there.

Conferences and workshops offer an almost unlimited number of resources for writers who want to learn about the craft and business of writing and who are willing to invest some time and money. But be careful not to fall into the conference trap: You can spend so much time going to conferences and workshops, networking and socializing, that you can lose sight of the reason you're having all of this fun with writers and other industry folks. Eventually you have to sit down and write. If you realize that you're just going from one conference to another, call a moratorium. Plant yourself in a chair, and face no one but your laptop or your notebook. I did this a couple of years ago when I felt like my networking had surpassed my writing production and I needed to recalibrate my priorities.

Always keep one eye focused on what matters, and use your resources wisely. Because conferences and workshops aren't worth anything unless you use them to help you put words on a page.

 HOW TO GET IN YOUR OWN WAY, METHOD 21: BREAK THE BANK ON CONFERENCES AND WORKSHOPS

By all means, go if you can afford it, but it's really okay if you can't. There's no golden ticket; you don't need anything to succeed but your own imagination.

—BILL FERRIS

READING PEOPLE (AND WRITING THEM, TOO)

Dig Up Humanity in the Details

LANCELOT SCHAUBERT

Well, the world outside my window is shaming me again/From the things I haven't seen cause I've been writing about them. That lyric from the song "Perimeter of Me" by Dividing the Plunder haunts me even now because the line often describes me. You, too, if I'm putting money down.

Let me explain. I sent the most recent novel I wrote to an agent I respect for critique. This agent went above and beyond the call of duty, kindly offering five single-spaced pages of notes and paving me a path to publication. The most troubling of the notes nailed something I've struggled with for some time: One said, "The dialogue is often meted out in abstractions," and another said, "We seldom get a glimpse of the inner lives of these characters."

He spoke true. My novel's problem had little to do with the prose, its narrative framework, or the interconnectivity of the lives of my characters. Its problem had to do with me sitting inside all day long typing, letting the world outside my window shame me for the things I hadn't seen because I'd been writing about them instead.

Is this you?

Do you find that you've spent so long in the books, so long worried about the craft, going to conferences, sifting through the notes of beta readers, paying library fines, and revising that you've actually written yourself out of your own humanity?

Man, I know I have.

DIG UP HUMAN DETAILS, DIALOGUE, AND CONFLICT DIRECTIONS

If you're not a good human, it really doesn't matter how good you are at writing, because the foundation below you is quicksand. Good writers are, by necessity, good humans. Cutting yourself off from the world outside won't help. An alternative exists. You can read *real* people and then write them—read their dialogue, read their defining attributes, read the direction of their relational conflict. Become a student of the masses.

Lucky for you and me, we're not the only ones in history to go through this. Hundreds of writers have found ways to reinvigorate their humanity. Hemingway, for instance, would take time every day to push himself into adventures. In his *Art of Fiction* interview with *The Paris Review*, Hemingway and *The Paris Review*'s interviewer made the following exchange:

INTERVIEWER

Archibald MacLeish has spoken of a method of conveying experience to a reader which he said you developed while covering baseball games back in those *Kansas City Star* days. It was simply that experience is communicated by small details, intimately preserved, which have the effect of indicating the whole by making the reader conscious of what he had been aware of only subconsciously …

HEMINGWAY

The anecdote is apocryphal. I never wrote baseball for the *Star*. What Archie was trying to remember was how I was trying to learn in Chicago in around 1920 and was searching for the unnoticed things that made emotions, such as the way an outfielder tossed his glove without looking back to where it fell, the squeak of resin on canvas under a fighter's flat-soled gym shoes, the gray color of Jack Blackburn's skin when he had just come out of stir, and other things I noted as a painter sketches. You saw Blackburn's strange color and the old razor cuts and the way he spun a man before you knew his history. These were the things which moved you before you knew the story.

His point moves beyond details. Often in MFA courses, my friends in such programs must go out into a busy part of New York—Madison Square or Battery Park or MoMa—and listen to dialogue, transcribing the weirdest things people say as fast as they can type. For many, those snippets become the first inklings of stories that end up in magazines like *The Paris Review* and *One Story*. People say *strange* things, troubling and astounding things. For instance, I transcribed the following *real-life conversation,* and it ended up in a story I sold to *Hatch Magazine* last year:

> "How'd things work out with the Columbian woman?"
> "She killed a guy," Frank said. "Who knows?"
> "She call you? She try to contact you?" Micky asked.
> "Nah. It was easy."
> "It doesn't get any better than that."
> "We'll know," Frank said.
> "Does the teacher want to be with you?" Micky asked.
> "She was so freaked out about it, with the other woman."
> "Does she want you closer?"
> "Yeah, but I want to be away."
> "Do you want that distance?"
> "Yeah. She has kids."
> "Kids, okay does she—"
> "She killed the guy, the father."
> "The teacher did?" Micky asked.
> "The Colombian woman."
> "She killed the guy and broke it off?"
> "Yeah," Frank said.
> "Oh, she killed the guy and broke it off."
> "Yeah the dog was just hanging there by herself. Had to take care of her."
> "Do you guys communicate well?" Micky said.
> "The dog loves me."
> "Not the dog!"
> "Ha!"
> "Get off the dog!"
> "I'm not on the dog!"
> "Ha! Stay off the dog, you old dirty bastard. Leave the dog. The woman. The teacher. You like her? You communicate well?"

Sure, kids say the darnedest things. But adults? Their conversations baffle me—I'm reminded of that Lewis Black comedy sketch in which he randomly hears a woman say, "If it wasn't for my horse, I wouldn't have had to spend that year in college."

As for digging up the humanity in the details, Mary Robinette Kowal suggests this method: Sit in a room, and describe everything you see *for thirty minutes straight.* At the end of those thirty minutes, you'll find yourself writing about the most human details—the things that Hemingway talked about in the interview, the things that show you where the stories are. I did this exercise once on the Long Island Rail Road, and after thirty minutes I noticed a splatter of blood in the shape of a cheekbone on one of the ledges. That was the most human part of the train—cut out half the details I transcribed and end the paragraph on that cheekbone blood, and suddenly you have enough curiosity to drive a story.

READ YOUR PEOPLE, AND WRITE WHAT YOU READ

Or maybe you need to learn some conflict. Maybe your dialogue is fine, and your details are human rather than abstractions.

In that case, your assignment is to truly read *people*—people as in their collective interactions with one another—to partake in "people watching" of the highest degree. If you see someone order a Chick fil A sandwich with a spouse, see if either of them hems and haws, shuffles his or her feet, or ignores the other person. Are two people being passive-aggressive? What does that look like when it unfolds before your eyes? In my own work, and in the work of most writers, there are far too many shrugs and sighs and smirks. Where are the stretched lips? Where are the tucked knees? The toe-point grinds? The palm-heel strikes? People are much more subtle than we write them. We only write them poorly because we read them poorly. Open your eyes and your ears, and wake up to all you've missed.

Let me encourage you: Take a break, grab a pen and a journal, and get into the world outside your window. Let it stop shaming you. Take a good week to listen to and see and read the people in your neighborhood and city.

You might be surprised at what you find. And, in the long run, so will your readers.

In fact, I'll bet by the time you return to the world inside your window and open your manuscript once more, you'll be ready to improve by learning from the story craft of others, from your own book, and from workshops, conferences, editors, and the rest.

Be a good human, and you'll find the big cornerstones have already been laid for you to become a *great* writer.

DRIVEN TO DIGITAL DISTRACTION

Why You Need to Deal with the Publishing Business

PORTER ANDERSON

> In the beginning was the Word, and the Word was with God, and the Word was God.
>
> —John 1:1, King James Bible

All authors ever since "the beginning" have needed to know about the business of publishing. This includes you.

Authors today need a Newer Testament, one that contains just two commandments:

1. Thou shalt not hide from "The Industry! The Industry!" as I call our ever-excitable business.
2. Thou shalt seize the digital tools and trade of tomorrow and thus prosper.

My father, the Methodist minister, always more theologian than pulpit pastor, would want me to tell you that the best verse in John 1 is this one: "And the light shineth in the darkness; and the darkness comprehends it not."

God knows it's hard for many authors to comprehend the benefits of the digital light that burns so blindingly into the farthest-flung reaches of modern publishing. Left to your own devices, you can't get a word in edgewise on your manuscript because the beepings and burpings, the pop-ups, the e-mails, the

Facebook follies, the towering tweeterie, the lurid Instagrams, and the uninteresting Pinteresting all make you want to back the car over your smartphone and microwave your tablet.

But technology is not known for marching backward. That "landline resurgence"? Yeah, not so much.

And like the Lord, the digital dynamic gives and it takes away. Yes, it has taken away some of our ability to focus, to lose ourselves in the reverie of our words, to "just write." It has also given us the power to know how many books we're selling, converse directly with our readers, and monitor and understand the complex, staggered, and reinvigorated industry in which we work.

Publishing has now entered a state of continual change. That *won't* change. In that change lies your best chance to succeed.

More and more, the token of professionalism among authors will be their knowledge of their industry. Whether you are trade or independent, sumptuously published or formatted on a shoestring, readers shall know you by your business savvy. Or they won't know you at all.

As Werner Erhard, founder of the *est* consciousness-training program, told us, it's easier to ride the horse in the direction it's going.

GO FORTH, AND MARKET THYSELF

In the beginning? The thundering beauty of the Book of John makes no reference to the holy literary agent, nor the celestial editor, nor the leather-and-gold-leaf cover design, nor the pearly royalty statements totted up by Saint Peter, nor even the Multitude of the Heavenly Host, to whom we refer today as Sales and Marketing.

But don't miss the fact that the Bible has been propelled into untouchable status as the planetary bestseller by the most successful word-of-mouth campaign in heaven and Earth. A mighty street team is Christianity.

The Wycliffe Global Alliance of Bible translation organizations reports that there are 554 versions of the complete Bible, with scriptures available in some 2,932 languages.[1] And yet Wycliffe also tells us that in the Bible's success, "God is accomplishing His mission through His power *and through partnership.*"

"Partnership?" You bet. Even His Holiness, Pope Francis, turned to the earthly powers of a publisher for his own first book project. Pan Macmillan's Bluebird imprint announced late in 2015 that it had secured the U.K. and Commonwealth rights to Oonagh Stransky's translation of the Pope's *The Name of God Is Mercy.*[2]

---

1 www.wycliffe.net/statistics
2 www.thebookseller.com/news/pan-macmillan-publish-pope-francis-315602

And there was much rejoicing in the boardroom, too. (Random House brought it out in the United States.)

And yet, on a day-to-day basis, you hear pushback on all sides from authors who "hate marketing." They blanch if you say the words *author platform*. They waste precious writing time participating in blog gossip fests about "how *hard* it is to sell yourself." Quiz those folks gently. You'll find that these are usually the same authors who are embarrassingly clueless on industry issues that affect their work and their livelihoods. They send you long-outdated blog posts from amateurs to prove a point. They tweet incessantly about their books—to other writers but not readers. They dash away—"my *Love in the Backyard* is calling!"—as if you're supposed to (a) know the title of their work-in-progress and (b) give a damn.

Please chant it now with me, the call of the amateur: "I *just* want to *write*." That's actually an excellent mantra. If you're a hobbyist.

If you want to sell the stuff, read on.

Ironically, business avoidance may be more pronounced today, in our so-commercial era, than in the past. Think of how much mythology gets passed around about "back in the day," when publishers were publishers and marketing departments jetted authors around for well-managed book tours on flying carpets of full-page ads in the *Times*. Right?

Wrong. The cult of "I *just* want to *write*" is all ours. More than five hundred years of *authorati* have known that they lived or died in the Kasbah, not in those sylvan Maxfield Parrish temples of androgynous creativity with the tall pillars and see-through togas.

"Capitalism *per se* and the market forces that both animate and pre-suppose it aren't the problem," writes publishing entrepreneur Richard Nash in his masterful *The Business of Literature*.[3] "They are, in fact, what brought literature and the author into being."

In the beginning, Nash tells us, meaning before Gutenberg invented the you-know-what:

> The role of the writer was … simply to transcribe. … Writers were not thought leaders, conjurors of other worlds, conjoiners of emotion and aesthetic. Writers were the machines through which the word of God was reproduced and disseminated. … The writer was the printing press.

Indeed, it was thought in the mid-1400s that the advent of the Gutenberg press would be "an economic disaster for the writer," Nash tells us. But in fact, he writes, "The supply of writers in no way withered. … The sixteenth-century

3 thoughtcatalog.com/book/what-is-the-business-of-literature

printers' shops became magnets for people with something to say, as would the eighteenth-century coffeehouses that followed."

CLASS UP YOUR ACT WITH SOME BUSINESS SAVVY

Writer Unboxed contributor Jane Friedman, in her keynote address at the 2014 Grub Street conference, The Muse and the Marketplace,[4] reminds us that Dickens was a tireless businessman. (Serials, right?) And she reminds us that Mark Twain made more money from the lecture circuit than from his books. Would that man have loved TED Talks or what?

It gets better: Twain had subscription agents going door-to-door to sell his books. The Morgan Library & Museum included one of the sample cases these front-porch sweet talkers used to tote Twain's writerly wares up and down the streets of America. Maybe you think you know Twain's writings, but it's not all river rafting and fence painting. I'll bet you've overlooked *The Successful Agent*,[5] 1865, which contains his instructions to the sales team:

> Keep the Book in Your Own Hands. Possession is power. Surrender the book, and you lose the power of showing it. … Books are seldom bought for what they are as a whole, but for some *particular feature* or *features* they contain. … If your book is published in several bindings, always sell one of the *higher priced* ones, if possible. … Canvass closely, thoroughly, *exhaustively*. This is the great secret of money-making in the book business.

In her keynote, Friedman quoted the nineteenth-century publisher G.H. Putnam: "When literary workers complain, it's because they don't understand the business of making and selling books, nor their actual rights and obligations."

FACE THE WALL

And while smart authors have always been scrappy businesspeople and the other kinds of authors have always complained, "I *just* want to *write*," there actually is a reason that all this seems so much more acute today: the Wall of Content. It's rising fast and stands in front of you, a sheer rock face made up, by some estimates,[6] of as many as 700,000 new self-published titles annually—before we even count trade titles—in the United States alone.

---

4 museandthemarketplace.org/index.php?id=5310

5 twain.lib.virginia.edu/marketin/salestlk.html

6 www.thebookseller.com/futurebook/futurebook-cha-cha-how-big-self-publishing

And e-books are forever. No more "out of print." It's all in your readers' faces. It's standing in your way when it comes time for your audience to find your books.

In the U.K.? Samira Ahmed, hosting BBC Radio 4's Front Row,[7] recently put it this way: In 2012, just one year, more books were published in the United Kingdom than were published in the eighteenth century, the nineteenth century, and the first half of the twentieth century *combined*.

Only perhaps digital photography can rival what's happening in digital publishing. As film and big cameras and expensive photo-finishing techniques have been overtaken, the point-and-shoot world has overwhelmed what had been a richly layered industry of craft and expertise.

And in publishing? I'm going to let Internet analyst and consultant Clay Shirky take the heat for me. As he says in his book *Here Comes Everybody*: "The future presented by the Internet is the mass amateurization of publishing and a switch from 'Why publish this?' to 'Why not?'"

I know, I know, I know. It's not considered appropriate in our fair culture to call people amateurs. And be assured that even if you're a newcomer to the field, if you're reading this book and seriously considering this discussion, you're on your way toward professionalism. Good for you, and stay with us. Professionalism is nonnegotiable. That's what it's going to take to rise above it all, because amateurs are buzzing like bees on a honeycomb on that Wall of Content. They are rock-climbing enthusiasts in the extreme, baby, and they'll kick you to the bottom of the hill. They have less to lose than you do—because it's not a career to them. It's just something they think anybody can do. Write a book? Piece of cake.

Don't tell them the truth. Self-publishing is easy. Self-selling is not.

It's the only secret you've got. Mass amateurization (to use Shirky's term) is upon us, and your ace in the hole is getting past that "I *just* want to *write*" thing and embracing the fact that if you don't get some business backbone, you'll end up in that big heap of amateurs at the bottom of Mount Content.

Dude, digital is your *answer*, not your problem. Digital is your friend.

EMBRACE THE DIGITAL DYNAMIC, EVEN BEFORE YOU PUBLISH

Here's how digital giveth and taketh away:

1. For authors, digital means that your mother can create a thing online that looks just as good as a book created by Penguin Random House almighty.

---

7 www.bbc.co.uk/programmes/b05w8dnv

You may know that what your saintly mom has written is tripe, much as you love her, but a consumer does not. If she can post a halfway-decent book cover thumbnail image, she can sell *The Book of Okra* to people who actually believe she's a chef.

2. For *smart* authors, digital means that they can track the following:
   - developments related to book retail, whether print or e-book, online or in stores
   - major initiatives or changes at traditional publishers
   - controversial articles or posts being discussed in the author community
   - new publishing industry reports and statistics
   - updates on lawsuits or legal issues pertaining to authors
   - new services or companies serving (or preying on) the author community
   - new sales to traditional publishing houses, which can help identify the movers and shakers in the agenting world and new trends in publishing
   - emerging developments in publishing strategies and successes

That list of good moves for modern authors comes from an informational piece that Friedman and I have created for savvy authors, the ones who know what they don't know. We put out a private subscription e-mail (digital!) newsletter, The Hot Sheet,[8] for authors who want to get down with their businessy selves and get exactly the industry news they need, the advice on what to do about it, with "no drama, no hype," as we say, no need to mosh in the blog pits of the Internet inferno trying to suss out a scrap of trustworthy analysis or news. And there are more assists like this in the digital realm, Horatio, than you may realize. *Professional* authors are pulling down vast knowledge and capability from the cloud every day.

Why do you think publishing houses are now scrambling to develop or upgrade author dashboards for their writers? Thanks to the Bezosian Beelzebub in Seattle (Amazon.com, for those not yet in the know), publishers have been pressured to provide actual sales data (*mon Dieu!*) to their authors. No longer is the royalty statement that even your agent can't read acceptable. Amazon proved long ago that technology can tell an author what sold, where, when, and for how much.

Now we're talking digital. And you're going to pass up that kind of information because "I *just* want to *write*"? Okay, but then don't forget that you can shut down all of those beepings and burpings with systems like RescueTime[9]

---

8 hotsheetpub.com

9 www.rescuetime.com

that let you close off programs and apps that interrupt you—for exactly the length of completely focused, uninterrupted writing time you crave. That's digital, too. Digital at your service.

Digital is the sensible readings from industry players like literary agent Kristin Nelson, whose Pub Rants series is full of no-nonsense, real-world advice, like when never to query an agent: "I can tell you right now that on our first day back [from the holidays] we get 600+ queries. Hard to stand out in that flux." (Did I mention the Wall of Content to you?)

And digital is marketing. At your fingertips.

Instead of spending an hour complaining with your friends on a Facebook page that you hate marketing, why not consider some of the advice that marketing smart man Pete McCarthy offers at Logical Marketing?[10] He'll tell you about finding "adjacent communities" to the themes in your work in an effort to reach out to likely buyers.

Take an online course on revamping your dated and badly designed website, monitor a webinar discussion from the Alliance of Independent Authors, or follow a site like Writer Unboxed, where assertions are tested in civil, friendly comment discussions you can engage with. Strategize a marketing plan for yourself; don't just upload and run.

"E-books! Throw 'em up on the Web!" is author and instructor James Scott Bell's line that makes rightful fun of that misguided approach to faux marketing.

"If you build it, they will NOT come," the agent Rachelle Gardner is telling her clients these days. "You must promote it."[11]

Are you thinking of self-publishing because you don't want to query agents and editors in the traditional publishing system? Then get your door-to-door samples case ready. Listen to Gardner again: "What would be the point of self-publishing a book if you have no intention of promoting it? Who will buy it? With *millions* of books available for sale at any given time, what's your plan for letting people know that yours exists?"

Look, many authors these days cling to an idea that the publishing industry is none of their business. Day and night, you can find them online, banging on about the unfairness of expectations that they "do marketing" and "be PR people." But the fact that you can get online and find those gripe fests means that you can also get online and find the resources, the people, and maybe even the crowdfunding you need to give your stuff a chance to punch through the Wall of Content.

---

10 logical-marketing.com/hubspot-research-hashtag-how-to-knowledge-graph-amazon-stores-mobile-email

11 www.rachellegardner.com/to-blog-or-not-to-blog-2

As the digital dynamic transforms the industry—of which you are a part, if you want to sell a book through trade or indie channels—business sense is your best currency. Publishers need author-partners, and that's one reason to be hopeful about the kind of contract reform that the Authors Guild, the Society of Authors, and other advocacy groups are agitating to bring about.[12] You can be an author-partner, a team player, an agent of your own success.

Because after the beginning, it wasn't enough for the Word to be only with God. It had to get out there. Your stuff has to get out there, too. And you've got an unholy Wall of Content to contend with if you have any hope of drawing attention.

Your career is your business, and "I *just* want to *write*" will make you forgettable before you even start. Authors-in-progress—before they have a single sentence ready to sell—need to come to terms with the truth: Life in the marketplace is success in the making. So stop resisting. Take your seat among the congregation of the professional, entrepreneurial authors of today.

Otherwise your career will never get past "In the beginning."

 ## PORTER'S POINTERS FOR INDUSTRY-WISE WRITING

Here are several resources you need to follow to prepare and maintain your position as a knowledgeable business operative in today's fast-changing marketplace.

General Resources

- The Hot Sheet: My colleague Jane Friedman and I have created this one-of-a-kind private, subscription-only newsletter with Wall Street's familiar industry-insider bulletins in mind. We provide expert interpretation of the most important industry news *expressly for authors*. Read us biweekly to get informed, briefed, and updated. Then you can get back to your writing, confident that your business brain is in gear. Our brand promise is "no drama, no hype," in direct contrast to all the emotion, agenda, gossip, rumor, and personality you encounter on writing blogs. Special offer: If you send an e-mail to us at editor@hotsheetpub.com and tell us you're a reader of this book, we'll send you back a code to use for a special one-time discount off our standard annual rate of fifty-nine dollars (at the time of this writing) to get you started, and we offer a thirty-day free trial.
- Publishers Marketplace (which includes Michael Cader's Publishers Lunch e-mails) is more expensive—starting at twenty-five dollars per month—but it's the other key paid site I recommend for authors because

---

12 www.thebookseller.com/futurebook/publishing-2016-between-writers-and-readers-319489

it's the industry's reporting hub on publishing deals and the activities of agents, publishers, rights specialists, business trends, and more.

- In addition to reading my fine fellow contributors at Writer Unboxed daily (free, emphasis on craft) and keeping up with blog and event material at Writer's Digest (free, emphasis on both craft and business), I recommend one more regular stop: literary agent Kristin Nelson's Pub Rants series at her agency site, free to read. Here you'll find some of the most direct, forthcoming, and aggressively informative insight into the business as it pertains to authors. Nelson tackles everything from how to keep your head on straight amid rejection to how to be sure your own agent is capturing all your royalties for you. Her fellow agents read this. So should you.

Major News Sites

- *Publishing Perspectives* provides a comprehensive view of the international industry. Remember that I'm the editor in chief of this free resource (who me, biased?), but we operate with the support of German Book Office New York and our affiliation with the Frankfurt Book Fair. We have the big picture.
- *Publishers Weekly* is the U.S. mainstay. Much of its best material is freely available to read online, or you can opt for a subscription if you prefer.
- *The Bookseller* is the United Kingdom's medium of record for the publishing industry and is top-notch on key issues. It's a subscription service (author discounts are available), but its blog/column sections and its digital-publishing focus, The FutureBook (for which I once served as associate editor), are free.

Author Memberships

- Self-publishing authors, be sure to look into membership with the Alliance of Independent Authors. Its offices are in the United Kingdom, but its membership is international, with roughly half in the States.
- I recommend Authors Guild membership for trade authors in the United States, and Society of Authors if you're in the United Kingdom. Self-publishing authors need to consider these memberships carefully as well. These organizations are developing a powerful network of international advocacy and beginning to make impressive advances in terms of bringing writers' working conditions to light.

PART FIVE

REWRITE

Know this to be true: Even the pros rewrite. In fact, they likely wouldn't be pros if they didn't. For this stage, "Serve the work" should be your mantra and your guiding principle. It's as simple—and as difficult— as that.

POWER DOWN

How (and Why) to Begin Reworking Your Novel Away from the Computer

KATHLEEN MCCLEARY

At one point while I was rewriting my second novel, I printed the entire book and spread it out, chapter by chapter, in a grid across the floor in my office. I had thirty or more chapters, plus blank pages to mark where yet-to-be-written chapters might go. I spent days deciding how to structure the book: what to cut, what to add, what to move from this part of the book to that part. I came home one day about two weeks into the process and found my husband in the kitchen.

"Oh, hey," he said. "You know that mess all over the floor in your office? I picked it up for you."

I stared at him, speechless.

"I'm kidding," he said. "I'm kidding!" The fact that my first reaction to his joke was the feeling that the bottom had dropped out of my life says something about the challenging, head-banging, but ultimately rewarding process of re-writing a book. Revising is "the hardest work there is," Ernest Hemingway told author Arnold Samuelson. (He also mentioned that he rewrote *A Farewell to Arms* "at least fifty times.") But learning to revise away from the computer—with markers, sticky notes, whiteboards, index cards, geographical maps, and even desk calendars—can give you fresh insight into your book and how to approach it.

I've revised three novels now (four, if you count the rewriting I've done already on my work-in-progress), and I've learned that working on my story *off* the computer helps enormously in focusing my attention on what needs to change, sparking ideas for new directions, and identifying what and where to cut. If you're ready to dive into your own revision, here are some off-line techniques to try.

PRO TIP

Once you finish the draft, take a break. How long is up to you, but you need to let your chapters simmer without interference, let your mind focus on other things, and let your spirit rest. I have taken a minimum of a month off from each book before tackling a rewrite and found that each time I came back to my book with fresh eyes and a much clearer, more objective sense of what worked and what didn't.

PRINT IT OUT

Print out your manuscript. Holding the entire physical book in your hands will give you a major sense of satisfaction. You made something out of nothing—how cool is that? Give yourself credit for your amazing accomplishment in finishing an entire novel, something few people actually do.

Also, reading on paper instead of on your computer screen will help you better see, understand, and track changes you want to make. A 2013 *Scientific American* article found that in multiple studies people were able to create better "mental maps" when reading on paper—they had a better sense of where in a book they read a certain scene or bit of information. This, in turn, helped readers better comprehend what they were reading.

"When we read, we construct a mental representation of the text in which meaning is anchored to structure," writes *SA*'s Ferris Jabr. These representations are like "the mental maps we create of terrain—such as mountains and trails—and of man-made physical spaces, such as apartments and offices." People often can remember where in the text they read something—at the top of a right-hand page, for example—just as they might remember walking past a watercooler before turning right to enter an office. Because reading on paper provides "more obvious topography" than onscreen text (left and right pages, eight corners, etc.), it's easier to make a mental map of what you're reading.

Reading through your entire book on paper will help your brain map your story—what occurs at what point in the novel, how far into the journey it is. And that helps you understand the pacing of your book as well as any components that might be missing or repetitive.

SPREAD IT OUT

Once you've printed your book, spread out all the manuscript pages across a large surface—a table, counter, or floor (my favorite). You can organize it in whatever way works best for you.

I lay the book out chapter-by-chapter across the floor, as mentioned earlier, going from left to right in a giant grid. This gives me an immediate sense of the story as a whole. I determine how many chapters are devoted to each character's POV, how the chapters compare in length (I don't want a book with some chapters of thirty pages and some of two pages), and I mark where, according to my outline or plot synopsis, transitional scenes (or more major scenes) are needed by putting a blank sheet of paper in the correct spot on the grid. This technique helped me enormously with my second novel, which included two POVs and chapters that frequently switched time lines. By laying it all out, I saw how much of the book belonged to one character and how much belonged to another, and where and when I needed better transitions between their stories. Where in that grid does the climax happen? When does the character move from the ordinary world into the journey that launches the novel?

 **PRO TIP**

The first time I taught a writing class at American University, one of my colleagues told me to use a green pencil to edit students' essays because it was less threatening than red. Well, when you're editing yourself, you can't be a wimp. Go for the red one.

Tish Cohen, author of five novels, including *The Search Angel*, prints out all the chapters and lays them "on the floor with giant stickies noting the narrative point of each, for a bird's-eye view." Try it. If one character's POV fills twice as many pages as another character's, does that make sense? Does the character who gets the most space deserve or need it? Similarly, is there a character or POV that deserves more space? You can pinpoint these issues at a glance.

And don't be afraid to chop up that grid of papers if you have to. Ania Szado, author of *Studio Saint EX* and *Beginning of Was*, wove together the present-day narrative of her protagonist with a time line from that character's past in her first novel. The memories didn't appear chronologically in the book, but Szado wanted to be sure information flowed in a way that made sense to the reader.

So she cut up the manuscript, split it into two stacks—present and past—and put each in chronological order. "I read through each one as though it was its own manuscript, reordered where necessary, and then put the whole thing together again."

MAKE A MIND MAP

Mind mapping is a visual form of outlining. After I finished my third novel, I struggled with the revision. I knew parts of the story didn't work, but I wasn't sure why or which parts. Finally, I got out a big piece of poster board, markers, scissors, and tape. The novel tells the story of two women, good friends, who both desperately want a baby. I cut out a photo of one of my daughters as an infant and taped it to the center of the poster board. Then I drew a branch from the center to represent one character and another branch (in a different color) to represent another character. I drew sub-branches off each branch, representing the important people in that character's life. I drew lines across the branches and scribbled in major events that happened in each character's story arc. This exercise helped me see the story in a completely different way.

You can find mind-mapping software online, as well as thousands of examples of mind maps and blank mind-map charts. The basic elements of a mind map are as follows:

- a central image (this should be a visual image, not words) that represents the main focus or idea, which, for me, is always the "want" that is driving the main character
- branches radiating from the center that embody the main themes (or characters)
- twigs shooting out from the branches to represent ideas directly connected to the relevant branch
- curved lines, images, color—visual stuff that excites your brain

You can put your character's goal or desire in the center of your map and work from there. Or you might put your character in the center, and the branches could represent the different obstacles or adventures the character faces through the course of the book. Experiment.

HANG UP A GEOGRAPHICAL MAP

My second novel took place in the San Juan Islands off Washington State's coast. I put up several large maps of the San Juans on the wall of my office as I was revising so I could see where the characters lived and worked and played, and so I could make sure that anything I wrote about the geography was accurate. Catherine McKenzie, author of six novels, including *Smoke*, put a large map of Cincinnati on her wall while working on her latest novel (*Fractured*, October 2016) so she could track characters as they moved around the neighborhood in which the book takes place.

OFFICE-SUPPLY THE HECK OUT OF IT

Whiteboards, bulletin boards, index cards, markers, magnetic boards, chalkboards, sticky notes, pens, thumbtacks, tape, and scissors are all your friends. While revising one novel, I bought a large magnetic whiteboard and lots of little magnet "tacks." I wrote a one-sentence summary of each scene on index cards, using green for scenes that were in one character's POV and yellow for scenes in another character's POV. Then I arranged the book scene by scene on the whiteboard by "tacking" each index card with a magnet. Seeing the entire novel on one space (a space smaller than the floor of my office) helped me see where it was dragging, where it got off track, or where one character was too dominant.

Writer Tish Cohen uses different-colored permanent markers and gigantic sticky notes to chart each revision task on her wall. For smaller details, she uses index card–size stickies. As she addresses the issue on each note, "I get a little thrill—okay, a big one—from balling them up and throwing them away," she says.

Catherine McKenzie has used a corkboard with giant sticky notes to "see POV, the number of scenes, and whether it's past or present narrative action."

SET IT IN TIME

You know those big desk calendars, the ones that are almost two feet wide and a foot and a half tall? Try using sticky notes and one of those calendars to help you plot out the time line of your story. This tip comes from Allie Larkin, author of *Stay* and *Why Can't I Be You*. She writes individual scenes on different-colored sticky notes and posts them on the calendar to track what happens when.

TRUST YOUR INSTINCTS

Michelangelo supposedly said, "The sculptor arrives at his end by taking away what is superfluous." (You'll find that quote online as "Sculpting is easy. You just chip away the stone that doesn't look like David," which is Michelangelo as interpreted by social media.) No matter how or if he said it, the point is a good one: You're honing your book into what is true and essential, and the ultimate best guide for that process is the instinct that led you to write that story in the first place. Trust it. You're a writer. You know what to do.

 FAQ

....

In revision, I could take my project in any one of four directions, and all would be good. How do I choose?

That situation may be indicative of a project that has poorly focused intentions. Why are you telling this story? For whom? What's its core appeal for readers? (I mean, what's the main reason they'll read it?) Most of all, is this the novel *you* want to read? Focus more on you and less on the market.

—DONALD MAASS

WRITING BY EAR

How Tuning into the Sound of Language Can Elevate Your Story

TOM BENTLEY

There's a passage in *Huckleberry Finn* where Huck is describing how he and Jim travel down the river at night, hiding at dawn on the overgrown banks:

> Next we slid into the river and had a swim, so as to freshen up and cool off; then we set down on the sandy bottom where the water was about knee deep, and watched the daylight come. Not a sound anywhere—perfectly still—just like the whole world was asleep, only sometimes the bullfrogs a-cluttering, maybe.

The entire passage is a marvel of cadence and rhythm, a singing vernacular that rolls through your mind. The reason I excerpted this particular paragraph is because it mentions sound—or its absence—directly and also uses an unfamiliar term—"a-cluttering"—that could, but doesn't, disrupt the reader. Rather, the word choice supplies the river's background music in the reader's ears.

Magic this might seem, but much more is at work. The author is acting as orchestra conductor: Conscious waves of the writing wand bring the word woodwinds in when needed, at the right volume. And note the piccolos of punctuation: a dreaded semicolon (think of Vonnegut's declaration that semicolons are "transvestite hermaphrodites representing absolutely nothing"), a brace of dashes, the wink of the comma before the "maybe" at paragraph's end. Those are the tiny adjustments in sentence pace and breath that resonate, quietly, in the reader's mind.

You're the writer: Those words, those adjustments, are yours to make. And you can make them best by reading your work aloud.

HEAR THE MUSIC OF WORDS

Henry James famously said that *summer afternoon* are the two most beautiful words in the English language. That's arguable, of course, but Henry could feel—could hear—that a certain succession of letters, syllables, and sounds are felt and heard in the reader's mind as being pleasing or painful. (James himself perpetrated paragraphs of such intricately curling phrase and clause that you couldn't locate the originating verb with a microscope, but on this summer afternoon in question, he's clear.)

The best way to find the summer afternoons or dodge the blistering thunderclaps in your writing is to read it aloud. Hear whether it flows or fumbles. Become conscious that a well-placed comma can invite a sentence to catch its breath or that the exclusion of that comma can spark an agreeable acceleration. Even complex sentences with potentially cumbersome clutches of words can be structured so that they are a series of smooth steps or, if need be, a graduated set of invigorating leaps. The artful mixing of Anglo-Saxon bread with Latinate butter, short words and long, ones with internal rhyme that gather tightly with their cousins, a two-word sentence next to a twelve worder—here you have a well-tuned orchestra of words, not dissonant squawking.

Oddly, reading writing aloud will often reveal holes in composition that are unseen (well, unheard) when the words are only read in the head. Speak it, and you'll know its truths and its terrors.

STRETCH OR SHRINK YOUR SENTENCES

Rivers can gush and splash, sometimes trickle and swerve, according to the contours of the land and the volume of their flow. So it is with sentences. Narrative stretches can comfortably flop out and languish, and, in context, sound just right. Dialogue can be spat out, surge in herky-jerky jumps, and still pin a reader to the page. But you won't know if your tale has just the right amount of molasses or could use more caffeine unless you hear the words and hear them spoken.

When you're editing your work on the screen or, better, on the printed page, you can get into a comfy, slumping numbness caused by the familiar beats and patterns of your own expressions. Reading the work aloud pulls you back, straightens the spine of your attention, so you know if your characters fall flat or light fires. The ears hear what the mind mumbles.

It's very important to note here that I'm not talking about producing writing that's contained and leashed, no hair out of place. Some writing needs to gallop, to career; other writing needs to simmer or smolder. By reading it aloud, you know if the tension you're trying to build in a scene doesn't actually flop. Hearing a fresh metaphor can give you a frisson that's a bodily rush, but the wording on a flat metaphor will leave your ears—and your mind—unmoved.

NOTE THE SHAPE OF SOUND

I'm a slow reader anyway, but when I see a sentence, or even a word, that touches me both visually and aurally, I'll say it aloud a few times, mouthing its syllabic shape. (Hey, there are no horses around to spook, so I'm safe.)

Consider that words have both aural shapes and textures that are felt and heard in the reader's mind, often at a visceral, emotional level. Writing that sounds ugly is less persuasive (unless you're playing with foul-faced words for effect, which is a different matter entirely). So pay attention to the sounds and the shapes of your words. Make them swim, spin, or sigh in the auditorium of the imagination rather than crash or clatter. Your audience will rise to their feet to applaud rather than to run.

In Huck, Twain managed to create a character whose expression is uncannily pure, using a dialect that doesn't rely on clumsy spellings or folksy twang but on a kind of raw immediacy. Of course, Twain took more than seven years to finish his *Adventures*—I suspect he kept reading it aloud to get Huck's voice just right.

You might not want to take seven years to get your words just right, but no matter if you use Hemingway's tight-lidded box of words as a model or Austen's more elliptical resonance, pay attention to how they sound. Make music in your reader's ears, and you'll make more readers.

 HOW TO GET IN YOUR OWN WAY, METHOD 22: THINK YOUR ONLY JOB IS TO FIX PROBLEMS YOUR BETA READERS FOUND

You could do everything your betas mentioned, and it still might not be as good as it should be. Only you can prevent forest fires *and* fully realize your book's potential.

—BILL FERRIS

LEVELING UP

Harnessing Revision to Make the Good Even Better

HEATHER WEBB

As a freelance editor, author, and avid reader, the revision process is near and dear to my heart. I like to think of the editing process as the point where we lavish our stories with love, pruning and fine-tuning our words so the manuscript ripens into a novel. As it happens, I just recently finished my third novel. Since I had pushed in a slightly new direction from my other two books, this story challenged me in ways I hadn't experienced before, resulting in a lengthy revision process. I tangled and toiled, reworked and reread. At times, I felt like I was wandering in the dark, unsure if I was headed in the right direction. But I did know one thing: I had to give myself the time I needed to revise properly, to revise *well*.

What does revising well mean? Regardless of where you are in your journey to becoming published, you can employ some useful tools and methods during the editing process to ensure your revisions are fruitful. Below are some of my favorites.

LEAN INTO YOUR STRENGTHS

What have your readers enjoyed most about your works? Embrace those elements, and look for other scenes in your manuscript where you can utilize them to make the prose sing. Perhaps you've been told you write fast-paced stories. Harness that natural eye for pacing, and integrate tension in a slower, more internal scene to give it zip. Maybe your critique partners have enjoyed your descriptions. Are there places you can thread in a bit more detail to ground the characters in scene or create a certain mood? If your strength is dialogue, use it wherever you can to convey subtext as well as highlight a character's voice.

Your strengths are a big part of your authorial voice. They're what make you unique as a writer.

The problem is, you've worked on this book forever and read it a hundred times. How do you find these areas in the manuscript where you can lean into your strengths or layer for depth? I've found the handiest method, in addition to working with multiple critique partners or an editor, is to read your chapters out of order. Keep track of what you've finished by making a list of the chapter headings on a piece of paper. Cross each one off as you go so you don't backtrack. To push this idea even further, print out the entire manuscript rather than reading it on your screen.

Reading in this way prevents you from getting caught up in the flow of story, breezing over the portions you know by heart, and essentially missing opportunities to polish, deepen, prune, and heighten tension. I like to think of this stage of revisions as putting a dollop of whipped cream on a sundae or a sprinkle of Parmesan on pasta; you know the dish is tasty already, but adding the final touches makes it spectacular. (I can't help myself; I love a good food metaphor.)

PRACTICE METAPHORS AND OTHER COMPARISONS

Speaking of metaphors, they're one of my favorite literary devices. Used properly, they can create a sense of tone, reveal a character's emotional space, and also foreshadow coming events. They add depth and beauty to a narrative that give it a sense of richness. Are there places in your manuscript where the main character's emotions shift? How can you use a metaphor to illustrate this shift?

I find one of the more interesting forms of comparisons is the use of parallels. Parallels link two contrasting characters through their very similar journeys. Not only can they shed light on each of the character's traits, motivations, and goals, but they can also be used as an element of foreshadowing about what is to come for the protagonist.

Writing metaphors and other comparisons are skills one obtains through plenty of practice and mindful reading. To hone your metaphoric dexterity, read poetry—the more the better. Poetry creates links in your brain that help you both discern and design metaphors and parallels, as well as grasp shades of meaning, rhythm, and style. Your mind absorbs all of these devices, all of these beautiful words, and begins to make connections that find their way to your pages.

USE SYMBOLS TO ADD MEANING

Using symbols is one of the most effective ways to elicit an innate emotional response or to convey meaning to a reader. Consider a crucifix, an American flag, a rabbit's foot, a dove; though these are common and simplistic, they are tangible, and all evoke immediate perceptions and emotions.

Let's look at one of these symbols. An assassin creeps through an almost-deserted office building late at night. He spies his target at a desk and peers through the scope on his gun. Just before he shoots, he fishes inside his shirt for his cross necklace. He kisses the cross, aims the gun, and shoots.

We learn a lot about this character by his simple action. Is he on some sort of mercenary errand? Perhaps he's a flagellant or a vigilante. His cross also tells us something about his possible ethnic background, depending on where the story takes place. Since he follows a religion, he might be sympathetic in some way. In any case, we get a strong sense that this assassin isn't your average CIA operative.

Develop your own symbols. Find ways in which these objects not only tell a tale of their own but also become a part of the protagonist's journey.

DROP HINTS, GIVE CLUES

Foreshadowing is a terrific device for deepening the narrative as well as creating tension. Once you have a complete draft or two, review chapter one. In what way can you thread in clues about the character's journey ahead? Where else might you be able to add a line or two of internal reflection or dialogue that offers a peek into the protagonist's future? Ponder the tone you would like to evoke, keeping in mind that foreshadowing often indicates impending doom. Tread carefully, too, as this device can be overplayed and therefore can lose its impact. Integrate it into the narrative with a delicate hand.

MAKE SECONDARY CHARACTERS COUNT

Secondary characters aren't just a part of the external action that drives the plot. They're a means to reveal facets of the protagonist's personality, motivations, and goals, whether positive or negative. These secondary characters shouldn't just fill a role; they should be useful and bring meaning to a scene or the story as a whole. They may act as mirrors of the protagonist, in which the two possess similar traits and complement each other, or they may be used as foils, in which the secondary character is vastly different to emphasize the protagonist's weaknesses and strengths. Finally, a secondary character may be used to reflect the protagonist's arc or change over the course of your story.

Let's look at a simple example. Jack leaves a cafe after a date with his lovely neighbor, Marilyn—a woman who hasn't given him the time of day until now. On his way down the street, he passes a shop window and notices his reflection. His shirt strains over a new bulge of muscle on his chest, determination is reflected on his features, and scruff grows on his chin, which makes him appear less vulnerable and perhaps more masculine. He feels alive, vigorous, and confident. This budding friendship with Marilyn (a secondary character) has helped him see himself in a new light. He must be someone worth knowing if she wants to spend time with him. Jack is changing, growing. In essence, a secondary character has triggered a shift in Jack's arc.

The delicate details Jack sees in his reflection seem unimportant, but they add up to a well-developed main character.

INTEGRATE QUIRKS, TICS, AND FLAWS

At times, the best way to deepen a character is by showing her quirks, tics, and flaws. What is the story behind this flaw? What makes this quirk endearing—or grating—to others in the story or to the reader? Drop hints about why a character possesses these idiosyncrasies throughout the narrative. Not only does withholding the information promise there is more to this character than first perceived, but it also adds a layer of tension that tempts the reader to turn the page.

REVISE IN DRAFTS, AND MAKE THE ROUNDS

We hear a lot about layering our manuscript, but what does this mean, exactly? I find the two best strategies to create well-developed, layered fiction are working in drafts and soliciting feedback in multiple rounds.

Begin by examining your process. How many drafts do you need to create a solid, salable manuscript? Do you muddle through each draft, juggling different points as you go? This can be frustrating and can also cause you to neglect certain elements of the story. For each draft, try editing with a specific purpose in mind.

Let's look at my system as an example. In draft one I simply get the words down on paper. In draft two I make sure all plot threads connect and make sense, add any necessary scenes to attain this goal, or condense or cut miscellaneous scenes that have no purpose. During draft three I print out the entire manuscript and check voice and character arcs. In draft four I read aloud for pacing and awkward dialogue. After this draft I send out the manuscript to my first round of critique partners. Once I have their feedback, I incorporate it for draft five. In draft six I apply the polish—descriptions, wordsmithery, metaphors, symbolism. Next, I send the manuscript out to one more round of readers. In draft seven I incorporate their feedback. Finally, I send it to my agent.

Giving your manuscript to readers at different stages allows you to test whether the changes you've implemented are working. For example, I mentioned above I distribute my manuscript to my first round of critique partners after my fourth draft. For this round, I ask them to read for plot, pacing, and character arcs. Asking specific, pointed questions helps me get a feel for whether my revisions thus far have been successful. It also helps the reader zero in on any possible problem areas. For the second round of feedback, I may ask a different set of questions surrounding pieces I've "fixed," or I may ask for general impressions so as not to bias their thinking while they read.

Working steadily and carefully and allowing yourself the time you need to process—staring out the window, taking long showers or drives, doodling in your notebook, plucking weeds—are imperative to shaping your manuscript into something rich and beautiful.

The bottom line is, whether you're a "pantser" or plotter, a three-draft person or a ten-draft person, all of that brilliance doesn't flow to the page in one go. Be systematic in your editing approach to eliminate unnecessary dithering. Utilize readers after various stages to check your work as you go. Be diligent. And above all, have patience with yourself. Your process is your process, and much of the time that means you need to give your mind time to work through the many puzzles that come with crafting a novel.

 **PRO TIP**

Smart cuts help the remaining parts grow even stronger, but that doesn't mean you should always leave them on the cutting-room floor. Sometimes cut parts make great bonus content for your website later on.

HAVE PATIENCE—WRITING IS ART

Consider how a painter works. A painter begins with a blank canvas. She sketches her ideas or outline on paper, perhaps even completes a watercolor of the picture she's envisioning. Next she primes her canvas. After each layer of paint, each detail added to the work, she must wait for the paint to settle and dry before moving on to the next. How do the color and the object appear after the paint dries? Does the image or hue need adjusting? After dozens of layers and many, many hours of careful strokes, the artist has produced a completed work. But what would happen if the artist didn't wait long enough for the paint to dry? The images might become obscured, the colors muddied. She might consider the painting a masterpiece—the very best she could do—or she could feel that it's not quite right and certainly not her best.

Now look at your process as a writer. You might brainstorm ideas, take notes, create an outline of some sort—whether your outline is a first draft or pages of organized notes on chapters, themes, and characters. Next you construct the story, word by word. After each draft, a bit of time away from the manuscript allows the story to settle and set before you go into the next round of layering.

As an artist, you need to allow your stories to ripen. Be patient with your characters and story arc. Give them time to reveal themselves to you. And most of all, be patient with yourself as you create and try new things.

GROW, EXPAND, AND REACH FOR THE STARS

Writing the same sort of plotline, characters, or worlds can cause your skills to stagnate. Push in a new direction. Keep things fresh, flowing. Making the good better involves both practice and stepping outside your circle of comfort. Be bold. Be brave. Be original. Refill your well often, challenge yourself daily, and create with all your heart. It will show in your writing, and you'll reach new heights.

When we stop growing, we're dying. That's my motto.

 HOW TO GET IN YOUR OWN WAY, METHOD 23: RUSH THROUGH REVISIONS

It's tempting to get so excited about releasing your book that you don't spend enough time and attention whipping it into shape. All that fame and fortune will still be there if you take another week or two—or even a few months—to give your book a final spit shine.

—BILL FERRIS

LETTING GO OF
THE REINS

When a Complete Rewrite
Is the Right Choice

STEVEN JAMES

We launch into our writing projects with so much confidence, so much reassurance that we know where things are going to go and what ground we're going to cover. So we climb onto the horse and begin to ride along the path, and when the ideas that start unfolding before us don't line up with what we had anticipated we would find, we keep yanking the reins back: *Stay on the trail, girl. Don't go off the path.*

Writing instructors and craft books often warn us about the dangers of writing ourselves into a corner or taking rabbit trails. So no matter how much the story whinnies or stamps its feet or tries to veer off and explore other paths, we make sure it stays steady and true on the one we've laid out for it, toward that destination we've already predetermined is the right one.

Now you be a good story. Obey me. I am your master.

I spent a year working on my novel *The Knight.* It was my most ambitious project yet—an intricate thriller exploring the question of what's more important, justice or truth, interwoven with a storyline of a killer who was reenacting crimes from a thirteenth-century manuscript that'd been condemned by the Catholic Church. Tense. Interesting. Lots of intrigue and moral quandaries. From the time I started writing the book, I was certain I knew the villain's identity. I was quite pleased with myself, actually, and constructed the entire story around the twist that would reveal who was truly behind the crimes.

However, getting that climax to work proved to be a challenge. No matter how I tweaked things, they just didn't feel right. The novel was due to my publisher on August 1, and I had to get an extension to September 1. Then October 1. Then November 10.

"We really need it by November 10," my editor told me.

"No problem," I assured her, just as any good author would, even as the story kept seeking another trail and I kept yanking it back onto this one—and kept not finishing the manuscript.

Finally, on November 7, I was at the airport to fly out to teach at a conference for the next three days. My plan: Speak during the day, and then furiously edit each night. It would be an insane schedule, but I told myself I could pull it off.

As I was walking through airport security, a crazy thought came to me: *Steve, you have the wrong killer. That's why this story isn't working.*

Then another voice, the rational one: *I'll find a way. I've known how this story ends for the past year.*

No, you need to change who the killer is.

Leave me alone.

As hard as I tried to wrestle the story over to the right, it kept trying to take me left. At last, I had to admit that if I kept things as they were, readers would bristle: *That's cheating. There's no way we could have guessed he was the killer. That came out of nowhere!* However, if I added more clues, it would become too easy to predict that he was the mastermind behind everything. I needed a different antagonist, one whom readers wouldn't anticipate but would accept: *Yes, of course. That makes total sense. Why didn't I see that coming?* The conclusion was painfully clear: To make things work, to make the story's end both unexpected and inevitable, I needed a different villain. And I knew exactly which character it needed to be. The bronco bucked, and I let it take me down a new path—a trail that I hadn't even known existed until an hour earlier.

I spent the flight jotting down what switching to a different killer would precipitate. Change after change, causing change after change. At the very least, I needed to add an entirely new storyline, alter relationships, change the clue progression, and recast the ending. Trail after trail, turn after turn, running all throughout the 125,000-word manuscript, and all of those pathways would be passing through up-until-now uncharted territory.

We landed in Cincinnati, and I phoned my editor. "Hey!"

"Hey."

"I have some good news."

"Oh. What's that?"

"This is going to be an even better story than we thought."

"Excellent."

"I'm going to change who the killer is."

There was a long pause. I got ready to argue my case, to unload all the reasons why I needed to make this change, but finally she just said, "As long as it'll be a better book, I trust you. Go ahead."

Rewriting the book took another two months. New paths, each one leading to another. But in the end, it really *was* a better book. My editor knew it. I knew it. And although readers had no idea about the change, I think if they could see how I'd veered away from my original plan, they would agree as well that this path was better.

A few takeaways from all of this:

- **LISTEN TO YOUR STORY.** Stop assuming, and start responding. Let the logic of the story guide you rather than imposing your agenda on it. Hand over the reins. Take those rabbit trails, and seek out the corners—because often that's where the best ideas will be found.
- **TAKE TIME TO PROCESS YOUR INSTINCTS.** A fresh perspective helps, so regularly step away from your work. Live a little between your drafts. Ask those tectonic plate–shifting questions, and don't muzzle your instincts.
- **TRUST THE CREATIVE PROCESS.** Over the course of time, I've finally realized that I need to place my confidence in the creative process, not in the decisions I make prior to embarking on the journey into the story.

There, off the beaten path, along that ridge that looks a little too intimidating and dangerous ... yeah, that's probably the route you need to take. The story wants to gallop in a new direction.

Let it.

 **PRO TIP**

Revising is not polishing. Revising is being willing to take the whole thing apart and put it back together again in an entirely different way. Or start all over again from scratch. Put in the work that the story demands.

—ROBIN LAFEVERS

PRO TIP

Create a file on your computer called "Experiment" to test extreme changes. The benefits are twofold. First, you'll have a preserved digital file of your old work in case you ultimately reject your new ideas. Second, the word *experiment* may embolden you to take additional risks that serve the work.

—THERESE WALSH

 HOW TO GET IN YOUR OWN WAY, METHOD 24: GET TOO ATTACHED

You know that phrase "murder your darlings"? It's not just that those darlings might be dead weight. The character or plot or setting or sentence you love might be actively getting in the way of taking your book to the next level. It's like that time you didn't get the summer job at Dairy Queen because of your pink hair.

—BILL FERRIS

A MECHANIC'S GUIDE TO REVISIONS

Consider Story Change as Skillful Overhaul

CATHY YARDLEY

You've completed a rough draft, which is cause for celebration. You've let it rest, just as so many writers have suggested. You've gone over it. You've let a few beta readers review it as well. You have a full toolbox: You're ready to mind map, mark up the manuscript with a colored pen, cover it with sticky notes, and even scissor-snip it if necessary. You've got Scrivener or some other nifty electronic tool that will let you shift scenes and add notes. You are prepared! Unfortunately you are also at a complete loss as to where to *start*.

You can think of your first draft in artistic terms: You're molding clay, throwing paint on a canvas, or allowing your creativity to run rampant to produce the raw material. This is where your most powerful prose and authentic and vibrant themes emerge.

When you get to revision, you've got all the material you need, more or less. What you need to do is take all that *stuff* and make it *go somewhere*.

So instead of artwork, think of your story as a car. Your job now is to be that car's mechanic. (And if you're not mechanically inclined, don't worry—I wouldn't know a carburetor from a crankshaft. It's just an analogy.)

 WHAT'S SCRIVENER?

Scrivener is a word processor on steroids. It lets you organize your writing, research, notes, pictures, and Web pages into a single project file for each book, and it is flexible enough to accommodate any writer's process.

Divide your manuscript into separate documents (e.g., scenes or chapters), building your structure as you go or planning it out in advance. Storyboard with virtual index cards. Write in or out of order, and easily change the order. Track your progress. Output to nearly any file type, including e-books. Back up your work automatically, and much more. Free trials are available online.[1] Why not check it out?"

—GWEN HERNANDEZ, AUTHOR OF *SCRIVENER FOR DUMMIES*

TEST THE ENGINE

The engine of your story is your character arc. Your protagonist(s) should be different at the end of the book than they are at the beginning. That's what readers want to see. These days, I would argue that all fiction—even the most action-packed thrillers or coziest mysteries—is character driven.

If your character hasn't changed over the course of your story, then your engine doesn't run.

If your character doesn't have a clear goal (preferably external and measurable if you're writing genre fiction), then your story is probably stalled in the driveway.

If your character doesn't have a clear reason for wanting said goal, one attached to a clear and painful consequence for failure, your story is probably stuck on the side of the freeway.

And if your character doesn't have strong and escalating conflict to prevent said goal from being accomplished, it's time to call a tow truck and haul that thing in.

MAKE SURE YOU HAVE ALL THE PIECES

If you find that your engine theoretically works but your car isn't going anywhere, then look at the overall system. Is the starter not working? (Does the story have a potent hook?) Is the fuel not getting to the engine? (Should the reader care?) Is something going haywire between the engine and the wheels? (Does the protagonist compel the reader to go on a journey with him?)

In short, something's not connected. An engine block alone isn't going to get you any closer to your destination; it needs a framework, a structure, and machinery that direct the energy and momentum in a useful way.

This is where you start looking at your *plot*. It's called the "Hero's Journey," after all, not the "Hero's Day of Navel Gazing." The story needs to illustrate,

---

1 www.literatureandlatte.com/trial.php

through gradually increasing conflict toward a well-motivated goal, how the protagonist evolves through the crucible of challenge.

That's what plot is: showing, not telling, how the protagonist changes.

MAKE SURE ALL THE PIECES ARE CONNECTED

The next step is to check your plot arc. Are all the major turning points connected? Do they make sense? If you're working with traditional three-act structure—the genre standard—then you probably know the elements you need:

- An opening act that establishes who the character is, what he wants, why he cares so much, why *we* as readers should care, and, finally, what he's up against.
- A second act that puts the character through her paces and causes her to transform—from wanting something very badly but having no clear idea how to accomplish that desire to gaining information, skills, and confidence as the opposition throws obstacles in her way.
- A final act that is a culmination of events. Will the character achieve the goal or not? If the character succeeds, it is through character growth and development. If the character fails, the growth itself usually turns out to be the true reward. Regardless, the ending needs to be both satisfying and logical.

TUNE UP YOUR STORY TO SMOOTH OUT THE RIDE

Okay, so your story is up and running. You've got characters doing important things that they are clearly invested in, all while facing formidable opposition. Everything seems to be going the right way.

As a mechanic, you know the thing's running, but it's running rough. There are splutters and stalls and unexplained bumps, and you don't know where the heck that knocking is coming from.

So you roll up your sleeves and start to test your components, step by step, scene by scene.

Traditionally this is known as the second pass—where you go more granular, making sure each scene contributes something meaningful to the whole.

Here are some places where problems usually crop up.

IF YOUR STORY STALLS ...

You probably have issues with your character's goal, motivation, and conflict (GMC). Every scene (yes, *every* scene) should connect to the GMC. If you're missing that connection, or if all of your scenes have the same level of intensity, then your story will stall out.

REPAIR IT: Write down the GMC for your protagonist in every scene, and give it a high-level once-over. Is the GMC present? Does it evolve? If not, revise the scene.

If you find your story stalling out at a certain point, odds are your problem started about two or three scenes prior. Setup makes all the difference. Make sure you didn't jump the story rails earlier, and don't try to fix things by simply adding more stuff to the problem scene. You're a mechanic, remember? Get in there, and get dirty.

IF YOUR STORY IS RUNNING TOO SLOWLY ...

Certain craft elements might be dragging down your pacing like a low-riding muffler. Ask yourself:

- Does the reader spend a lot of time in the character's head?
- Are you showing, not telling?
- Worse, are you reiterating what's being illustrated by spelling it out in the character's thoughts?
- Are you going through every detail in excruciating minutiae? (Does the reader *really* need to know that your protagonist put on his lucky socks, got on the crosstown bus—number 71—and then meandered to the local coffee shop for his usual double latte and copy of the *Times*?)

REPAIR IT: Pretend the story is a play. Make sure that the actions and dialogue do most of the story's heavy lifting. Also, make sure that the details you include are there for a reason.

IF YOUR STORY IS RUNNING TOO FAST ...

You may be revving a little too hard with that plot of yours! This creates what a friend of mine calls "falling asleep at the edge of your seat." It's not just about breakneck pacing, lots of set pieces, action scenes, and ridiculous stunts. Both comedy and action benefit from taking a breather between dramatic moments.

If your story takes a breather, this doesn't mean those scenes lack GMC, by the way. But your writing can get more circumspect.

REPAIR IT: If your characters have been acting, pursuing, and striving, give them moments to ruminate. Show them questioning their motivations. Show what they have to lose, in stark relief. Show the results of their actions in triumph; give them hope. You're probably going to obliterate that hope again anyway—which will increase conflict and tension.

IF YOUR STORY HAS A FLAT ...

This is slightly different than a story that's running slowly. The story structure itself is sound, and the pacing would be fine, except that something isn't working as it's supposed to. It's flat.

This issue usually links to character—either the characterization itself, the dialogue, or the voice.

You can test for characterization problems by asking the following: Would your character believably respond in this way, given this set of circumstances? If no, then the flatness probably comes from a forced plot device. Figure out another way for the character to resolve the situation that rings true.

If your character's actions do feel authentic, then your character may not be well rounded. How much do you know about this person, anyway? You don't need to show it all on the page, but further exploring your character's history and choices will help align your story and add greater depth. A deeper look at backstory here, a shading of words there, can build dimension and color. (For more on backstory, see the essay "Story First, Plot Second" by Lisa Cron.)

Do both of those things check out? Then it's time to look at dialogue. Does everyone sound the same? If you pulled out a section of dialogue and put it on a page, would you be able to tell which lines belong to which characters?

Finally, does the internal voice of your character reflect his unique dialogue? Your point-of-view characters may sound too homogenous, too staid. Don't be afraid to imbue your scenes with personality. It will help readers fully immerse themselves in your character's POV.

IF THERE'S A PROBLEM WITH THE STEERING ...

You may need to check on the driver. Did you choose the right POV for this story? Ask yourself whose story you're telling, who has changed the most throughout the story, who has the most to lose or the biggest stakes. These are things you don't often see until after you've finished the first draft, even though you thought you knew what you were doing all along. (Stories do that sometimes—take a hard right when we meant to go left.)

If your story has multiple POVs, have you handled them all clearly? The reason editors shy away from "head hopping" is because it can confuse readers; it's like teleporting them from one vehicle to another with no time to adjust.

Every time they need to reorient themselves and figure out whose POV they're in, the flow of the story hiccups.

REPAIR IT: Check each scene's POV. If you shift POV within a scene, make sure that you haven't done so too frequently, that you have a good reason, and that a primary character's GMC still directs the action.

Remember: Your POV character is the vehicle through which your reader experiences the story. The deeper readers can immerse themselves, the better.

 **PRO TIP**

Omniscient POV tends to put distance between the story and its readers. By necessity, there's more narration, more explaining. It's like being driven by a cabbie who decides to tell you about the local sights rather than driving yourself and figuring it out as you go. Use with caution.

IF YOU CAN'T SEE OUT THE WINDOWS ...

It's dangerous to move the story forward if your reader can't tell what's happening or where you're going. Make sure to anchor your reader in the here and now! This is, fortunately, a fairly easy fix.

REPAIR IT: Somewhere near the beginning of the scene, let your reader know how much time has elapsed since the previous scene and where the characters are. Also, show the scene goal.

DO SOME BODYWORK

Your story is running like a top and purring like a tiger. Unfortunately it still looks like a hoopty. Here's where you make it shine.

- **POUND OUT THE DENTS.** Check for continuity errors. These can be jarring details, like a hero having blue eyes in the first chapter and brown eyes in the sixth. Or naming a character Phil, only to have him become Terrance in the third act.
- **CHECK FOR LOGIC ERRORS.** There is nothing more embarrassing than to plan an exquisite and intricate escape scene, only to have a reader point out, "Why didn't he just go out the window? It was open."

- **GIVE IT A PAINT JOB.** Setting. Description. Voice. These are the colors of your writer's palette. This is what brings vibrancy and texture to your story and prose.

  - Make sure that the setting is more than just a bare stage, even if you want readers to focus on actions over environment. Emphasize and enhance locations that contribute to the scene's purpose.
  - Be specific in your descriptions when they matter to the story you're telling. There's a big difference between "he stood by a blue car" and "he stood by a rusted, slate-blue sedan."
  - Finally, voice. This is where your individuality, your soul as a writer, comes through. Be as authentic as you can. If it scares you, either because you feel too vulnerable or you're worried about how people will respond, then you're probably going in the right direction. (See the essay "Your Unique Voice" by Robin LaFevers for more on this topic.)

TAKE IT TO THE CAR WASH

Time to clean it up, inside and out. Fix typos, word choice, and any slight errors.

REPEAT AS NEEDED

Revisions don't have to be scary; they're just part of the process. While great revisions can create amazing works of soul and beauty, revision itself is more craft than art. Focus on the mechanics before you rather than your fears, and you'll find it a lot easier to dive in, make decisions and adjustments, and ultimately have a story you'll love.

 HOW TO GET IN YOUR OWN WAY, METHOD 25: WORRY ABOUT MESSING IT UP

This is the digital age. There's no change you can't undo. Save a hundred different drafts if you like; you can always put your albino unicorn back in the book later.

—BILL FERRIS

DO YOU NEED A PROFESSIONAL EDITOR?

Weighing the Pros and Cons

JANE FRIEDMAN

Writing and publishing advice can sometimes feel obvious or like common sense: *Have a fresh concept. Cut everything that's boring. Keep the reader turning pages.* But being able to truly see if you've been successful in writing a compelling work requires objectivity and distance that can be hard to achieve on your own—and this is where a professional editor comes in.

There are three primary reasons to hire a professional:

1. **THE LEARNING EXPERIENCE:** You'll grow as a writer by working with an expert who can point out your strengths and weaknesses, and give you specific feedback on how to take your work to the next level. Sometimes if you have an excellent mentor or critique group, you can learn the same things, but the process takes longer, and often there's more confusion and doubt due to conflicting opinions. When you pay a professional, you're partly paying for distance and objectivity. But you're also paying to receive trustworthy and meaningful feedback *and* learning how to apply that feedback. This is a skill you'll use again and again. You'll begin to develop an intuitive understanding of what kind of attention your work needs and at what point in the writing process you need feedback. (There are different types of professionals, which we'll cover in detail later, who work with you at different stages of the writing and revision process.)

2. **THE INDUSTRY ADVANTAGE:** The right professional editor typically offers industry insight, experience, or perspective in your genre that critique partners don't have. Assuming you work with someone with industry experience, you'll increase your understanding of what a quality editorial process looks and feels like. Once a writer has experienced the work of an editor who can make her work dramatically better, she often sticks with that editor for as long as possible. It becomes an invaluable career relationship.

3. **SUBMISSION PREPARATION:** The question of whether to hire an editor almost always arises just before or during the submissions process as a way of increasing the chances of a book's acceptance. For better or worse, this is the key motivation many writers have in seeking an editor. The learning experience goes unacknowledged or becomes a side effect.

In query letters, I see more and more writers claim their manuscript has been professionally edited, and it's no surprise. People inside the industry are known for emphasizing the importance of submitting a flawless manuscript. However, when evaluating professionally edited work, I find that it tends to be of *lesser* quality. This is quite paradoxical. Shouldn't this material be much better?

Unfortunately writers don't always understand what type of editor to use or how an editor is supposed to improve their work. This results in surface-level changes that don't meaningfully affect the chances of publication. Less experienced writers tend to be more protective of their work and less likely to revise. This is also true of early-career self-published authors, who may fall prey to "it's good enough" thinking or simply not have enough resources to invest in a professional edit. This can be a serious, career-stopping mistake. If the editing has been sloppy or haphazard, you'll see that reflected in readers' reviews. Even worse, if a reader has taken a risk on your work and been disappointed, he may never return.

APPRAISE YOUR EDITING NEEDS HONESTLY

When writers ask me if they should hire a professional editor, it's usually out of a vague fear that their work isn't good enough. They believe or hope that it can be "fixed" by a third party. While a good editor can help resolve problem areas, their work on the manuscript often requires the writer to do just as much work in order to improve the manuscript.

If you're hoping an editor will wave a magic wand and transform your work into a publishable manuscript overnight, you'll be disappointed by the results. But if you feel you've reached the limits of your own ability to improve the work, you're more likely to benefit. Writing teacher Richard Gilbert once advised, "The more frustrated a writer is with his own piece—meaning he has struggled hard with it on all levels and has turned it into an external object, a misshapen piece of clay he's almost angry at—usually the more help an editor or teacher can provide." I couldn't agree more.

Before you hire *anyone* to edit your work, you need to first understand the different stages of writing and revising, the different types of editing available, and what an editor can and can't do in terms of making your work publishable. One challenge is that the terminology used to describe editing can be subjective and therefore may differ from editor to editor or from service to service. This may seem strange, given that we're talking about an industry that specializes in language, but unfortunately it's a gray area you'll have to deal with. Before hiring an editor, it's critical that you're clear on exactly what level of editing or service will be provided. The first rule to remember: Never hire a copyeditor until you're confident your book doesn't require a higher level of editing first. Perhaps it seems obvious, but I see writers do it all the time. And doing so is like painting the walls of your house right before tearing them down.

Here's another way to think about the editing process: Don't hire a rules-based editor—someone who will look for sentence-level errors—when what you really need is a big-picture editor, who will identify strengths and weaknesses in the work. Some editors can provide all levels of editing, but it would be a mistake to hire an editor to perform *all* levels of editing in one pass.

UNDERSTAND THE ROLE OF HIGH-LEVEL EDITORS

Developmental editing, content editing, and book doctoring fall under the broad category of high-level editing. This process inevitably leads to revision and significant, substantive changes in your work. It would be nearly impossible for a writer to work with a high-level editor and not end up doing rewrites. Even if the editor can assist in rewriting the manuscript to fix problems, the writer should not expect validation or praise but rather an extensive editorial letter and manuscript notations with detailed advice so he can successfully revise.

A thorough developmental or content edit from an experienced professional is expensive and sometimes cost prohibitive for writers. An alternative to this type of edit is a more general manuscript assessment, in which an industry professional reads and assesses the strengths and weaknesses of your manuscript. You won't get page-by-page advice on revision but a broad overview of how to improve the work. Fortunately some high-level editors also provide assessment services in addition to more intensive editing work.

Developmental editors (DEs) are most commonly used for nonfiction work, especially by traditional book publishers. DEs focus on the structure and content of your book, and if they work for a publisher, their job is to ensure the manuscript adheres to the vision set out in the book proposal or the contract. They get involved early and while the writing process is ongoing.

Content editing has more or less the same purpose as developmental editing—it's focused on structure, style, and overall development, for both fiction and nonfiction. However, content editors don't often work on your manuscript while it's still in progress. You'll sometimes hear the term *book doctor* used in connection with this type of work. A book doctor is someone who performs developmental or content editing on your manuscript, usually after you have a completed draft.

In his essay "Developmental Editing," Paul McCarthy writes, "A successful collaboration allows the author to feel sustained and liberated by knowing that she doesn't have to bear the burden of creation, development, and refinement alone." Either a developmental or content editor gives you someone else to trust and lean on. This editor's goal is always to produce the best book possible for the reader, and her suggestions are made with an eye on producing better sales. She'll be concerned with the narrative arc, pacing, and missed opportunities. She'll do her best to troubleshoot and offer solutions to any inconsistencies or structural problems.

However, authors can be sensitive to feedback that suggests changing the book's structure or eliminating entire chapters. As a result, they can find this kind of editing very uncomfortable, even though it tends to be the most valuable form. A thorough high-level edit requires you to let go of things that may be important to you personally but might not belong in the book from a market-driven perspective. It can be hard to see or accept the bigger picture of what the editor is recommending.

Whether you can overcome your discomfort will largely depend on two things. First, if you trust your editor, then you'll be more likely to listen to his ideas and accept that he may see things more clearly than you can. Second, writers who see the editing process as a means of professional development—to improve their own abilities and perspective on their work—often tackle revisions with a more accepting and enthusiastic frame of mind.

KNOW WHEN TO EMPLOY A SURFACE-LEVEL EDITOR

Earlier I discussed writers who claimed to have their work professionally edited, yet their manuscript quality didn't reflect a professional's involvement. In many such cases, a writer has hired a line editor, copyeditor, or proofreader, which all encompass sentence-level or surface-level types of editing.

The task of line editing focuses on sentence structure, word use, and rhythm. Its goal is to create smooth and streamlined prose. Copyediting is generally more focused on correcting errors in grammar, syntax, and usage. Some copyeditors also fact-check and seek out inconsistencies or lapses in logic. Proofreading comes at the very end of the editorial process, sometimes after the book is already typeset. At this late stage, an editor would only be looking for typos, formatting mistakes, and other egregious errors that shouldn't make it to publication.

Unless you have serious recurring problems with grammar and punctuation (which is sometimes the case with nonnative English speakers), it's not usually necessary to hire a surface-level editor before submitting your manuscript. Here's the rule of thumb I use: If you have some "oops" errors here and there, it's not a problem, but if the agent or editor can't read for more than a page without getting distracted by surface-level problems, you need to fix them.

CONSIDER THE RIGHT EDITOR FOR YOU

Knowing what type of editor to hire requires some level of self-awareness—you must know where you're at in the writing and revision process and what kind of help you would most benefit from. Unpublished writers who keep getting rejected may need to hire a high-level editor to receive an honest and direct appraisal of how to improve big-picture issues. Some writers mistake a technically correct manuscript, one that follows all the rules, for the goal of editing. While the polish helps, no polish can make a flawed story shine.

Let's return to the reasons you might want to invest in a professional. The three reasons are to learn and grow as a writer, understand the role of the editor, and become better at the editing process. Yet your true motivation may be to get closer to a publishing deal. Unfortunately not even the best editor can guarantee you'll get an agent or publisher based on their work. There's no editorial formula that will transform your book into a bestseller.

Ask yourself: Will you be okay spending several thousand dollars on a high-level edit if your work doesn't succeed in getting published? If the answer is no, then you're probably not in a good position to hire an editor. If you're comfortable spending that much on long-term career growth—if you're okay investing in improving your work—then you're in a better and more appropriate mindset for this sort of thing.

If you are in a position to hire an editor, then the next question is: How do you find one? Start by asking other writers who write in your genre or category; word of mouth can lead you to someone who is qualified and has happy clients willing to recommend him. If that doesn't lead anywhere, take a look at the freelancer listings at publishersmarketplace.com. Freelancers who are members of this site are likely more knowledgeable about the industry by fact of keeping an updated profile at one of the most trafficked sites in book publishing. They might also be actively working with traditional publishers and agents, which is a good sign.

You can also search through established associations of editors, such as the Editorial Freelancers Association in the United States and the Society for Freelance Editors and Proofreaders in the United Kingdom. These organizations also provide helpful information about what rates to expect, what freelance agreements might look like, and more.

EVALUATE FREELANCE EDITORS

Whether you search for an editor through a database or an organization, or conduct an online search for freelance editors, you'll likely have dozens if not hundreds of options, and you'll have to learn how to evaluate them based on what information they make available online.

First, it's okay to judge them by their website. If you don't get a sense of professionalism and confidence from the site, keep looking. You should be able to find a range of testimonials from happy clients—or if not testimonials, then success stories. If you can't find any, ask. Avoid hiring an editor who can't provide evidence of quality work.

Most experienced editors specialize in specific genres or types of editing. You'll get the best results by hiring an editor who has a long track record of editing within your category of work. That means that if you're working on a romance, avoid hiring a nonfiction editor, and vice versa.

Also, most experienced editors will work with you on a sample to ensure their style is a good fit and you know what to expect. Sometimes this sample work is done for free, and other times you'll be charged; both practices are normal. I recommend not hiring an editor until you feel confident the match will work out; it's a big investment, and you want to reduce the possibility of a surprise at the end.

Avoid any kind of editing situation where you don't know the name of the editor you'll be working with. This can often be the case for writers who obtain self-publishing services or other packaged services. It's important that you're able to communicate directly with the person editing your work. You should be able to ask questions and have confidence in the qualifications of the editor. It's not often possible to do this with a middleman obscuring who's really doing the work.

Sometimes during the submissions process, you may hear back from an agent or publisher who recommends you retain the services of an editor and asks you to resubmit after you pay for the revision. You may be sent to a very specific service or freelancer they trust. While some agents and publishers do this in good faith in an effort to be helpful, others receive kickbacks for business they send to freelancers. So be cautious and always independently vet any recommendations you receive. It is generally considered a conflict of interest and inappropriate business practice for the publisher or agent to recommend *his own* editing services for a fee.

One of the biggest mistakes you can make is assuming a friend or colleague who has an English degree or is an English teacher is qualified as a professional editor. Editing isn't about academic credentials or having a good eye for typos. Book editing is a specialized area of expertise, and your average English major has never been exposed to either the book publishing industry or what professional book editors do for a living.

However, to save money you may be tempted to hire someone who has less experience. This might be acceptable if you're looking for a rules-based edit or a polish, but ask yourself: Do you really want your book to serve as a practice project for someone else?

I recommend you seek a professional with a clear record of book-related experience who is willing to share the specifics of her writing and publishing credentials. It's also a good sign when an editor is selective about what projects she takes on and doesn't have immediate availability. Quality editors are in demand, get repeat business, and have their schedules booked well in advance. For that reason, you'll have to be realistic about who you'll be able to hire. The editors of best-selling books might be perpetually unavailable or out of your price range. They're also more likely to turn down writers or manuscripts they don't think are ready for their level of expertise or involvement. They'll straight up tell you if they don't yet see a strong enough foundation in place for you to benefit from a high-level edit.

Unfortunately it's far more common to encounter the opposite situation: There are plenty of unqualified editors out there offering services and trying to sell you on how they can make your work more publishable. No formal accreditation process exists for freelance editors, so anyone can call himself one, and many set up shop with little experience or qualifications. Plus the growth of self-publishing has increased the number of people who are putting out their shingle. This means that freelance editors can quite easily point to published works they've edited, which may not reflect high-quality work.

REVISE, BUT AVOID ENDLESS EDITING

So begins the long journey of learning how to improve your self-editing skills, perhaps among the most important you will ever have. The most common advice you'll receive from any writer or editor is *revise, revise, revise*. Revision is what separates the serious writers from everyone else; professional authors revise their work multiple times, with and without professional advice. If you expect to get anywhere in your writing career, you'll need to find the right process or method for revising. The editing process is one each writer develops on her own through experience and trial and error.

But be warned: It is possible to overedit. If you find yourself rewriting everything again and again or going through a series of editors for your work, you might be using editing as a means of avoiding potential rejection. Sometimes it's more important and helpful to get finished pieces into submission in-boxes than it is to spend endless time refining the same manuscript over and over. Most writers, though, are far more likely to be hurt by too little editing than by too much.

PART SIX

PERSEVERE

Writing can be such a slog. You have to muster a lot of belief and heart-sweat for something that may never truly pay off. You complete a draft, finish a revision, look for more feedback ... and then what? Back to rewriting. Wash, rinse, repeat.

This is the stage when many writers quit. Here's how to endure.

RESIGNATION LETTERS

Coming to Terms with the Psychology of Resistance

SARAH CALLENDER

Roughly twenty times a year, I try to quit being a writer. Sometimes I quit for a few hours. Other times, when I am feeling especially morose and inept, I quit for an entire day. I'm not sure whether the Thing requesting my resignation letter is a force inside or outside myself, but I am certain it can hijack any artist's creative journey, no matter how skilled or experienced she is.

Let me repeat that: *Any artist. No matter how skilled or experienced.*

So let's talk about it. Let's also name that force "Resistance," just as Steven Pressfield does in his beautiful, inspiring book *The War of Art.*

With little to no warning, Resistance enters stage left. It has no cue. It has no script. It needs no lines or even a dance number. But I know it has crashed my show when any or all of these realizations occur to me: *I have no creative talent. I can't write a story. Every word I have written should be tossed. People will laugh at me. People* are *laughing at me. And now they're casting looks of pity upon me! If I ever do manage to publish a book, I will sell three copies, two of which will be purchased by my mother.*

That's the first thing that happens when Resistance invades, and then occupies, the stage of my story.

Here's the second thing that happens: Because Resistance is persistent and smarmy, the perfect used-car salesman, I also start believing at my core's core that the feelings about my dearth of skill and the magnitude of others' guffaws are true. I muck about the Internet, searching for regular jobs where someone will pay me. I don't care what the job is. I just know it cannot require fiction-writing skills because I ain't got none of those. I gussy up my résumé, churn out a few cover letters, and e-mail the designated HR contact, typing *APPLI-CANT* in the subject heading.

Here's the third thing that happens: With the job search underway, I text my critique partners and my husband to share the news. *I have quit writing, and I have found five excellent jobs for which I may or may not be the perfect candidate!* I feel free, relieved, empowered, all fired up.

Hearing the news, my husband says, "Okay." He has witnessed this progression of events before. He knows better than to argue.

My critique partners know better than to pretend they have never felt the exact same way. "Me, too," they say. "But let's not. Let's keep going."

Crumb. Their words deflate me.

I sit back and look at the clock. I have wasted several hours applying for weird jobs that will make me miserable. If there were such a thing as a writing referee, he'd make a stiff, unambiguous gesture with his arms and penalize me at least one thousand yards for unnecessarily poor time management, excessive use of drama, and inappropriate submission of ridiculous job applications. Resistance, the sneaky fellow, has helped me waste yet another chunk of writing time. I grumble and make huffy sighs. Then I get back to work.

BE A GEOLOGICAL MOVER AND SHAKER

Can we talk about waterfalls for a moment? On a drive through the Cascades in western Washington State, my children were delighted to see waterfalls, thick streams tumbling off rock ledges. Hardly fancy or hi-tech, a waterfall is simply a group of water molecules moving where it will.

Water is beautiful in its power and its relentless determination to flow, seep, carve. Whether a trickle or a tsunami, water makes its mark on the world, always aware that if it stops moving, it will become swampy and algae covered, encouraging bacteria and mosquitoes. A water molecule knows that all the best gigs involve chutes and white water, ocean spray and ancient, snaking rivers. If water were added to the game of Rochambeau, it would win every time—water submerges rock, water dissolves paper, water rusts scissors. A possessor of great power, water is also the epitome of patience.

If writers are water molecules, they are the ones that long to join the sea rather than fester in a bog, and we must expect that Resistance will set up the ultimate obstacle course: dams, boulders, a bottomless crevasse or two, "No

Trespassing" signs, dense forests that (Resistance hopes) will block our storytelling journey. We water molecules are the geological movers and shakers.

The most insidious thing about Resistance? It always seems so reasonable, so eager to protect us, so willing to be our trail guide, our rescuer. And because Resistance has a walk-in closet full of disguises, it's a good idea to stay on high alert. Make no mistake; Resistance hits most spectacularly when we are humming along, feeling fabulous about our work.

RECOGNIZE RESISTANCE IN ITS MANY FORMS

With that in mind, shall we spend some time looking at Resistance's go-to guises and shticks?

UNHELPFUL REMINDERS

Raise your hand if anyone has ever said, "I want you to go to college so you can major in fiction writing!" Or "Sweetheart, why can't you find a nice novelist and settle down?"

When we pursue the writer's life, we choose a journey that is, for 99 percent of writers, professionally unpredictable, unstable, uncertain, and largely unprofitable. Our families and friends, people who love and want the best for us, can serve as Resistance's henchmen, questioning our decision to pursue such a silly dream.

Another truth makes Resistance's job even easier: Writing is *hard*. Even the most skilled art makers find it nearly impossible to translate the colors, emotions, and ghosts of our imagination into words and stories; words are pitifully wimpy compared to the limitless expanse of our imaginations. Ink and paper, that's all we get. Some days, that doesn't feel sufficient for crafting a grocery list, much less a novel.

Resistance attempts to convince us that if we were meant to be writers, then the stories, ideas, and words would flow naturally. The prose in my favorite novels certainly seems effortless, the story organic and natural, surprisingly inevitable. When *I* am writing, however, I toil and struggle. Very little feels effortless.

Why, then, Resistance whispers, *would you choose to do something that feels impossible? Why not focus on something that comes naturally?*

There are certainly moments when writing a story feels effortless, and there are ten times as many moments when it feels like swimming in a faux fur coat. Resistance delights in reminding us that we are choosing an endeavor that often makes us feel like we are drowning.

DISTRACTIONS

Resistance wears the disguise of distraction, arriving when it occurs to us that our bathroom tile grout needs cleaning. Or that the junk drawer needs organizing. Or that our ears need swabbing. My dad recently came over and said, "Guess you've stopped cleaning your house?" A writer can receive no better compliment! When we are writing, the house is a mess, the in-box is terrifying, and our to-do list fills us with overwhelm.

When I feel it is more important to clean my ears than to write, I am honing the art of silly prioritizing and procrastination. When I feel like it's more important to click on a link promising *50 Celebrity Nose Jobs!* than to write, Resistance is taking the form of distraction. Even writers we deem successful are not immune. Thoreau didn't have the Internet, but I bet it took him hours to find a proper to-the-woods outfit. Hemingway found diversion in stiff drinks and large fish. Tolstoy distracted himself by fighting in the Crimean War, losing loads of money in card games, and wooing an attractive wartime nurse.

Writers are masters at locating and creating distraction, and when we do, when we waste minutes on silliness, Resistance wins.

SILENCES

We face Resistance in the comments, real or imagined, of others. The publishing industry tells us what we can and cannot write. Our family tells us we must not divulge family secrets—*the skeletons! the closets!* Our life partners wonder why we spend so much time on a hobby when we should be looking for a full-time jobby. Without encouragement from those around us, we have a hard time writing even the quietest words.

And when we share our stories, feedback can shut us down. When I was a newer writer, I did not believe in writer's block. Then I shared a bit of my writing with a close friend, just a scene or two, from what would turn into my first novel.

"She's annoying," he said of the child narrator, a kid I loved as much as I love my real children.

I gave a nervous laugh. "She's what?"

"Annoying. She's annoying."

I could not write for roughly three weeks after he spoke those words. Resistance carries with it a roll of duct tape to press over our mouths and bind our hands. And often we forget to fight back or even utter a few words of protest when it arrives.

TAUNTS AND SHAMES

I have named my Resistance "Ron." Ron is a mealy, mean-voiced fellow who sits on my shoulder and whispers sour words: *You think you have what it takes? Ninety-nine percent of writers never get published; you think you're in the 1 percent? Writing is too hard and so silly; get a real job.*

Ron's also a master of the What Ifs: *What if you fail, tank, can't write a second book? What if your friends hate your work? What if you are a one-hit wonder? What if you're slammed by* Kirkus, The New York Times, *Goodreads, and Amazon reviewers?*

I have a friend whose first book was a *New York Times* bestseller. While setting up dates and venues for his book tour, one bookseller, whom I'll call Ron, gushed, "I just loved this book. Seriously, I can't see how you will ever write another book this good."

My friend wrote roughly zero words during the next month. It's so hard to write when there's a Ron perched on your shoulder, taunting and shaming you. So say hello to him, and then flick him off.

COMPARISONS

Do you have a literary nemesis? Someone who always succeeds more successfully than you? That's okay. All literary superheroes do. Your nemesis might enjoy cutting you down to increase her own height. She might always manage to get a better contract the day after you get yours. She might be awarded a residency—the same residency *you* have tried to get for the past eight years.

It's all right to have a nemesis. It's not comfortable, and we need to determine the best way to limit her influence over our focus and self-confidence, perhaps by avoiding her at parties or on social media, possibly by T.P.-ing her secret hideout and tying up her henchmen when they are playing poker. But it's all right to have one. A nemesis ensures that we keep up our game, stay hungry. A nemesis reminds us why we need to don our capes every day as we sit down to write.

Resistance also tells us that there are only so many pieces of the literary-success pie. That's a lie, of course. Art and creativity ascribe to the mentality of "the more, the merrier." As there is no shortage of literary opportunity, there's no need to compete with other writers; we are free to support and encourage our fellow artists. Or to just ignore them while we buckle down and write.

QUESTIONS OF OUR SKILL

Too often I have a deep and clear sense of the texture, energy, and flow of my story, but capturing that in words is impossible. I'm in good company. Ann Patchett, in her Kindle Single, "The Getaway Car," says the story in one's imagination is like a butterfly. To get that imaginary story on paper, she says, "I must reach into the air and pluck that butterfly up ... press it down against my desk, and there with my own hand, I kill it." Patchett doesn't want to kill this butterfly, "... but it's the only way I can get something that is so three-dimensional onto the flat page."

We must kill the butterfly to write its story. How horrible! How messy. How true.

Poet Stanley Kunitz notes similar frustration. "The poem in the head," he says, "is always perfect. Resistance starts when you try to convert it into language. Language itself is a kind of resistance to the pure flow of self. The solution is to become one's language."

CONQUERING RESISTANCE

Kill butterflies? Become one's language? I hear that, and I reach for my laptop to update my résumé. We have only words and imagination. When the truth of that statement halts and paralyzes us, Resistance wins. We cannot let it win. How then, do we disarm it?

NAME IT

"Oh, hello jerk wad. It's been a while. I was wondering when you'd show up. And now that you are here, please let me escort you to the edge of this very high cliff. Oops, careful! Oh, such a shame ..."

Give your Resistance a name, or assign it an image. A slug or a fruit fly, perhaps, or some other squashable creature that is irritating but not at all threatening.

Understand that Resistance is simply fear. In *The War of Art*, Pressfield explains how Hitler was a painter. A frustrated painter. A *failed* painter, who apparently surrendered to Resistance. Pressfield makes the point that it was easier for Hitler to start World War II than to stare at a blank canvas. A blank canvas is scary, yes, but when people succumb to fear, even scarier things can happen.

Resistance is also unhealthy doubt. Healthy doubt drives us to hone our craft. It keeps us fresh; it creates in us a sense of wonder and perplexity. Perplexed wonderers like Lewis and Clark, Einstein, and Earhart didn't have the easiest lives. In fact, Einstein claims he experienced "years of anxious searching in the dark." Healthy doubt leads us to delve into questions and pursue greater understanding. Unhealthy doubt, a.k.a. Resistance, convinces us to stop writing.

CREATE A MANTRA

Keep it simple. Make sure it's no more than seven words long. Want to hear mine? *Just tell the damn story.* Five words. One of my critique partners likes to remind me of her mantra, especially when I want to quit writing. *Trust the process*, she says.

Commit your mantra to memory. Ask your partner to remind you of your mantra when you forget it. Tattoo it on the back of your hand. Write it on your bathroom mirror and the window out of which you stare when you are supposed to be writing. Mantras are powerful enough to give Resistance the stiff-arm or, if necessary, a karate chop to the groin.

FIND A DAILY ROUTINE

I don't deliberate about whether I should put in my right contact lens before my left or enjoy a cup of coffee when I wake up. I just do it. I don't question whether I should put on underwear or wear my seatbelt. I just do it. When we don't question sitting down at our computers or notebooks, we don't leave room for Resistance. Habit and routine are the bouncers that keep Resistance standing outside the club. Make daily writing a habit.

DON'T WAIT AROUND FOR THE MUSES

If your creativity package comes with "muses included," you are one of the luckies. But know that muses only arrive when you aren't expecting them, and they hardly ever come when you are staring at a blank sheet of whiteness. They see blank paper and say, *Ha! No way, José. I'm out.*

Muses only insert themselves into a project, right in between words and sentences, when they see ink on that formerly blank page. They like to see *us* do some hard work first. Then, if we are lucky, they might decide to join us, riding in on their magical elephants and bunnies and skateboards. Sometimes they come in disguise, as they did for Carl Sandburg. "When I was writing pretty poor poetry," Sandburg says, "this girl with midnight-black hair told me to go on."

Some of us have muses with midnight-black hair. Some of us get stuck with the summer-intern muse (who's about as unhelpful as you might imagine). We who are muse-less must fly solo. Regardless, we mustn't expect or rely on anything other than our own imagination and creativity. That's where muses are born, after all.

Resistance doesn't come for us because we have less talent or tenacity than a *New York Times* best-selling author. It comes for me and for you because it comes for all artists, for anyone who toils to create something original from words, colors, or musical notes. It tries to convince us, *There's nothing new under the sun. Why even bother writing a new story when everything's been done before?*

The good news? Feeling the push or pull of Resistance proves we are artists; the stronger we experience that Resistance, the more worried it is about the mischief we are stirring up. Resistance is fear; Resistance is also fear*ful*. If it didn't fear our tenacity and creativity, it would go pick on someone else.

Most of us are not born literary Mozarts, but we can develop our ability to work, persevere, work, hone our craft, work, work, work. Most of us who make art are just regular folk, ordinary drops of water. That's not a bad thing.

"Water is patient," Margaret Atwood writes in her novella *The Penelopiad*. "Dripping water wears away a stone. Remember that, my child. Remember you are half water. If you can't go through an obstacle, go around it. Water does." Let's do that, my watery writer-friend. Let's keep going. Let's be that patient, steadfast molecule of H_2O—perhaps taking the form of shower steam or a slippery icicle, perhaps a drop of the Pacific that crashes onto the shore, turning rocks, shells, and lava into silky grains of sentences and stories.

 COMMUNITY CONVERSATION

The Writer Unboxed community weighs in online. Please consider adding your voice by visiting Writer Unboxed via this QR code or link to the site. Join the conversation at writerunboxed.com/resignation-letters, and use the password "aip" (all lowercase).

Writer Unboxed is a moderated community, but comments that evolve a conversation in a positive manner are always welcome.

RON ESTRADA: I, for one, am very fond of Ron. I find him intelligent, helpful, and ruggedly handsome.

Let me show you my Resistance issues from another perspective. I didn't start my life as a writer. I started it as the polar opposite. I'm an engineer. Not the really cool kind that design lasers or drive trains, either. The manufacturing type, the ones who make pretty darn good money but often find themselves staring longingly at meter readers and dreaming of such an exciting career.

My Resistance is my reasonable nature. My wife and I live well. I could easily plop myself onto the couch every afternoon when I get home, flip through my *Field & Stream*, and then watch *Keeping Up with the Kardashians* without losing a penny of my retirement fund.

Writing, however, requires that I come home, sit at yet another desk containing another computer monitor, rip my mind out trying to come up with a better verb than *plop*, and somehow find the time to send soon-to-be-rejected queries to agents. I'm telling you and Ron (heck of a guy) both: Sometimes I want to burn the desk and do normal human things.

Here's what breaks through the Resistance: Inside me is a little voice—I shall call her Sarah—that says I have, at best, ninety years on this planet, assuming my wife is only bluffing. Those ninety years are a gift. They will not last. Most are already gone. Sure, you can work and be comfortable, but life is supposed to be embraced, latched onto like a five-year-old on a hot streak at Chuck E. Cheese's.

What I've discovered about myself, as is the case with so many of my writing friends, is that we find true peace through the process of creation. Yes, even while it feels like someone set our brains on "frappé," we can be at peace. People weren't meant to stagnate. I believe my greatest work is one I will never be paid for or be paid very little for. But when I'm closing in on that ninety-year mark, I really won't care about the money I have or have not made. I'll only find comfort in the knowledge that I've left the world with as much of me as possible.

And, as we all know, you can never have too much Ron.

SARAH CALLENDER: This is beautiful, Ron (heretofore known as Good Ron).

Years ago, when I started writing more seriously, I forced myself to tell people that I was "working on some fiction." Since then, I have regretted my decision to out myself many times, because there are the kind people who ask, "How's the writing coming along?" On the days that it is tempting to give up, I realize I can't. I have simply told too many people. The idea of giving up (and having so many people know I have given up) is too mortifying.

Good Ron, you are right; there are some days it would be so much easier *not* to be a writer, and I know you agree that there are far more days when being a writer feels like the best gig on the planet.

Lucky us. We have the ability to leave bits of Good with the world.

BARBARA MORRISON: I can find all kinds of distractions to avoid writing. It's not because I'm waiting for a muse or suffering Ron's taunts about my lack of skill or success (the not-ruggedly-handsome Ron, that is).

It's because plunging into that emotional stew is hard. There are days I'm not sure I have the stamina for it. That's where a routine helps, as you've noted.

My mantra—not just for writing but for a tough project at work, painting a room, running, anything—is *Just Start*. I know that if I start, I will quickly become absorbed in it, habit and practiced skills will take over, and I'll get some good work done.

SARAH CALLENDER: Yes, Barbara, *Just Start!*

And you have hit on an idea that resonates with me: the emotional-stew element. I don't know that nonwriters understand how mentally and emotionally demanding it can be to embody characters and live in the stories of others.

I imagine it's similar to how actors feel; when they are playing heavy-duty emotional roles, they are removing themselves from their real lives and submerging themselves in that of another.

As I get older and more forgetful, I like to blame *not* my age but the necessity of living in two worlds: my real one and the one inhabited by my characters. Too much jet lag! Too much adjusting to new cultures and customs. And when we have only small snippets of time to write, we are landing in Bangladesh or Beaumont or Bavaria for only forty-five minutes ... and there were only peanuts for the in-flight meal. And the guy in the seat beside us has snored the whole time. But, oh, isn't Bavaria beautiful at Christmastime?

LJ COHEN: My Resistance comes in the form of a disembodied voice whispering, "Who cares?" It's that terrible belief that what I write has no meaning and doesn't matter. What keeps me writing is remembering the books I have read that mattered to me and continue to matter, even years after I've read them.

While I've never sent out résumés in my moments of despair, I do look back at my long prior career as a physical therapist and think about walking into my local hospital and asking for a per-diem position.

Then I get back to work on the story.

SARAH CALLENDER: I have felt that many a time, LJ. Who cares about this small character in her small life and her small desires and only-slightly-bigger inability to attain her desires?

We do. We care. Isn't it amazing how much we can care for someone who doesn't even exist?!

I often tell myself I'm not so crazy. If I care about this motley crew of characters, and if I tell their story properly, then others will care, too. And then I, like you, get back to the story.

BERNADETTE PHIPPS-LINCKE: I love your comments about water. About its patience, its depth. You know what else I think is water? Childhood. It is a time when we are effortlessly connected to the universe.

When I was a child, I knew I was a writer. I accepted myself, and because I did, grown-ups and children alike did. I won story and poetry contests, and I had my work on the bulletin boards in my classrooms. I never had writer's block because there was nothing and no one to block my writing.

I stayed a child for a very long time.

I lost my childhood when I decided to start writing seriously and went back to school for it. That was my big mistake. Not going back to school but writing *seriously*. Because when you are pursuing a *serious* writing career, you encounter so much gobbledygook passing for the gospel of writing that you can't help but lose sight of the river. I am now thoroughly convinced that a lot of stuff taught about writing is the antithesis of the creative process.

I've learned that, for me, the only way to hone my craft consists of getting rid of all the voices in my head and sorting the wheat from the chaff in expert advice by trusting my gut. And with that renewed trust in my own creative juices, the river has started to flow again. As uninhibited as a child.

SARAH CALLENDER: You are a beautiful writer, Bernadette, and your points about the freedom of childhood are spot-on. I do wish it were easier to maintain that childlike mentality. But don't you find that it returns (at least a little, at least for some of us) as we get beyond our forties? That's a gift for sure.

I am glad you have shaken the crummy stuff you were handed in Writer School. It can certainly take a while to shrug off the voices of teachers or anyone else who offers unhelpful feedback. It's a bit like a snake shedding its dead skin; we all must shed the dead words of the Unhelpfuls.

ALISHA ROHDE: I've been wrestling with Resistance all week. It shows up every day, and many days I say, "Yes, yes, that's nice," and keep going. But then there are those days where Resistance took its vitamins and got a better night's sleep than I did and it follows me around with more persistence than my cat at dinnertime.

Sometimes I find I'm better off not investing the mental energy in analyzing Resistance—why feed it?—but this week I realized I have the "butterfly" problem: I'm reluctant to kill the butterfly. Okay, afraid to kill it. It's so pretty, flitting about; why must I smoosh it onto the page? I know why, of course. And no one else can enjoy the butterfly or appreciate its beauty until I work up the nerve to put it on the page.

So. I'm going to go track down the Ann Patchett piece you mentioned, work on arm wrestling the Resistance, and remember that there will be more butterflies after this one. I might even get a bit better at snaring and pinning them.

SARAH CALLENDER: Yes, Alisha! And there are some butterflies that even land *on* us. It's as if they want to be caught and turned into something that can land on everyone—in the form of a story, of course.

I used to have a recurring dream as a child, and it scared me to death. It was a weird one: a mean eagle beating a drum, and the beating started slow and got faster and faster, kind of like the *Jaws* music. But even creepier than the visual was the feeling I experienced the next morning, sometimes for the whole day. I couldn't articulate it, but it was so real and visceral.

Writing can be like that. I feel it, that slippery tone I want to create, but man, it can be so hard to articulate.

We should really give each other butterfly nets and spritz ourselves with nectar ... and see what beauty we can find.

 ## HOW TO GET IN YOUR OWN WAY, METHOD 26: WORRY YOU'RE NOT GOOD ENOUGH

Some literary geniuses think they're terrible. And some hacks delude themselves into thinking they're the next J.K. Rowling. The common denominator is that authors are uniquely unqualified to judge whether they're any good. Your energy is better spent on your work.

—BILL FERRIS

ENVY

How to Tame the Green-Eyed Monster

KRISTAN HOFFMAN

They say envy is a green-eyed monster. We've all felt the bite of its fangs and the seep of its poison. That mix of resentment, frustration, and longing can be toxic.

But there's good news: Envy does have an antidote, and over time we can build up immunity. In my experience, it's even possible to transform envy into a positive influence. Getting to that point is a practice and a process—one I'm constantly working on—but I believe that the rewards are well worth the effort.

PUT AWAY THE MEASURING STICK

They say comparison is the thief of joy. I know this to be true because I have spent far too much time stealing happiness from myself.

Like most modern writers, I rely on the Internet for information, camaraderie, and outreach. It's an amazing resource and basically serves as the industry watercooler. However, the Internet also feeds my doubts and insecurities. Every week, new deals are announced. Starred reviews are awarded. Bestseller rankings and film options are shouted from the rooftops—as well they should be. But if your accomplishments are of the quieter sort, all that noise can make you feel inadequate.

How do you stop measuring your worth against other people's high points? I have unfollowed blogs; unfriended authors, agents, and editors that I didn't know personally; and given myself permission to be less informed and connected. The result is that I have more positive energy to focus on my writing. And whenever I do poke my head into the publishing den, I find that little has changed. My absence does not plunge me into ignorance or obscurity.

We face a million distractions, a million drains on our time, enthusiasm, and well-being. Envy doesn't have to be one of them. Keep your eyes on your own path. Guard against thieves—especially the sneakiest thief of all: yourself.

SAIL WITH THE TIDE

They say a rising tide lifts all ships. Envy wants you to believe the opposite: that when another writer floats to the top, you sink to the bottom. But publishing is not a zero-sum game, so don't let envy's lies become your truth.

The next time a book hits big—like *Orphan Girl with a Da Vinci Secret: The Life-Changing Memoir of a Reality TV Star*—remind yourself that it will bring thousands of readers to the shelves. People are hungry for great storytelling, but with television, movies, apps, and everything else competing for their attention, books often fall to the wayside. Anything that generates excitement for the written word benefits us all.

When you hear about an author snagging a seven-figure multibook deal at auction, remember that she wrote her manuscript the same way you write yours: one word at a time. And she probably did so in between loads of laundry, maybe bleary-eyed at the break of dawn, possibly even with a baby crying in the background. It's impossible to know every writer and the trials they face— but it *is* possible to remember that no writer succeeds without putting in effort and facing occasional setbacks. Not a single one.

It's normal to wonder, "Why not me?" when you see your dream coming true for someone else. But the real question is: "Why *not* me?" There is no reason at all why it can't be you. You're a boat, they're a boat, we're all just boats, bobbing on the same waters. So embrace the tide, and keep sailing toward your vision of success.

BORROW LIGHT FROM OTHERS

They say it is better to light a candle than to curse the darkness. Though envy tries to blind us by casting deep and bitter shadows, I've found that wanting what someone else has can actually serve as a flame of inspiration to light the way forward.

When someone I care about works hard and does well, I feel joy and admiration. I celebrate her wins and try to learn from them. Knowing that she has gotten to a place I want to go makes it feel more doable. I am encouraged, motivated, reinvigorated. I don't want to take anything away from her; I just want to create a version of it for myself.

Why should that be any different for someone I don't know? Envy and admiration are two sides of the same coin, so whenever I start to feel jealousy, I flip it around and look for things to respect and emulate. Maybe I can integrate something from that person's process into my own. Maybe her editor is someone I should submit to in the future. Maybe it's as simple as soaking up her wonder and gratitude, and using that as fuel for faith in my own journey.

Rather than begrudge the successes of others, we can choose to celebrate and learn. If they catch fire, we don't have to burn with resentment. We can use their light to illuminate our paths.

WALK AWAY FROM THE MONSTER IN THE MIRROR

They say envy is a green-eyed monster. But it doesn't jump out at you from cobwebbed corners. Envy is a monster that lives in the mirror. It is the ugliest reflection of ourselves.

With all this talk about what other people are getting or achieving, it's easy to think of envy as an external issue. But it's not really. Envy is about us. It's about the distance between where we are and where we want to be. So the best way to undermine envy is to take a step, no matter how small, in the direction of our dreams. One step at a time. That's how we close the gap. That's how we get away from the monster. That's how we get anywhere worth going.

 PRO TIP

One of the best ways to combat envy is to take a look at an early draft of your work to see how much it's evolved. Keep going. Those authors you're envying? They did.

 **HOW TO GET IN YOUR OWN WAY, METHOD 27: WORRY ABOUT HOW YOUR PEERS ARE DOING**

When other writers get a big slice of cake, that doesn't mean there's less available for you. Literary success is not a cake; it's a bottomless-steak-fries deal at Red Robin. There's plenty for everybody.

—BILL FERRIS

THE HEALTH AND MAINTENANCE OF WRITERS

What You Need to Know to Stay *You* for as Long as You Are Able

JAN O'HARA

I know what you're thinking: *An essay on health in the middle of an inspirational and informational writing book? Isn't that like biting into a Parisian-made madeleine cookie and discovering a filling of pureed Brussels sprouts?* The above was my initial reaction when I was asked to use my background as a former family doctor to write this essay. But as soon as I wrapped my head around the concept, I recalled 5,110 excellent reasons to pair health and literary ambition. It turns out that if you consistently incorporate the following four habits into your life, you'll gain an average of fourteen extra years. For those of you who complete a novel biannually, that's an extra seven books you can add to your backlist. (Not to mention the additional books you will write with the productivity boost inherent in these measures.) Furthermore, the same health changes give you a good chance of avoiding disabilities that dog many Westerners: dementia, diabetes, ischemic heart disease, stroke, cancer, erectile dysfunction, and so on. It's estimated that 65 percent of these conditions are preventable through lifestyle intervention. So invest in the four following habits, and harness your brain's best efforts on creative pursuits rather than fight the fear and frustration of doctors' visits.

EDITOR'S NOTE

This essay should not be construed as medical advice. Lifestyle medicine is strong medicine. Please consult your physician before embarking on these or any other changes to your health plan.

ADD COLOR TO YOUR PLATE

Virtually every writer I know likes to believe she is an original thinker capable of thumbing her nose at society when the prevailing culture proves unworthy.

Virtually every writer I know associates a productive writing session with a specific snack.

How would you like to demonstrate your countercultural chops *and* gain an extra three years of life by simply adjusting what you consume? The habit is straightforward: Eat a minimum of five servings of minimally processed fruits and vegetables each day. (A serving size of green, leafy vegetables is one cup. All other fruit and vegetable servings, whether fresh, frozen, or cooked, are a half cup in size.)

Notice the words *minimally processed* in the preceding paragraph. They require emphasis because of the current situation in the Western world in which we are surrounded by food that has been ground, dehydrated, and doused in sugar, oil, and salt.

Is there any wonder we overeat? Is there any wonder we can fall into the pattern of writing while snacking on hyperpalatable foods?

Minimally processed fruits and vegetables, on the other hand, offer many health benefits. They are a symphony of vitamins and minerals we cannot hope to replicate through supplements or "nutritional" shakes. Thus they help address a common problem in the modern world in which we are overfed yet undernourished.

Also, they are comparatively calorie dilute. Human beings are designed to stay trim by eating the same *weight* of food each day rather than the same amount of calories. Unprocessed fruits and vegetables retain fiber and water. They displace less healthful, more calorie-dense foods. By incorporating a good quantity and variety of them into your diet, you will automatically maintain a slimmer waistline than you would otherwise.

To reach the minimum of five servings per day, the basic advice is to incorporate fruit and vegetables in each meal. For example, add a banana or berries to your breakfast oatmeal. Consume a cup of vegetable soup with your noontime sandwich. Add a salad and carrot sticks to your dinner entree.

But snacking writers have an extra weapon in their arsenal: automaticity.

If you're going to nibble while you work, make it easy to do the right thing. Put a fruit plate on your kitchen counter or your desk. Wash vegetables, cut them into bite-size pieces, and then place them in a clear container at eye level in your fridge. Begin a work session with these foods within reach, and watch how mindless consumption finally works in your favor instead of against your waistline.

With a little advance planning, it can be easy to get in a minimum of five servings. Chances are, if you do, your daily word count will finally exceed your weight.

For references on healthful eating patterns and other lifestyle changes, go to writerunboxed.com/additional-material-on-the-health-and-maintenance-of-writers.

MOVE YOUR FEET, GROW YOUR BRAIN

We've only just met, but I'm willing to bet you are fond of your neurons and plan to keep them around and functioning at maximum capacity for as long as you live. In this regard, moderate exercise is your friend. Besides three extra years of life, moderate exercise (defined below) provides brain benefits essential to creative types.

Let's begin with what movement does for mood: By replenishing your neurotransmitters and increasing endorphins, exercise helps you weather the discouragement of rejections and the stress of meeting deadlines.

It stimulates the growth and regeneration of neurons, especially those that preserve long-term memory.

Exercise has proven, positive effects on attentiveness. Newer studies show it enhances imagination. It also helps slow the cognitive decline associated with aging.

In other words, move more and you can extend your life, be more productive, master new writing-related skills faster, and stay at the top of your game longer than you would have without exercise.

To gain the benefits of exercise, it's not necessary to run a marathon! Simply work a minimum of 150 minutes of moderate exercise into your weekly routine—ideally distributed over several days with each session lasting a good ten minutes. (Thirty minutes of exercise five times a week is a fantastic schedule to strive for.)

To determine whether an exercise counts as moderate, use the Rate of Perceived Exertion scale. A score of 0 indicates that you are doing nothing more strenuous than pecking at the keyboard. A 10 is full-on effort that cannot be maintained for more than sixty seconds. Aim for a level of 6 to 7. Generally speaking, that means you will be perspiring and have the capacity to talk in sentences, though singing proves impossible.

For extra brownie points—or should I say "strawberry" points?—incorporate twice-weekly resistance exercise into your regimen. This will help counter the bone-melting effects of prolonged sitting. Circuit training qualifies, so make a few of your sessions a series of squats, push-ups, lunges, chin-ups, and rows.

I'm a fan of activity trackers. They eliminate self-deception and subtly reinforce the movement habit. For most people, a basic step-counter is sufficient, but when sorting through the wide variety of trackers available, keep these factors in mind: cost, whether the device is water-resistant or waterproof, whether it can measure and record the type of exercise you do, and whether it requires frequent recharging or operates off long-lasting watch batteries. Avoid simple clip-on trackers, as they're easily lost. And unless the device uses a chest strap, don't bother with one that includes a heart rate monitor; at this time, they aren't sufficiently reliable. Lastly, consider a tracker that prompts you to move every waking hour. *Any* amount of exercise is beneficial, and the 150 minutes I mentioned before is the minimum recommendation.

If you decide to take up the exercise mantle, know that you'll be in good writerly company. Charles Dickens was known to walk up to twenty miles a day. Multipublished author Susan Shapiro conducts office hours while speed walking with her writing students. Haruki Murakami, author of *1Q84*, runs ten miles a day when he's not preparing for triathlons.

Common sense tells us that our bodies fare better if moved on a regular basis. *Science* tells us that exercise helps build and preserve new circuitry in the brain. If you want to master the art of dialogue or scene transitions, go for a brisk walk between writing sessions.

DELETE THE DAIQUIRIS

I can already hear the admonitions about the threatening title of this section. "Back off, lady. Booze helps me relax when I write. And what about the French paradox? You're the one talking about living longer. Doesn't alcohol protect you from heart disease and the ravaging effects of a high-cholesterol diet?"

Sadly, after further investigation, the French paradox transforms into the French mirage.

The French appear to escape ischemic heart disease for two reasons: inaccurate medical coding at autopsies in which heart disease deaths are attributed to other causes, and the French diet, which isn't uniform. In fact, in substantial portions of France, the diet is a far cry from the fat- and cholesterol-laden cuisine of the capital. When health statistics take regional differences into consideration, it becomes clear that success in escaping heart disease occurs despite alcohol rather than because of it.

Unlike carbohydrates and protein, which contain four calories per gram, alcohol contains seven calories per gram. Our bodies easily convert it to fat, putting us at increased risk for obesity and all its associated illnesses.

Alcohol consumption is a risk factor for a huge number of cancers, including leukemia and malignancies of the head and neck, lung, cervix, bladder, esophagus, pancreas, stomach, and colon, to name a few.

As little as one ounce of alcohol per day has been found to raise blood pressure by 10 mmHg (the amount by which most medications can lower blood pressure).

Because of alcohol's deleterious effects, by abstaining altogether you can earn an average of three to four additional years of life. But if that is too much to ask, women should limit their intake to no more than four drinks per week, and men should imbibe no more than seven per week. On any given day, limit yourself to a two-drink maximum.

VAPORIZE THE SMOKES

Conjure an image of the quintessential writing figure. Did any part of that picture include lazy smoke rings and cigarettes? I wouldn't be surprised; much of the romanticism and mystique concerning writers involves a hard-living lifestyle.

Here's the reality, gleaned from a few moments of research: Rod Serling, writer and director of *The Twilight Zone*, smoked four packs a day, and he was dead at fifty-one of heart disease. T.S. Eliot, author and poet, died at seventy-six with emphysema. Ian Fleming, author of the James Bond books, was dead at fifty-six from a heart attack. Dashiell Hammett, author of such classics as *The Maltese Falcon*, died of lung cancer at sixty-seven. F. Scott Fitzgerald, author of *The Great Gatsby*, died of a heart attack at forty-four.

 **PRO TIP**

Secondhand smoke occurs when you breathe air contaminated with another's cigarettes. Thirdhand smoke exposure occurs when you touch an object contaminated with the toxic by-products of cigarettes.

When I was a family doctor conducting yearly checkups, I considered it a minimum standard of care to tell smokers that the best thing they could do for their health, bar none, was to quit smoking. An astonishing number of patients informed me that I was the first doctor to make this declaration. In an effort to make up for the system's gross deficiencies, allow me to make an unequivocal recommendation: If you smoke, quit. If you can't quit, please cut down.

You've heard of the robber-nun metaphor when it comes to guarding the till? (I owe this mode of explanation to Dr. Caldwell Esselstyn.) If you are a shopkeeper experiencing employee-generated theft, which would be the wiser strategy, assuming people run true to stereotype: Hire more nuns, or fire the robbers?

Smoking is an indisputable health thief. Freeing your body from its influence will add an average of four to five years of life, not to mention help you avoid an astonishing number of long-term illnesses. (While you are at it, avoid secondhand and thirdhand smoke.)

Now, much like the idea that all you need to do to complete a publishable novel is insert butt in chair and write, there is a vast distance between understanding the dangers of smoking and quitting. The average smoker who quits permanently manages to do so on his twelfth attempt, meaning that some succeed on their first try, others on their hundredth. If you're edging toward the higher end of the spectrum, that's okay. With each successive effort you will have learned more about your strengths and vulnerabilities, and what you require to find success as a nonsmoker.

The good news is that the moment you stop reinjuring yourself with a toxic substance, your body will throw all it has into its best healing effort.

How should one quit smoking? Statistically speaking, the highest success rates belong to those who've worked through a behavioral program prior to making any changes. This allows you to rehearse what you'll do after meals, how to handle empty hands and mouth, and so on. Talk to your family doctor or general internist. Besides pointing you to local smoking cessation programs, they can explain medical options to deal with nicotine withdrawal, some of which may be covered by your employer or insurance.

Writers are gifted with two known superpowers: imagination and persuasion. Use these talents to pull off an inside job. Imagine yourself free of tobacco, and persuade yourself to try and try again until you succeed. Unbridled health is the source of true sexiness.

CREATE AN EXCEPTIONAL BRAIN HOUSED IN AN EXCEPTIONAL BODY

I doubt any of the previous advice came as a great surprise to you. What might astonish you is how rare it is for Westerners to observe all four habits consistently yet how often we persuade ourselves our health isn't at risk. In one study of 42,847 men, only 4 percent accomplished the recommendations in this essay and maintained a body mass index (BMI) of 25 percent or less. That's one in twenty-five people.

 **PRO TIP**

Chronic disease isn't reserved for our twilight years. A full quarter of all chronic illness exists in the under-sixty crowd.

Can writers fare any better given the sedentary nature of our calling? Why not?

Writers are detail oriented. We learn to persist on our chosen path despite setbacks and chronic discouragement. Our work requires us to observe human nature and obtain self-understanding.

In other words, the very attributes that encourage you to park your posterior in a chair are the qualities that will enable you to rise from it, eat your fruits and vegetables, and minimize your exposure to two known health robbers.

 HOW TO GET IN YOUR OWN WAY, METHOD 28: NEGLECT SELF-CARE

Writers' neuroses don't appear on their own; we have to nurture them with a constant supply of interesting hobbies and the company of friends and family. Writing involves sitting a lot, so it wouldn't kill you to go for a walk, either.

—BILL FERRIS

FUELING YOUR MIND

How External Stimulation Can Fuel Your Creative Life

LIZ MICHALSKI

"Tell me, what is it you plan to do with your one wild and precious life?"
—Mary Oliver, *The Summer Day*

Stop writing. I mean it. Step away from the computer, put down your pen, and do something else. The best way to write well is, well, to *not*. At least for a while.

I discovered this by accident when I was writing my first novel, *Evenfall*. I'd gotten about one-third of the way through the story when I became stuck. I put it aside, and then life happened, by which I mean that I had a daughter, and then a son, on top of a fairly busy freelance calendar and a barn full of horses to care for. The novel got pushed to the side.

And yet, I found myself thinking about the characters, about where they were going, about how they would have looked against the background of Connecticut's rolling hills, how they would have behaved in the old farmhouse I'd been hired to write about for the real estate section of a local magazine. When I was finally able to pick up the threads of that story again, I found I had something to say.

I'm not suggesting that for the sake of your art you have kids, as entertaining as I have found mine to be. Instead I'm suggesting that, for the sake of your art, you develop a life.

In some ways and compared to many other jobs, writing is a cakewalk. But it is also lonely and hard and discouraging and draining. Too many days in a row spent struggling to piece together your imaginary world will leave you gray around the edges, in dire need of recharging.

But therein lies the rub. For most of us, writing fiction is something we do on the sly, crushed in between the demands of real life and basic human needs such as food and maybe sleep. How can we possibly take any more time away from it, especially to do something as frivolous as feed our souls?

It's not frivolous. I've found that if I don't fill the well—find a way to replenish what I've put on the page—my writing becomes stale. I struggle to find the words, and my work loses vitality. I can only get it back by disconnecting from my imaginary world and spending some time in the real one.

If writing fatigue is hitting you, here are a few suggestions on how to refuel.

MAKE ART

I've found that when I'm blocked or tired of writing, working with my hands in a different medium can help me reset. Expressing yourself in ways other than with words can be powerful. What you make doesn't have to be museum quality; it just has to be something you enjoy. My preference is for activities that pose enough challenge that my brain has to engage but aren't so difficult that I become frustrated. Over the past few years, I've tried knitting (a disaster), photography (I love it, but I'm not good at it), and paper crafts (a small success). Even jigsaw puzzles can be enough to refresh my brain.

SUPPORT ART

Visit a museum. See a show. Watch a dance performance. Get inspired by how and what other people create, and use their energy to feed yours. It doesn't have to be the Louvre to be interesting—almost every community has something to offer. In the past few months, for example, I've visited a local museum and learned the role immigrants played in the area's textile industry, watched a modern dance performance, and caught a high school musical. In all three cases, I've come away amazed by the efforts of fellow artists, and my creative spark has been renewed.

EXERCISE—HARD

Jan O'Hara's essay, "The Health and Maintenance of Writers," includes a comprehensive roundup of reasons exercise is important for writers, but it's worth saying again here. Putting your body through its paces can take the focus off your brain for a bit and give your subconscious a chance to work. There's nothing wrong with a leisurely stroll, but I get the most benefit when I'm doing something that requires concentration. Activities that have been successful for me include horseback riding (if you don't pay attention, you fall off); fencing (if you don't pay attention, you get stabbed with a sharp, pointy thing); and dancing (if you don't pay attention, people get angry when you crash into them). Even following a new exercise video from the library can work, so long as it engages your attention.

I have writer friends who swear by yoga, but for me it's too easy for my brain to wander. If it works for you, that's great. The point is to try different activities until you find one that's absorbing, and then switch it up on a regular basis so your brain can't cheat and go on autopilot.

SPEND TIME IN NATURE

Observing the natural world is one of the most powerful ways I've found to refill my writing well and refresh my soul. Without a regularly scheduled hike or walk in the woods, I become cranky and overwhelmed. On the trails, my brain tends to unknot tricky plot problems and character dilemmas without my attention. And since the natural world plays a big part in my writing, I often stumble across a detail or setting I can use later.

If you don't live near the woods, there are still plenty of ways to interact with nature. Some museums have gardens or butterfly habitats you can visit for a fee. A greenhouse at a garden center is a wonderful (and warm) place to visit in the winter. Even watching birds at a feeder can be soothing.

 **PRO TIP**

If you have an old battery-operated baby monitor, seal it in a plastic bag and put it outside. Keep the receiver by the window and you'll be able to both watch and listen to your feathery visitors.

VOLUNTEER

As writers, we spend hours inhabiting a solitary world. How to advance the plot, where to put the punctuation, whether we'll ever be published, whether we'll ever be published *again*—the worry can become all-consuming. It's easy to forget that we're surrounded by a whole world filled with real people.

An hour or two a week spent volunteering never fails to put my own writing struggles in perspective and remind me that the universe is bigger than what's on the page. Whether you offer your service at a school, a library, or an animal shelter, find something you are passionate about and lend a hand.

 **PRO TIP**

Consider volunteering in a capacity other than writing. The point is to stretch your brain in other ways.

Will following this list make you a best-selling author? I can't guarantee that, but based on my own experience, it is likely to make you a happier, more fulfilled one. And, paradoxically, time spent doing other things may actually improve your writing. As important as it seems to us when we are in the throes of it, writing is just one aspect of the writing life. The fuller the other parts of our lives, the more we have to draw from when we create our stories.

After all, as Steve Jobs said, "Creativity is just connecting things. When you ask creative people how they did something, they feel a little guilty because they didn't really do it. They just saw something. It seemed obvious to them after a while."

So stop writing—at least every now and then—and go live your one wild and precious life.

 HOW TO GET IN YOUR OWN WAY, METHOD 29: GET STAGNANT

We all get stuck in a rut. Changing things up can give you a boost of energy. Work on a different chapter for an hour, go write in the park on a sunny day, or just change out of your pajamas and get dressed. Maybe not in that order though.

—BILL FERRIS

Guest Contributor

TIRED WRITER, TAKE CARE

How Vulnerability Can Increase Over Time, and What You Can Do About It

VICTORIA STRAUSS OF WRITER BEWARE

EDITOR'S NOTE: Victoria Strauss has been illuminating publishing scams for writers via her website, writerbeware.com, since 1998. We're honored to present her guest essay here, which nurtures a street-smart sensibility to counter the natural susceptibilities of the author in progress.

• • •

The digital revolution has transformed the face of publishing. From the incredible growth of small presses to the new viability of self-publishing, writers have more options than ever before.

Some things haven't changed, though: the challenge of finding an audience and the hard work of building a career. And where the road to success is steep, the way will be crowded with opportunists who will promise you the world but really just want to snake a hand into your wallet.

The industry is filled with many wonderful, reputable agents, publishers, self-publishing services, and others. But schemes and scams also abound. Inexperience is a major risk factor for falling victim to them: Too many writers rush into the publication search without taking the time to learn about their chosen career path. If you don't know how things *should* work, it's much harder to recognize shady ventures when you encounter them.

Just as dangerous is fatigue. You've been querying agents for months and have gotten nowhere; in fact, half the time you don't get any response at all. You've lost count of how many publishers you've approached and been rejected by. You're bewildered by the multitude of self-publishing options—which are reputable? How much (if anything) should you pay?

Frustration and exhaustion can spur bad choices. You may be tempted to settle for less (the track-record-less agent who loves your work, the publisher who tells you that success is all about purchasing your own books). You may be more vulnerable to misleading hype (the costly self-publishing service that touts its connection with a traditional publisher, the high-entry-fee contest that promises exposure but is actually just a way for the sponsor to make money). If you're feeling worn down, it may become easier to ignore your gut feeling that something isn't right.

You *can* protect yourself by taking a few simple precautions.

I can't stress enough that these need to be done *before* you start your publication journey. It's very hard to learn on the fly—plus, if you've already experienced a lot of rejection, even a bad offer may be hard to refuse once it's made. Better to inoculate yourself against the bad actors from the start.

First, *educate yourself.* Others in this book have discussed the importance of being in the know, so I'll just reiterate how essential it is to take the time to learn about the wide world of publishing. Knowledge is your number one weapon against schemes and scams.

Second, *research the people and companies you want to approach.* Look for evidence of professional competence, as well as for problems and complaints. Order books from the publisher or self-publishing service so you can assess their quality. Contact watchdog groups (Preditors & Editors[1] and Writer Beware[2]), and consult writers' forums (such as the Bewares, Recommendations, and Background Check forum at the Absolute Write Water Cooler[3]).

Third, *know the warning signs.*

ASSESS AGENTS

When my friend Ann Crispin and I founded Writer Beware in the late 1990s, agent scams were common. Now that the agent-to-traditional-publisher route is

---

1 pred-ed.com

2 www.writerbeware.com

3 absolutewrite.com/forums/forumdisplay.php?22-bewares-recommendations-amp-background-check

just one option for pursuing a writing career, they've become quite rare. They're still out there, though—as are amateur agents, who pose less of a threat to your bank account but will waste your time just as thoroughly.

Watch for these warning signs:

- **THE AGENT HAS NO (OR A TINY) TRACK RECORD OF SALES.** A worthwhile agent will have a record of professional achievement—verifiable sales to publishers you've heard of. Be wary if most of the agent's "sales" are to non-advance-paying presses that accept manuscripts from writers. The whole point of having an agent is to get you through doors you can't open yourself.
- **THE AGENT IS NEW (ON THE JOB FOR LESS THAN A YEAR) AND HAS NO RELEVANT PROFESSIONAL EXPERIENCE.** Agenting is not an entry-level job. It requires specialized expertise and contacts within the publishing industry. New agents are more likely to succeed if they've worked in publishing or trained at a reputable agency. People who come to agenting without that background are at a major disadvantage.
- **THE AGENT CHARGES FEES OR SELLS SERVICES.** No matter what the fee is called, if it's due up front, it's a red flag. Fee charging violates the basic premise of the author-agent relationship: a shared financial interest in selling the author's manuscript. If your agent makes money only when you do (via a commission), she'll be highly motivated not only to sell your book but to make the best possible deal. An agent who makes money before a sale diminishes his incentive to pursue legitimate publication. (Note that most agents do expect authors to reimburse some submission costs, but these are usually nominal and paid only after they are incurred.)

Another red flag is any recommendation to use the agent's own paid services. Increasingly this is a gray area, with more and more agents branching out into editing, consulting, and even publishing. But an ethical agent will separate her agenting from her adjunct activities—agency clients will never be referred for paid services, and clients of the paid services will never be eligible for representation. Beware if the paid service is a condition of representation or carries a promise of special consideration.

PONDER PUBLISHERS

Once upon a time, it was difficult and expensive to start a publishing imprint. These days, all anyone needs is a website and an Amazon account. This has made possible some truly amazing small presses. Unfortunately, it has also fueled an explosion of amateur scammers.

Be wary of the following:

- **THE PUBLISHER EXPECTS YOU TO "INVEST."** A reputable publisher (as distinct from a self-publishing service) doesn't require authors to pay anything or buy anything as a condition of publication. If you must hand over cash in order to be published—whether it's for some aspect of production or to buy finished books—you are dealing with a vanity publisher. Vanity publishers may claim that your "investment" funds only part of the expense of publication and that they will pick up the rest. But it's far more likely that your fee covers not only all costs but the publisher's overhead and profit as well. Some vanity publishers maintain the appearance of traditional presses, with writers only discovering that money is due after submitting. But if the publisher deceptively presents itself, how likely is it that it will deal with you honestly?

 **PRO TIP**

Watch for these code words that are synonymous with *vanity*: *partnership*, *co-op*, *joint venture*, *collaborative*, *subsidy*, and the newest, *hybrid*.

- **THE PUBLISHER'S STAFF HAS NO RELEVANT PROFESSIONAL EXPERIENCE.** Hopefully the publisher will provide staff bios on its website. (Be wary if it doesn't.) A publisher staffed by people with no previous professional publishing, writing, editing, or design experience is far more likely to have problems: bad contract language, inexpert editing, unprofessional cover art, poor marketing support, and more.
- **THE PUBLISHER OR SELF-PUBLISHING SERVICE IS NEW.** There's a high failure rate among new small presses, many of which start up without a business plan or adequate funding. Such publishers often go out of business abruptly, leaving writers high and dry—especially if the publisher doesn't bother to revert rights before vanishing. It's a good idea to wait on approaching a new publisher until it has been issuing books for *at least* a year. This gives time for problems to surface and also allows you to assess things like quality and marketing.

SUSS SELF-PUBLISHING SERVICES

Like publishers, self-publishing services have proliferated over the past decade. Some are excellent and cost-effective (or free), others are inefficient mom-and-pop operations, and a few are unscrupulous profit engines that overprice their offerings and use hard-sell sales tactics to convince writers to buy extras they don't need.

Be cautious if you come across these scenarios:

- **THE SELF-PUBLISHING SERVICE PRESSURES YOU TO BUY OR TRIES TO UPSELL YOU.** Even the free self-pub platforms sell additional services, but you should never be pressured to buy. Be skeptical also if the service tries to get you to purchase a more expensive package than you originally planned or contacts you repeatedly to urge you to buy marketing services. Most marketing services sold by self-publishing companies are overpriced, of dubious value, or both. Unscrupulous self-publishing services may try to dazzle you with visions of book sales, worldwide distribution, and all the other things writers long for. Never forget that you're not a writer contracting with a publisher but a consumer buying a product. Be a smart consumer: Don't be swayed by sales pitches.
- **THE SELF-PUBLISHING SERVICE IS NEW.** As it is for new publishers, early failure can be a problem for new self-publishing services, especially if the service is an effort of tech entrepreneurs to cash in on the self-publishing boom. The same warnings apply.

APPROACH CONTESTS WITH CARE

Now more than ever, one of the major hurdles of a writing career is finding an audience. Dozens of contests and awards programs promise to help with that, claiming to provide prestige and exposure to winners. Many, though, are nothing more than profit-making schemes that cash in on desperate writers' hunger for recognition.

Watch out for these red flags:

- **THE CONTEST CHARGES A HIGH ENTRY FEE.** Profit-making contests charge sixty dollars, seventy-five dollars, ninety dollars, or even more. Reputable contests' entry fees are typically much lower.

- **THE CONTEST OFFERS DOZENS OR SCORES OF ENTRY CATEGORIES.** Some profit-making contests offer more than one hundred entry categories to maximize income.
- **JUDGING IS PERFORMED BY ANONYMOUS INDIVIDUALS.** Judges are described as experts, but their names aren't provided. In fact, the judging may be done by the contest's staff, who may simply pick winners at random.
- **YOU WIN "FAUX" PRIZES.** Moneymaking awards offer cheap prizes that don't cut into their profits: press releases, website listings, features in self-owned publications, and so on. Some offer little more than the "honor" of winning.
- **THE CONTEST GIVES YOU PLENTY OF OPPORTUNITIES TO SPEND MORE MONEY.** Profit-making contests vigorously hawk extras: stickers, certificates, critiques, plaques, and more.

WEIGH WRITERS' SERVICES

As the self-publishing and small-press worlds have grown, so, too, have the number and variety of services for writers—from freelance editing to cover art and illustration to e-book creation to publicity and marketing. Writers can also pay for review services, author website creation services, blog tour services, services that promise to get your small-press or self-pubbed book into libraries, services that will run your social media for you … the list goes on.

These services run the gamut from worthwhile and professional to outright scams. Here, again, research is your friend. Make sure the person you're thinking of hiring actually has professional expertise. (A freelance editor should have verifiable editing experience, for instance.) Carefully assess quality (artists and illustrators should have portfolios; PR services should provide sample campaigns). Ask for references, but also try to contact other authors with whom the individual or company has worked. If the company or service makes a promise, don't take it at face value: Look for proof that it actually delivers. Search for complaints.

It's just as important to ask yourself if the service is a good use of your money. Could you get as much benefit from approaching book bloggers as from buying a Kirkus Indie review? Wouldn't your social media be more, well, *social* if you managed it yourself? Is a blog tour worth the work if your book appears only on low-traffic blogs? Make sure you know why you're buying the service, and have a solid idea of how it may benefit you. Don't be swayed by sales pitches—and remember: If it sounds too good to be true, it probably is.

BE CAREFUL OUT THERE

Writing is a tough career, and you're bound to make some mistakes on your publishing journey. But along with the bad, you'll come across plenty of good. If you fortify yourself with knowledge and keep an eye out for the warning signs, you should be just fine.

 PUBLISHING CONTRACT PITFALLS TO AVOID

by Susan Spann

Dangerous contract language comes in many forms, from overreaching grants of rights to predatory publisher requests for fees and copyright transfers. Always have an industry professional—an agent or lawyer who works for you—review your publishing contract before you sign. That said, here are a few of the most common contract pitfalls that authors should look for and avoid:

- **COPYRIGHT TRANSFERS TO THE PUBLISHER:** A legitimate publishing contract will *never* include a grant of copyright ownership to the publisher. Contracts involve a *license* of publishing rights (and, often, certain subsidiary rights), but the author should always remain the sole owner of copyright to the work.
- **AUTHOR PAYMENT OF COSTS AND FEES:** Traditionally, the publisher is responsible for the costs of producing the author's work for sale. Legitimate contracts should never require the author to pay (or reimburse the publisher) for artwork, publishing, distribution, marketing, or other costs. This also means the publisher shouldn't deduct these costs from sales receipts before calculating the author's royalty share.
- **MANDATORY BOOK PURCHASES OR MARKETING CONTRACTS:** Most publishers give the author free copies of the finished work and allow the author to purchase additional copies (usually at a discount). However, legitimate contracts will never *require* the author to buy any copies of the finished work. Similarly, the contract should not require the author to pay, out of pocket or otherwise, for marketing services provided by the publisher or affiliated companies.
- **INFINITE TIME TO PUBLISH:** Publishing contracts should give the author the right to terminate the agreement and regain all rights if the publisher fails to publish the work within a stated period (normally twelve to twenty-four months) after delivery and acceptance of the manuscript. Without this clause, the author has no recourse against publisher delays.

- **OUT-OF-PRINT STATUS TIED TO "AVAILABILITY":** Before e-books, publishing contracts often declared the author's work was "in print" and under contract as long as the book remained "available" for sale. That language is inappropriate now because it lets the publisher keep control of the author's work as long as an e-book listing remains on even a single sales website—including the publisher's own! Insist on contract language that declares the work "out of print" (and allows the author to terminate the contract) if the publisher fails to make more than a stated number of royalty-bearing sales during a given period of time (no more than six to twelve months) at any point after initial publication.
- **FEES FOR REVERSION OF RIGHTS:** All rights to the work should revert to the author immediately and automatically when the contract terminates—regardless of the reason for termination and without the author paying any fees or "reimbursements of costs" to the publisher. Also, the contract should not require the author to buy the publisher's remaining stock of the work in order to terminate the contract.
- **NONDISCLOSURE CLAUSES:** Nondisclosure clauses prohibit the author (or sometimes the author and publisher) from public discussion of the contract terms and/or their experiences with one another. These clauses are not standard in publishing contracts. However, some publishers use them as "muzzles" to control and silence authors. Beware of any publisher that wants to put a muzzle in your contract.
- **UNLIMITED OPTION CLAUSES:** Well-drafted options can benefit both authors and publishers, but the option must be limited in three important ways: (1) It should apply to the author's next book-length work in the same series only; (2) the publisher should have the right to review and attempt to negotiate a publishing contract for the optioned work—but *not* to extend the current contract to cover the optioned work; (3) the option must not place any limits or restrictions on the author's right to sell the work if the author and publisher fail to reach acceptable contract terms for the optioned work.

Be aware that this isn't a complete or exhaustive list of dangerous contract language or terms to avoid. Never sign a contract without arranging for review by an agent or publishing attorney, and trust your instincts; if something seems wrong or "too good to be true," it probably is.

Insist on fair, industry-standard contract terms. You and your work deserve them.

ON QUITTING

When Moving on May Be the Right Choice

SHARON BIALLY

It's a familiar mantra: "We write because we must." We write for our characters, whose voices would otherwise go unheeded, and for their journeys and destinies. Yet few would deny that we also write for ourselves.

At the intersection of these two forces lies the motivation to continue—or, I believe, the reason we quit. Just as our characters' flaws, desires, conflicts, and inner struggles must somehow get revealed, resolved, or foiled as a story unfolds, so, too, must our own demons be confronted, our urges satisfied, our personal yearnings fulfilled through the process of bringing our stories to life. In the absence of meaningful fulfillment, frustration and discouragement take root.

For fifteen years, I poured my energies into that space where nurturing my characters went hand-in-hand with nurturing myself. While drafting a first novel in the late 1990s, my personal desire to develop a writing career and generate income wove itself into the fabric of my inspiration. To write, I had left behind a profession, an income, and financial peace of mind. With enough dedication to my craft, I mused, it would all come back to me again through writing. My husband and I would once again be able to travel and perhaps to afford a house with enough space for not one child but two.

Soon my young family underwent a profound and unexpected change: We relocated from the south of France, where we lived at the time, to the Boston suburbs. My husband, a French national, was able to make a long-overdue career change, and I found part-time work. We settled into a house with space for four. That the longing for change and improvement I'd projected onto this novel had been satisfied by other means helped soothe my nerves as the rejection letters poured in—and even after the manuscript landed in the hands of a young agent who promised a contract but then headed off to grad school, leaving my book with a colleague who ultimately passed.

EXAMINE YOUR YEARNINGS—AND WHAT SATISFIES THEM

One mentor told me it had taken her two years to find her agent and advised me to be patient, to just keep sending out more queries. But without the specific hunger that powered the creation of that first book, the prospect of riding the roller coaster of hope and disappointment for an indefinite period of time simply didn't seem worth the uncertain rewards. Choosing to move on from that first book—quitting, some would say—proved immensely liberating.

Pregnant by then with my second son, I turned my energy instead to a new idea: a series of children's books drawing on the mythology of the Marshall Islands, where I'd spent my childhood. Today the Marshall Islands are best known for being at imminent risk of disappearing into the Pacific Ocean's rising waters. A new yearning came to settle atop the continued desire for a writing career: one for excitement, engagement, and interaction with the world at large. Children's book series were all the rage. The environmental and cultural context would surely resonate far and wide; this series could become a bestseller, get made into a movie—or three, or four! Enough sitting quietly in a corner.

My time to emerge came, indeed, though through a completely unanticipated plot twist. While still deep in the process of drafting the series, I met the owner of a small PR agency. He offered me a job. I threw myself with gusto into this new endeavor, exhilarated by the fast pace and constant stream of results. The energy, the interaction, and the engagement I craved had found me even before I sent out a single query.

EMBRACE CREATIVE FULFILLMENT, WHATEVER ITS FORM

By the time I wrote my second novel, *Veronica's Nap*, my deepest and most urgent longing was for a reconciliation of the three sides of myself that coexisted without truly intersecting: publicist by day, writer by night, and mother during the infinite spaces between. I'd learned to keep my inner fiction writer hidden while at work and even at home, where the topic had become somewhat touchy after years without a breakthrough. I was bursting for permission to step out of this closet at last and shout, "I am a writer!" This desire infused every word I wrote.

When the manuscript was complete, a mentor introduced me to her agent. The introduction filled me with hope. Upon receiving the agent's rejection note, I knew beyond all doubt that I could no longer bear the process of querying, gnawing my fingernails, waiting for a stranger or some turn of events to determine my future. The future was mine and mine alone to write. I stopped querying and opted to self-publish instead, giving myself a version of the permission I yearned for. Rarely had I felt so empowered.

The following year, *Veronica's Nap* was picked up by a small press and republished. By then, however, this bit of success seemed anecdotal. I had let go of the dream. Having channeled my energy back into the very endeavors that were, in reality, yielding the results I craved, I found myself at the helm of a literary PR agency, BookSavvy PR, which technically I'd founded but in fact had grown organically from the synergy between my writing, my professional experience, and my literary connections. I took up dance and voice lessons, finding a new and formidable creative outlet in movement and sound.

Stepping back, I became aware of the pattern that had emerged: Fueled by a desire for fulfillment, I'd forged ahead relentlessly on the path toward a writing career. Yet the path kept splitting off. "Writing career" lay in one direction, and "fulfillment" lay in the other. The choice was baffling but clear.

Still, I scribbled. Short stories, mainly, many of which I never completed, and one of which I sent to a respected creative writing teacher I knew. His comments were positive, save for a few minor issues to iron out. He offered to take a look again once I'd reworked it.

Again, I never did. I had said what I wanted to say. I had learned what I needed to learn about my craft and myself. More firmly entrenched by then on the path toward fulfillment, I knew that the best way for the act of writing to serve its purpose for myself was to embrace that fulfillment, whatever its form.

ASK THE HARD QUESTIONS, AND ROUND OUT YOUR IDENTITY

"A professional writer is an amateur who didn't quit." These words by Richard Bach were once my daily prayer. Yet I have quit in every way a writer can, from abandoning drafts in the middle and giving up on querying to leaving writing behind altogether—at least for now. In doing so, I have learned to ask myself the hard questions most writers must ultimately face and have found the answers surprisingly easy:

- Do the benefits of writing with a career in mind outweigh the material and emotional costs?
- What inner goals does writing represent to me, and is writing indeed helping me reach them?
- If I never succeed as a writer in the ways I'd hoped, would I still feel that the sacrifices had been worth it?

I have also discovered other richly satisfying sides of my identity. A well-rounded identity is crucial to a writer's survival. When the relative importance of non-writing aspects grows and these begin vying—or nagging—for attention, we owe it to ourselves to pay heed.

After all, rather than a "career" in any traditional sense of the word, writing is a *path* with a life of its own—one that can't be crammed into a set of preset dimensions or made to conform to a particular definition. Who's to say that, having quit, I won't start again tomorrow? Or that twenty years from now, I won't complete—and publish—a third novel?

Quitting is no more a sin than continuing for all the wrong reasons: peer pressure, blind acceptance of social constructs that define our objectives, or a hunger for validation or glory, perhaps. In this era where a love for words quickly triggers dreams of recognition, grandeur, fame, and fortune, let us reclaim the essence of what writing *is* from amid the hype of what we, as writers, should *become*.

COMMUNITY COMFORT
Why You Need a Writing Tribe, Even If You Think You Don't

VAUGHN ROYCROFT

I have a friend who wants to write fiction. As in, the writing bug has bitten him and he's fully infected. We recently attended a writing conference together. Sure, there was a lot of instruction, lots of insight into process, which my friend—who's struggled with how to start—appreciated. But it was the stuff in between sessions, at the meals and in the bar at day's end, that made the difference to him.

It was during those in-between times that my friend met and got acquainted with other writers at various stages of their journey. We spoke to dozens of every sort, from an eighteen-year-old newbie at her first conference (with her mom attending as a chaperone) to a veteran with more than forty published novels. My friend was able to see that none of us has the secret formula, that each of us has to find our own process, and that none of us ever perfects it—that writing is all about ongoing practice and refinement.

This, I believe, is what my friend needed to experience through others in order to accept and embrace an imperfect start. Interacting with a community of writers was the key to overcoming his inertia.

FEAST ON THE (SOMETIMES ELUSIVE) BENEFITS OF COMMUNITY

I'm guessing you have some idea of what might be gained by associating with other writers: critique and beta-reader feedback, maybe a mentor. These things are the meaty chunks in a hearty stew, both nourishing and rewarding. But community is more substantial than that. Community is the culmination of those in-between moments my friend experienced at the conference and more. Community is the stew's broth—warming, flavorful, and sustaining.

In my years of talking to other writers about community, I've found that it's difficult to describe the benefits reaped, not just because community manifests in such a personal way but because its rewards vary over time and by circumstance. In the hopes of shedding light on the elusive, we asked members of the Writer Unboxed Facebook Group[1] to describe what community has meant to them. We received too many great replies to share them all, but hopefully a sampling will convey an appreciation for the multifaceted gem community can be.

> I recently reached a panic moment, a feeling of all of it being too hard. When I reached out to my community, members rallied around me to offer sound advice and perspective until I saw clearly again what kind of writer I want to be. I see now that the right community is vital.
>
> —Lana Billman

> My writing groups validate me: My confidence crises are not unique, and I am not alone in working out the writing/life balance issues that many writers face. I'm not alone in my struggles or my triumphs. … [Community is] like a great engine to keep us moving toward the fulfillment of our dreams. Not to mention the emotional and mental benefits, the thrill of being able to show others the way.
>
> —Lara McKusky

> I love being able to "nerd out" about writerly things without seeing anyone's eyes glaze over. It's wonderful knowing I can … connect with someone more experienced. I can get direction from people I care about. Community is like a flashlight on a long, dark road.
>
> —Risa Pedzewick

> One of the things I enjoy about writing is being alone with my characters. But since I started connecting with other writers, I write more, I'm more humble, I'm more accountable, and I'm bolder in approaching agents and publishers. I'm more confident in my ability to say the words "I am a writer." Some of my best moments come when I'm alone with writing, but a surprising amount come when I'm with my writing friends.
>
> —Julie McCarroll Duffy

---

1 writerunboxed.com/facebook

I can't imagine going through this whole writing process without my online friends. My learning curve has been much quicker than it would have been otherwise, and it's nice to have friends who can commiserate with me. I'm glad to know I'm not the only crazy writer in the world. We're a special breed.
—Valerie P. Chandler

A community is the group of pilgrims with whom we travel, the ones who challenge us, who inspire us, who give us strength. They're the ones who help us face our fears, the ones who give us reason to come back from the brink when we're ready to throw in the towel. And after a while, the bonds formed are so strong that the community becomes something more. It becomes your tribe.
—Mike Swift

I didn't believe I was a real writer or that I would be one. I was incredibly intimidated but thought if I was accepted as part of a group, I could learn and perhaps some magic would rub off on me. Through watching my inky cohorts, I grew and found a little courage. I flopped more than a few times, but I had a safety net. My tribe. They met me where I was with compassion, jokes, and examples of where they, too, failed and then triumphed. I know I'll fail again, but I'm a writer. It's what we do until we don't. With aplomb.
—Tonia Marie Harris

The Writer Unboxed community is filled with writers who empathize with other writers. We've all written bad first drafts. We've all struggled with revisions. We've all faced days when the words won't flow. We've all questioned what we're doing. People in communities care for one another. They pick up one another when one struggles. They understand it's not constructive to tear others down.
—Chris Blake

As someone who isolates by nature, I've found the Writer Unboxed community to be a vital link for both my writing and personal growth. I lurked for a long time before mustering the courage to post. Being part of this group is like being a member of a large extended family. There is a deep level of trust. And there is a great deal of laughter and loving.
—Brin Jackson

My writing friends have challenged me to employ my imagination in ways I wouldn't have on my own. They've pushed me to make my stories and my writing better. Not to mention the intelligent conversations and stupid jokes and laughter even in the midst of tears. It isn't just that my writing is richer but that my life is.
—Natalie Hart

As you can see, community's benefits are elusive because they reach beyond what's tangible and quantifiable. They're born of the feelings incited by the flow of others around us on our journey: those who are climbing beside us; those out ahead, shining a light for us to follow; and those behind us, to whom we can lend a hand.

You likely won't comprehend what you'll receive in return for your investment in community until you have it. And even then it will continue to change and grow in surprising ways.

FIND YOUR TRIBE

Discovering your community is easier than you might think. And although I once feared writers would be distant and judgmental, I've found them—almost without exception—to be kind, warm, and inclusive. Starting your search might be as simple as inviting an old friend to a conference. Or checking your local library and bookshops for writing clubs, groups, or classes. Or, easier still, searching the Internet.

There are all types of online writing groups with levels of involvement that run the gamut. Look for groups that feel inclusive and welcoming. Don't force it—not every group is a natural fit.

At the onset of my own search, I tried a few genre-based groups in which I felt awkward, and I was unable to be myself. In contrast, I eased naturally into my involvement with Writer Unboxed. I moved from commenting on the blog to joining the Writer Unboxed Facebook Group to interacting almost daily and swiftly cultivating my tribe. The process felt like coming home.

So be patient; follow your head and heart to your tribe. Once you've found it, be attentive and give of yourself as much as you take.

I came to writing a bit later in life, and I'm surprised by how significant and meaningful this journey has become. Community plays a huge role in making it so. It provides a steady source of support, encouragement, and camaraderie—the very fuel I need to persevere. But beyond the tangible benefits I find through my association with my fellow writers and amidst the comfort of my tribe, I've discovered community's most essential element: friendship.

The friendships I've found on my publishing journey have played a vital role in making it the most rewarding of my life. That's a special gift. I'm grateful. So my last and perhaps most important bit of advice? Don't miss your opportunity to share it.

> **☞ PRO TIP**
>
> Take care that social networking doesn't become your sugar fix—an unhealthy fuel that takes you away from your work and becomes addictive in its own right.

BATTLING DOUBT

How to Push Beyond Your Final Barriers and Finish Your Book

JOHN VORHAUS

AUTHOR'S NOTE: While working on this piece, I had a dream that I'd been assigned to write a book about snakes. I wonder if there's any connection.

• • •

"Writing a book," said Winston Churchill, "is an adventure. To begin with it is a toy and an amusement. Then it becomes a mistress, then it becomes a master, then it becomes a tyrant. The last phase is that just as you are about to be reconciled to your servitude, you kill the monster and fling him to the public."

We'll be skipping over the fun parts here—writing as toy, amusement, and mistress—and going right to the master and tyrant parts. These two are the last steps a writer faces before the *real* fun of killing the monster and flinging it to the public. Since these final steps are so fraught with doubt, we'll look at some specific strategies you can use to know *when, how,* and *whether* your beast is ready thus to be slain and slung.

And we're going to start, strangely enough, with a quick review of how to make a bed.

SMOOTH THE RIGHT WRINKLES

You know how to make a bed, right? You throw a sheet on the mattress in some random fashion, grab it by the corners, and then throw it again in some slightly less random fashion. You do this two or three times until the sheet is relatively in the right place, and then you move on to local fixes: tucking it in, pulling it taut, and smoothing the wrinkles away. That's where we are right now, in the "smoothing out the wrinkles" phase. The manuscript is pretty much done. The tens and hundreds of thousands of words are on the page. The story basically works. The thing is a *thing*, by and large. All that's left are those last few wrinkles. But why are they so stubborn? Why is it so hard to get to closure? Because we're up against a tough question: *How done is done?* Here are a couple of strategies to answer that.

First, don't sweat the small stuff. If you're looking at a phrase in the text and can't decide whether it should be "it is" or "it's"—or worse, if you're switching from "it is" to "it's" and then back again—guess what? Let it go! Whatever choice you make at this point, the reader will assume that it is (or it's) the choice you wanted and intended. When your operations become local (changing words) and no longer global (changing the book's DNA), you know you're done.

If you still can't let it go, invoke the twenty-year rule, which proposes that if it won't matter in twenty years, it doesn't matter now. Will it matter in twenty years whether you used "it is" or "it's?" Of course not. So smooth out those wrinkles to your heart's content, make any choice that feels right, and then move on. Your energy and critical eye are better spent elsewhere.

TO TRUST YOUR "YES," HAVE A RELIABLE "NO"

So that's what to do with tiny, unimportant decisions, but what about big, important ones? Suppose at this late date, for example, you start to mistrust your ending. You've rewritten it four, five, six times, and you're still not sure it's right. You know that it's too big an issue to ignore—this *will* matter in twenty years, damn it!—but you don't know how to close the book on your book. Fortunately I have a strategy for this, too. It's a little tricky to master but worth taking on.

When we work as editors of our own work, especially when we're coming to the finish line or deadline or any other sort of line we see looming in the middle distance, we have a strong tendency to examine our creative decisions through the *filter of hope*. We *hope* the ending works. We *hope* the tone is pleasing and consistent. We *hope* the funny stuff is funny. We *hope* we haven't radically overused the words *ameliorate* or *spleen*.

So we hope, but we don't *know*. Why? Because we're frail and we have egos. We want to be done so badly that we know we can fool ourselves into thinking we *are* done, even when significant issues remain, hidden to our eyes and ready to blow up, spectacularly and destructively, once the book is out of our hands.

We fear that we're lying to ourselves and we seem powerless to stop. What can be done about this?

Here's what: Have a *no* you can trust. Pour all your energy and objectivity into looking at your work and words and saying, "Nope, not good enough," and again, "Nope, not good enough," and yet again, "Nope, still not." All these times of saying no will send you back into the manuscript, back to fixing things you know need fixing, because you've been honest enough with yourself to say so. Then one day you wake up and—*mirabile visu!*—you see that you've fixed the things that needed fixing. If you're looking at a page of prose and you can't find anything wrong with it—and you trust your reliable *no*—then you can say yes with confidence and move on.

Filtering judgment through hope is a problem almost all of us face, especially late in the game, when we're so close to the work—so intimately engaged—that we've lost perspective. The way out of this trap of doubt is to be hard on yourself when called for so that when you finally feel like you have things right, you'll know you're telling the truth.

SQUEEZE OUT THE STUPID

Okay, so here's where you're at: You have a mature manuscript that you know basically works. You're operating on the final fixes, and you're going at it with clarity: You know you can stop making decisions that don't matter, and you know you can trust your judgment on the ones that do. What comes next? For me, it's my favorite part of the process: what I call *squeezing out the stupid*. I like this part so much because it's not about struggling to add new words that work but, simply and quite easily, subtracting the ones that don't.

So what's "the stupid"? It varies from writer to writer. Redundancies are common culprits. Overuse of words like *ameliorate* or *spleen*. Inconsistencies of tone, dialect, or character voice. Clumsy or unclear thoughts. Sentence fragments. For me it's a big deal to locate and eradicate anything that sounds like me, the author, and not like the characters or narrator. I'm a pretty self-indulgent writer—I like my inside jokes—but I strip away all those self-indulgences at this stage. Basically I'm looking for anything that "takes me off the page," that is, gets me thinking about the author and his choices rather than the characters and their journey.

Apply this test to your own work. When you're doing that final quality-control pass through the material and you're wondering whether something doesn't belong, just ask yourself if it takes you off the page. If the answer is yes, get it out of there. Now note that when you're asking a targeted, precise question like "Does this take me off the page?" you're not asking a vague and useless question like "Is this good writing?" At this stage of the game (and, really, at any stage of the game) the question of whether the writing is any good isn't helpful. The helpful question is: "Does this writing do the job I intend it to do?" If the answer is no, fix it. If the answer is yes, move on. By evaluating your revisions in terms of simple utility, you step outside the whole trap of *value judgement* and reach a point where you can actually kill the beast.

KILL THE BEAST

Some people never finish what they start. They might have a manuscript that's 99 percent ready to go, but they just can't bring themselves to deliver it to an agent or editor, e-publish it, or print it up on parchment scrolls for distribution to family and close friends. If you ask them why, they might say something like "I want it to be perfect, and it's not." Mostly what they mean is: "I am afraid." *I'm afraid that if I kill this monster and fling it to the public, the public will fling it right back to me, wrapped in the day-old newsprint of their scorn and disapproval. I'm afraid of rejection—so afraid that I resist putting myself in a place where I might have to face it.*

Well, guess what? Rejection is your fate. There's bound to be somebody who doesn't like your work—and will find a way to tell you. And this will be true whether you spend five months or five years applying the final gloss. There's no such thing as perfect. The pursuit of perfection is really just procrastination, and procrastination is really just fear. You have to get over that because the worst that can happen—that your work is ignored by the world—will *definitely* happen if you never send it out. Measured against this benchmark, then, any outcome—any response whatsoever—is better than what you'd receive if you never killed your precious beast and gave it the ol' heave ho.

I used to spend about four minutes of fretting for every one minute of real writing. Twenty-five books on, I've reversed the proportion: Now it's about one minute of worry for every four minutes of craft. That's not bad. I'm happy with that ratio. But I'm also realistic: I no more expect to be completely free from fear in my writing process than I expect to stop overusing *ameliorate* or *spleen*. Fear is natural. In a way, it's even useful. It tells you that you're working in the fruitful territory between your comfort zone and the interesting unknown. Fear—yes, fear!—tells you that you're growing as a writer. So embrace your fear, acknowledge it as a legitimate part of your creative process, stare it down, and then walk on by.

TAKE THE WIN

Every time you finish writing a book, you achieve two goals. First, of course, you've written your book. You've gotten your story out of the fragile and ephemeral vessel of your brain and into the slightly less fragile and less ephemeral vessel of e-book or print (or parchment scroll). So that's one win. Here's the other: You've improved. You have improved your writing to the exact tune of all the research, rough drafts, rewrites, edits, revisions, polishes, and squeezing out of stupid that you invested in the work. That's not nothing. In fact, it's everything. It means that next time your process will be more efficient. You'll do it better, faster, and with less angst, especially in the end game, because now you have the tools to blast doubt to smithereens. You now know how to do the following:

- Smooth the right wrinkles.
- Trust your yes.
- Squeeze out the stupid.
- Kill the beast.
- Take the win.

Especially take the win. I do. I do it with every book I write. After I'm done, I pause to reflect on the challenges I faced in the writing, the discoveries I made about myself and my craft, and, above all, the fact that I have completed this large, improbable, stunningly difficult to contemplate, yet somehow mysteriously and magically executed thing called a book. I take the win. I congratulate myself on work well done or at least on work, well, done. I let that good feeling wash over me, and I definitely make time and space to enjoy it. Sometimes I take myself out to dinner. I worked so hard to finish a book that the least I can do is pat myself on the back.

The least you can do is to take the win. Your book is done. It had its challenges, but you met them. It had its problems, but you solved them and got it done. So take pride in that because what you've done now separates you from the almost eight billion people on the planet who will never write a book. You're a storyteller ... an *author*. You are a breed apart. Gosh, you're Winston Churchill!

And if that's not mighty, I don't know what is.

FAQ

I wasn't planning to create a series, but one of my secondary characters is begging for his own book. Should I tie up his thread as planned or leave an open door? Is there any one right answer?

A series features the same character; a spin-off puts the spotlight on other characters. But that's a technicality. Whether a series or a spin-off, the real problem is that follow-up books tend to be weaker than the original. (Not always, but frequently enough to be notable.) Don't create a spin-off just because it's an easy idea or because fans are asking for it. Create it because it's a compelling story. Look at it this way: Would you write it regardless of whether you'd written the original? If so, great. If not, there's some risk.

—DONALD MAASS

 ## HOW TO GET IN YOUR OWN WAY, METHOD 30: IGNORE DIMINISHING RETURNS

There comes a point when you're not making the book better; you're just making it differenter. Recognize when it's time to move on to your next book. And catch up on laundry, which you've been neglecting as well.

—BILL FERRIS

THE TORTUROUS WAITING

How Waiting Becomes a Part of Writing

JULIA MUNROE MARTIN

Last year I was briefly represented by an agent, but it didn't work out. So I'm back to querying ... and waiting. The truth is, even when I had representation, I was waiting. *Then*, I was waiting for the agent to let me know if there was any word from editors. *Now*, I'm waiting to hear from agents.

"The torturous waiting," one of my writer friends calls it. Another writer I know has never submitted anything he's written (nor does he plan to, and he's written eleven novels), but most of us *want* external recognition. We're waiting for someone out there to deem our work worthy, a success, to acknowledge in some way, shape, or form that we have not wasted our time.

I've been at this for so long that not only do I have e-mail folders of digital rejections, I also have a yellowing file folder full of paper rejections. One of the manuscripts I'm querying came from an idea I had seven years ago; I first queried it three years ago. In other words, it can take a *really* long time. But when it's your first time out of the gate, it's easy for waiting to take on a life of its own as you check your e-mail every other second.

What if I told you there was a way to wait that didn't involve torture—or at least not as much?

DE-EMOTIONALIZE THE PROCESS

Avoid the pitfall of thinking "they" hate it and that's why it's taking so long. In fact, try to avoid too much navel-gazing. I was talking to a writer friend the other day who said one of her critique partners never got back to her with comments on her most recent manuscript. Let's face it: Sometimes we never *do* hear back. It's not you; it's them. Okay, bad joke. But it's really not us; it's the process. Even when you (a) land the agent, (b) get the book contract, (c) get your novel published, or (d) self-publish a novel, it doesn't mean you won't wait. It's a cycle, and in one way or another, we're always waiting—even seasoned pros are waiting. For editors. For literary agents. For reviews. For sales numbers.

What about when or if you *do* get rejected? Rejection is part of the writing cycle. It happens to all of us. As hard as it is, try to view your work objectively. Not everyone can like what you write.

TAKE ACTION WHILE WAITING

There are times when you might want to give up—I've been there plenty—but that's exactly when you should spring into action. Write something new, better, different. Avoid the trap of thinking you'll never have another good idea or that you don't know what to write next. One of the great things about writing fiction is that there's always another story right around the corner. And if I'm simultaneously submitting manuscripts, and sometimes nonfiction essays and short stories, too, I always have something out on submission. I'm not waiting for one e-mail but for multiple responses—which helps make me feel a little more in control of the process.

Sometimes as we wait we receive feedback. Most often in dribs and drabs but sometimes in a landslide, from critique partners or in the form of "revise and resubmit" letters from agents. Even if someone doesn't like what you write, you may get feedback you can use—something that will help you improve your work and grow as a writer. Consider a rewrite while you're waiting.

Now could also be the perfect time to take a class. Join a writer's group. Develop your social networks (without wallowing or whining). Take time to research the market: agents and readers, book clubs and advertising venues. Read. Not only is reading a way to refresh your brain and cultivate new ideas, but while you read you can keep your eyes open for an author who could blurb your book or for a book that's a good comparison with yours—this is especially useful if an author's agent is someone on your querying list and you can mention that book in a query.

The important thing is to keep evolving. Keep the wheel turning. Write more. Write again. Write often. It's all we can really do. That and wait. But if we do it right, the waiting doesn't have to be torturous. Just remember not to view silence as a judgment of your worthiness, and whatever you do, resist the urge to see waiting as an end game—it's not! Maybe it can even be turned into the most productive part of the writing cycle—moving us one step closer to launching our writing out into the big, beautiful world.

 PRO TIP

Many writing experts advise authors to stimulate the writing habit by making time to write every day, whether you feel like it or not. Find an accountability partner. She can be a sounding board for waiting, too. Someone to check in with when it feels like it's been "too long." Is it time to nudge? Or is it better to wait a little longer? Another writer can help decide.

 HOW TO GET IN YOUR OWN WAY, METHOD 31: WAIT AROUND

Editors know when you're freaking out about your submission. This makes them nervous, and they scurry under the slush pile to hide. Probably. Whatever it is they do, it's gonna take a long time, so you may as well get started on your next project.

—BILL FERRIS

SURVIVING "NEARLY THERE"

How to Thrive When You're *This Close* to Publication

ROBIN LAFEVERS

One of the hardest stages of the writing journey—one that will take the most dedication, commitment, and self-exploration—is the "nearly there" stage. This is the stage where your critique partners love your work, you're getting personalized rejections from agents or editors and highly complimentary reports from your beta readers, and yet … no sale or offer has materialized.

Remember those old cartoons where the character is walking in the desert, hot sun beating down on him? The ones where he's covered in dust and nearly perishing of thirst as he slowly drags himself to the enticing oasis that is just over the horizon—only to have it disappear just as he reaches it because it's *a frickin' mirage*?

That's what the "nearly there" stage feels like. Especially if you've been stuck in it for more than a couple of years. And here's a dirty little secret: "Nearly there" isn't just for pre-published writers. Many published authors find themselves stuck or stalled out on the midlist for years, their careers never taking off and slowly spiraling downward. For the self-published authors, "nearly there" might mean lackluster reviews and few sales.

However we arrive at this point, the "nearly there" stage is a vital, absolutely critical part of our development as writers. In fact, many agents and editors would argue that this is exactly the stage that is missing from so many aspiring authors' journeys and their ultimate ability to break through. So I'm going to talk about how to not only survive but *thrive* during this stage.

Yes, I said "thrive," because the truth is, if you take your focus off the finish line for a while and throw yourself into the spirit of experimentation and improvement, the "nearly there" stage can be a gift. It's a chance to strengthen your writing so that when you do get published, you have a greater chance of being published *well* rather than simply being published. Because yes, there is a difference. Just ask any of those languishing midlisters I mentioned.

The critically important tasks of the "nearly there" stage involve mastering those areas we have control over: the stories we tell, how we tell them, and our relationship with our writing.

TRY THIS RATHER THAN QUIT

Most of us expect to take some time to master our craft. A year or two, maybe three. But when our apprenticeship starts to draw out far beyond that, it can become dispiriting and discouraging, making it all too easy to throw in the towel.

The most widely circulated publishing success stories usually involve someone so naturally talented that she sat down and wrote a book in six months—her first book, mind you—and had it published to great fanfare. Those stories get retold so often that they feel like the expectation rather than the true outliers they are.

Far less exciting is the idea of long years of hard work spent mastering the craft one component at a time until you become proficient enough that your work simply shines.

This is not only true of the nuts and bolts of the craft of writing but also of the very stories you choose to write.

VOICE, TAKE TWO

It takes a while to recognize your creative vision, let alone to trust or believe in that vision enough to fully embrace it. It is easy to see your creations as too weird or romantic or irreverent or outlandish or creepy or mundane. But they may actually be none of those things. It may simply be that you are too close or too afraid of sharing it to see it clearly. Sometimes the stories you give yourself permission to tell aren't the stories you are truly, ultimately meant to write. Sometimes you have to work toward those more urgent and vital stories inch by painstaking inch as you get comfortable with your own truths. This, then, is one of the most vital tasks of being "nearly there."

It can help to look for a deep, personal connection to the themes to which you're drawn. Are you longing for forgiveness? Is there someone you should forgive but can't? Has someone in your life shown great self-sacrifice that inspired or benefited you in some way? If so, you know these themes well and have the ability to weave one or several into your book in a way that no one else can. Doing so will imbue your story with power.

In fact, this is the perfect time to return to my essay "Your Unique Story" and to double down on giving voice to your creative vision. Especially revisit the questions in the Finding Your Most Authentic Voice and Now Dig Deeper sections. After months or years of working on your writing, you've learned much about yourself—what thrills you, delights you, bores you, or sets your creativity on fire—and the answers to the questions in those sections will most likely be different now than when you first tackled them.

That is to be expected. After all, you send your characters on a narrative journey, knowing it will force them to change in fundamental ways. So, too, does the actual act and practice of writing force you to grow as you peel away your external shell and persona one layer at a time and come to know yourself better.

ADVANCED CRAFT

This "nearly there" stage is the perfect opportunity to work on some advanced elements of craft. Instead of starting a new manuscript with the intention of creating a marketable story, start with the intent of mastering certain aspects of the craft. Don't just refocus on the obvious elements, like plotting or point of view. Branch out, and look for other aspects of craft—compelling description, evocative subtext, nuanced language, layered characters, the subtle art of pacing, microtension—that aren't talked about quite so much. Give yourself permission, for just this one manuscript, to ignore plot or conventional structure, or to concentrate on plot and structure, if you normally avoid them. Not all of your million words need be in pursuit of one goal. I actually argue that they shouldn't be.

Once you've spent long hours perfecting the craft, play with it! Experiment. Color outside the lines. Be daring. Be brave.

It can be helpful to reassess your manuscript with this new skill set, but also accept that some manuscripts aren't salvageable. They were born flawed and will only ever be a fabulous learning opportunity. *And that's okay.* Nothing is wasted in writing, especially not words you put on the page, even practice words. (Remember what Catherine McKenzie said in her essay "Do You Need an MFA?" about ten thousand hours!) Learning what doesn't work is an important precursor to learning what *does*. Sometimes simply starting a story with a new understanding of your voice and creative vision can unlock your writing in unexpected ways.

RETHINK YOUR PLACE IN THE MARKET

Once you've honed your skills, then what? What if you build it—and improve it—and nobody comes? What if the stories you're driven to tell are quiet ones? Or don't hit the current market's sweet spot?

Sometimes the inescapable fact is that the things we love to write don't sell. When this happens, one approach is to rework your stories to create a larger welcome mat.

This is not about selling out on your artistic vision in order to get a contract. Nor is it about watering down artistic integrity in order to reach readers. It's about finding the largest, widest doorway into your story so that you can draw in as many readers as possible and then tell them exactly the core story you're driven to tell.

There are a variety of things that allow a book to stand out and find a wide audience: a gripping plot, stunning reversals and sleight of hand, compelling characters, a unique and original voice, exquisite language, and a story that explores the vulnerabilities and universal truths of the human heart.

If you write quiet books or books that go against current market conventions, that doesn't mean all is lost. It simply means that some of these other aspects of your work will act as the wider doormat for your potential readers. And the good news is that widening that doormat does not have to radically alter the story you are hungry to tell.

Also remember that just because your writing or storytelling style is understated doesn't mean the emotions or issues you're exploring have to be as well. It can be hugely effective to explore emotional upheaval with a quiet sucker punch as well as high drama.

ANALYZE THE LANDSCAPE

Another way to play with the *oomph* of your story is through the interior landscape. Can you ramp up the emotional stakes in your manuscript in some way?

Explore a deeper theme? The emotional stakes of your characters aren't only conveyed by your actual writing at the scene level but also by the brainstorming and story choices you make early in the process.

With quieter books and subject matter, the trick is to make them so utterly human that readers connect almost in spite of their inclination to dismiss a book as quiet. This is where your skill and finesse at plumbing the human spirit and heart will really have a chance to shine.

CONNECT WITH A BIGGER (MORPHING) PICTURE

Experiencing failure is an important part of the creative journey. Our characters don't change or grow unless they are forced to do so by the events of the story, and neither will we. Rejections, bad reviews, lackluster sales, and painful critique feedback are all necessary lumps on the road to your objective. You need to be humble enough to hear what that feedback is telling you. Sometimes the feedback won't be the obvious kind—a rejection or editorial letter—but rather a lack of progress on your journey. Keep your eyes peeled for that kind of subtle hint the universe likes to taunt us with.

Oftentimes the reason you started writing won't be the reason you continue writing. You might feel that doing something as daring as writing stories or becoming an author is a hard thing to admit. You are shocked by your own audacity. So your creative self tells your more rational self the necessary lies to get you moving in the right direction: *I can make a lot of money writing books. I will be famous. I will be respected. I can write a better book than this one I just paid ten dollars for.* And on and on and on. Eventually though, that hunger to be published or make it big should morph into something else: a love affair with writing, a personal quest, a creative outlet, a way to keep sane, a simple joy, or the thrill of finally—*finally*—capturing the wonderfulness of an idea on the page.

This is where the rubber meets the road. Are you truly committed to this writing thing? Even if it takes more than two or three years for you to achieve your goals?

There is no wrong answer. Writing might be something that only holds a certain amount of appeal for you, an appeal that will evaporate when it does not come easily or quickly, or when that need to express yourself is fulfilled in other ways. (See Sharon Bially's essay "On Quitting.") Or maybe it runs so deeply in your blood that you will write, published or not, until they pry the pen from your cold, dead hands.

You must come to terms with why you write and who you are and where the two of those intersect. Some people do write for validation, and no matter how much they wish that away, it won't change. This is fine as long as they are aware of the risks involved in that mind-set and how it shapes both their journey and their frustrations. Others write to better understand the world, to make connections, to explore the issues that haunt them, or simply because they can't *not* write. It is vital to know into which category you fall.

SHIFT THE FOCUS

Sometimes all you can change is your attitude or how you approach something. You can learn to release your death grip on the outcome, let go of your desires, and simply exist in the moment and enjoy the process. Okay, I know that is much harder than it seems. Believe me, I *know*. So here are some practical steps:

- Take the long view.
- Practice being in the moment and enjoying the stage you're in rather than assuming the grass is so much greener elsewhere and pining to be someplace you're not. As with life, each stage of the writing journey is full of valuable lessons and opportunity for growth, if only you let it teach you.
- Find a way to get more process minded. Try to remove the onus of "publishing equals success." I highly recommend Julia Cameron's *The Artist's Way* or Elizabeth Gilbert's *Big Magic* to find help in shifting your perspective.
- There are so many ways to define success! Challenge yourself to identify ten milestones of achievement that have nothing to do with being published.

This "nearly there" stage is equivalent to the "Dark Night of the Soul" in a character's journey, when you feel that all is lost and your efforts have been in vain. Just like a character in a novel, you will have to dig deep, take a leap of faith, and recommit.

You may even have to quit writing for a while if you decide it is taking up too much of your life or distracting you from other things that require your attention. But there is a good chance that the writing monster has already sunk her long, seductive claws into you and that you will not be able to leave her behind as easily as you thought.

And once you discover *that*, you realize that publishing really is only one piece of the creative life. That recognition can allow you to take a deep breath and step back from the sense of urgency that nips too often at your heels. Or, at the very least, it can give you the perspective and patience to cheerfully slog your way forward.

 PRO TIP

Submitting to agents invariably results in rejections. Most of the time, you should shrug them off. Every high-powered agent has turned down plenty of books that later won prizes or became bestsellers. But sometimes you'll get a rejection from an agent that includes a thoughtful commentary on how you could change the book to have a better shot at publication. If an agent takes time to do that, you should consider her opinion seriously. If a bunch of people all say the same thing—say, they have a problem with how the story concludes—then you should definitely consider rewriting. And take heart—if agents feel compelled to comment on your work, then they're seeing something special.

—MARGARET DILLOWAY

 HOW TO GET IN YOUR OWN WAY, METHOD 32: GIVE UP EASILY

You spent two years writing your book, but you wanna quit after five or six rejections? You owe it to your work to subject yourself to this torture at least one hundred times.

—BILL FERRIS

PART SEVEN

RELEASE

Congratulations! You've authored a novel. Sometimes publication provides unexpected twists that are more common than you might have guessed. Read on for a short course on what you might find beyond "The End," and be sure you take time to celebrate your major achievement. We knew you could do it.

LETTING GO

How to Cope with Empty Writer's Nest

ALLIE LARKIN

A week before my first novel came out, I stood in line at the post office with an armload of early copies to mail and was struck hard with something akin to stage fright. My pulse quickened. My knees went weak. The flop sweat was significant. I wanted to flee, but I was smack in the middle of a long roped-off line and didn't think I could calmly work my way out. I stayed put, the knot in my throat tightening every time the line moved forward. When it was finally my turn, I stumbled through the necessary explanations and payment, embarrassed by my sweaty fluster. I ran outside, jumped in my car, and cried the whole way home.

People were going to read my novel. People I knew. People I didn't know. People I only sort of knew. The possibility of the kid who once sat behind me in high school algebra reading my words was the most strangely frightening prospect. My book was entirely fiction, but I still felt exposed. I was saying to the world: *This is what I think about. This is how my heart feels.* I hadn't yet realized that it's brave to write. I wasn't expecting to feel so vulnerable.

In addition to having stage fright, I was sad. The characters I'd spent most of my adult life imagining were gone. For me, their story was over and it was time to share them. Of course, that's the point. That's why we finish and then publish books, but it was never why I wrote one. My novel was a labor of love. A compulsion. A need to spend time with incredible people who would not otherwise exist. Letting them go created a sharp, unexpected feeling of loss, and I didn't know how to move to the next stage in the process. Everyone around me wanted to talk about the happiness of having a book published, but I wasn't wholly happy. I felt ridiculous for holding sadness in my heart over an accomplishment, but I missed connecting with the people I'd created now that their story was over.

There's an intimacy to the time we spend with our characters. Our books are most appealing when we put our whole hearts into them, fully embody the feelings of the people we've made up, and fall madly in love with them. It's silly to think that letting go would be easy. Like leaving high school and going to college, the transition from one book to the next is not without tearful good-byes. Acknowledging our feelings—all of them—is the best way to move on.

IF IT HURTS LIKE A BAD BREAKUP, EMPLOY BREAKUP RULES

Give yourself time to mourn the loss of a constant in your life. Play your writing playlist one last time. Watch movies your main character loves. Eat her favorite foods. Be gentle with yourself.

REACH OUT TO OTHER WRITERS

You may want to consider carefully whether you'll tell the nonwriters in your life that the loss of imaginary people inspired your pajama-and-ice-cream wallow fest, but other writers will understand. Much comfort can be found in talking it through with people who have been there.

CHEAT

Going through the process of letting go of the characters from my first book was a bit easier because I'd left myself room for a sequel. "Goodbye for now" is easier than "goodbye for always." Even if you never plan to write another book with the same characters, it's okay to daydream about what they might do next or what they did before your book began. It's not like drunk dialing an ex. There's no rule against checking in with them.

ENJOY READER FEEDBACK, BUT KEEP IT IN CHECK

Hearing a reader's story of connection is amazing. Knowing someone else understands and even loves your characters is a deeply rewarding experience. You are not alone! You created a story that speaks to readers! Unfortunately sometimes the search for positive feedback can also yield some dissenting opinions. Remember that nothing anyone else says about your work, good or bad, changes the experience you had with your characters. During the first fragile book launch days, have a trusted friend filter feedback for you. Knowing you have that filter in place can help quiet your nerves.

CELEBRATE

Toast to your characters, your hard work, and the accomplishment of finishing what you started. Even if part of you feels the loss, the part that relishes your success is also allowed to come out and play.

On launch day, I stood in my favorite bookstore, reading to a crowd of people I knew, people I didn't know, and people I only sort of knew. My stage fright dissipated quickly because I realized that I was in a room full of readers. I was sharing my characters with people who wanted to meet them. I talked about how I came to write my first book, the places and events that inspired the story, and what the characters meant to me. I teared up while reading a passage, and it was a good thing, not a blunder. When I looked out at the audience and saw their kind, supportive faces looking back at me, I realized that it's okay to show people how much you care. That's what we're here for. It's a beautiful experience to share the way your heart feels, and we are deeply fortunate to have that opportunity.

When it came time to mail early copies of my second book, I made it through the line at the post office with dry armpits and a normal heartbeat. I shed a tear or two in the car on the way home. I knew I would miss those characters, but this time, I also expected the feelings that came from sending a book out into the world. Giving myself room to miss those guys also made room for happiness, and sending them off made room for the new cast of characters I was about to meet.

 HOW TO GET IN YOUR OWN WAY, METHOD 33: FORGET TO CELEBRATE

Finishing your book is a big @#$%-ing deal. So is the first time you send it to an agent and the day you start a new one. Writing is a lonely, grueling slog full of disappointment and rejection. For the love of God, give yourself permission to enjoy it once in a while.

—BILL FERRIS

Author In Progress

Guest Contributor

GREAT EXPECTATIONS

What to Do When Dreams and Reality Collide

M.J. ROSE

EDITOR'S NOTE: *New York Times* bestseller M.J. Rose (www.mjrose.com) has written more than a dozen novels. She is also the founder of the first marketing company for writers, Author Buzz (authorbuzz.com), which makes her an ideal guest for this book. M.J. has witnessed firsthand the collision of many an author's dream with reality and learned how best to cope with the aftermath.

• • •

I think one of the real problems we authors face is that in order to write a book—to do all the research, to juggle day jobs and family and make sacrifices to find time to write, to sweat over words and paragraphs and characters, to sometimes bleed on the page—we have to believe what we are creating is not only wonderful and amazing and worth what we are giving it but that there is no other book like it.

We have to be huge optimists. We have to believe in the impossible.

Certainly we each think our books are good. But in reality, there are hundreds of good books published every month and thousands and thousands every year. And no matter what we tell ourselves to stay motivated, we know the truth.

We don't write miracles. We just tell stories.

Yes, they are often fine stories. But are they wake-up-in-the-morning-and-shout-from-the-rooftops-no-one-has-ever-written-a-book-like-this-before-oh-my-god-stop-the-world stories? No, they're usually not. And that's where the problem lies.

HOPE FOR THE BEST, BUT BE REASONABLE

The contracts we are offered and the reception our books receive, no matter how good, almost never ever match our expectations. That's because what we had to believe in order to write the book involved putting it on a tall pedestal—where it almost never belongs.

Simon Lipskar, president of Writers House, has this to say on the topic:

> There is a difference between hopes and expectations. Hopes are naturally, fundamentally irrational, and we are irrational creatures who always hope for wonderful things. And we should always embrace and cherish our hopes. But expectations are different; they need to be rational and rigorously grounded in reality. Once identified, we should never, ever accept anything but the most vigorous effort from ourselves or our business partners to meet those expectations, as long as we've set reasonable ones. We should also, however, never, ever see failing to meet hopes as 'failure.' One can hope to win the lottery, but one can't expect to; you can hope that your fifth novel will be your first *New York Times* bestseller, but all you can fairly and reasonably expect is that you and your publisher will make the efforts necessary to deliver on shared expectations, which may or may not include hitting the list.

Having reasonable expectations make sense. But still, most authors I know are disappointed, including many who make seven figures per book and/or are on the *New York Times* bestseller list and/or get wildly positive reviews. There's always something you aren't getting.

Who is satisfied? Those few authors a year for whom true lightning has struck, for whom the lottery has been won and who hit *Water for Elephants* or *Gone Girl* level. The rest of us? We moan and try to drown our great expectations in chocolate or wine—pick your poison—and curse the writing gods and feel sorry for ourselves.

Those runaway successes can happen, but how often? How realistic are they? Why hold up those exceptions as plausible outcomes and set yourself up for failure?

ACKNOWLEDGE ONE THOUSAND SHADES OF SUCCESS

New York Times bestseller Christopher Rice offers this advice:

> Get honest about how you define success. Separate your definition of success from your parents' definition of success. Or your sixth-grade English teacher's definition of success. If you'd like to sell a million copies of every book, set that as your definition of success, but learn to accept the sacrifices that come with that path; writing to market as opposed to your heart's desire, putting out at least one, possibly two or more books a year. Or accept that for you success means forming a deep and lasting connection with a small but dedicated group of readers regardless of whether or not the resulting sales will give you the kind of picture-perfect suburban lifestyle you saw idolized on television growing up. Success for an artist has a thousand different definitions; find yours, and commit to it.

The fact is, writing is an art and publishing is a business, and if you tie your happiness to the business instead of the craft, you are bound to be disappointed. That's because no business is kind. It's a corporation that needs product and profit to keep itself going. And as much as we like to think we are making art, once that book is delivered to a publishing house, it's a product. And the score in that game is mostly kept in dollar bills.

Randy Susan Meyers, author of *Accidents of Marriage*, suggests that it helps if you become knowledgeable about the business:

> You can become more realistic if you know the average sales of novels. Online you get answers like this: 'The average book in America sells about 500 copies' (*Publishers Weekly*, July 17, 2006). And average sales have since fallen much more. According to BookScan, which tracks most bookstore, online, and other retail sales of books, only 299 million books were sold in 2008 in the United States in all adult nonfiction categories combined. The average U.S. book is now selling less than 250 copies per year and less than 3,000 copies over its lifetime.

To stay sane in this business, Meyers also suggests "becoming enmeshed with a group of writers who are honest, funny, and are the best of cynicism and art."

MARRY YOUR HAPPINESS TO YOUR CRAFT

There is hope.

Tie your happiness and expectations to the writing—the one thing you actually do control. Be thankful for a talent that takes you on great escapes, that gives you pleasure and makes you feel more alive than almost anything (except maybe sex). Crafting that story is accomplishment, one that should not be ruined by what others may or may not do with that story.

What to do when you get overwhelmed by the biz, the hopes, and the dreams? Here's what three authors had to say about it.

Alyson Richman, author of *The Lost Wife*, says:

> I force myself to take a step back and say, "Why are you doing this?" The answer always saves me. I'm writing books because I have a story to tell. It has to be the intellectual curiosity and the creative impulse that propels me. Not the financial rewards, as grateful as I would be to have them! We'll never be able to control the publishing success of a book, so it's important to reinforce the positive—the fulfillment of creating the novel from the first sentence to the last. I also feel very grateful for having a creative life. It is not always easy. But I can't imagine doing anything else.

Steve Berry, *the New York Times* bestseller of more than a dozen books, adds this:

> It's amazing to me how people all over the world can sit down and read your story, becoming enthralled and entertained, losing themselves in your imagination. That's something that definitely keeps me going. And just to be able to do it again. That, to me, should be the real goal of every published writer.

New York Times bestseller Lexi Blake shares this insight:

> I came into this business as a people-pleasing-want-everyone-to-love-me Southern girl, and now I'm pretty thick-skinned and can take a punch. Why? Why put up with bad reviews? Why put up with people yelling at you that you don't write fast enough? That what you write isn't good enough? Or worse [receive] no reviews at all because no one read the damn thing? Because this is the best job in the world. Because I get to feed my family while I feed my soul. Because I spend the majority of my day creating worlds and going on journeys most people only dream of—or read about.

As for me, I live for the writing. I get intense pleasure from the stories I create. And I love coming to the end: writing that last word, knowing I've finally completed the creation. Expecting to *write* is totally within the writer's realm. It's precious and wonderful and can only belong to us.

When you tie your happiness and expectations to the writing, you can revel in it. And if you can do that, it becomes much easier to let the business just happen, even if it never matches up to those great expectations.

HOW TO GET IN YOUR OWN WAY, METHOD 34: BELIEVE YOU'VE GOT IT ALL FIGURED OUT

Every book is different. Like a video game in which bad guys get progressively harder, each new book you write will humiliate and drive you crazy in its own infuriating way.

—BILL FERRIS

WRITER AS PHOENIX

When It's Important to Remember Your True-and-Always Freedom

SOPHIE MASSON

You've probably heard the inspiring myth of the phoenix, which rises, renewed, from the ashes of its former self. But if you go to the Wikipedia entry, here's how the phoenix is defined: "a long-lived bird that is cyclically regenerated or reborn."

That's a rather sobering view of the spectacular phoenix image, but a better metaphor couldn't exist for the long-lasting, successful writing life. For it's not only about the capacity for regeneration of your career and refreshment of your craft but also understanding that there are cycles in publishing and that those cycles come and go, no matter what. That's the nature of the beast.

A couple of years ago, I conducted a series of interviews with many established authors in Australia, New Zealand, the United Kingdom, and the United States. I asked each of them about their careers and how they'd managed to stay published for so long. Not one of them said that it had been easy or that they had always successfully ridden publishing cycles. All spoke frankly of experiencing professional difficulties of one sort or another over the years, though looking in from the outside, you might have thought that these writers led charmed lives and brilliant careers without a single flaw. Yet though they had gone through ups and downs—sometimes spectacularly so—what distinguished them all was a capacity for regeneration: for taking stock and taking action.

Over the twenty-six tumultuous, occasionally hair-raising years since I first became a published, professional writer, that's the lesson I've learned, too: Never take anything for granted. Neither the positives nor the negatives are forever, and things can change with bewildering rapidity. You can't necessarily predict them—you just need to be ready to act if you want to stand a chance of being a long-lived writer-phoenix.

Well, that's the big picture. But what about the nitty-gritty? How *do* you prepare for that phoenix life and build your capacity for regeneration?

To put it in a nutshell, it's all about being a "keeper."

KEEP YOUR OPTIONS OPEN

Think of yourself as a writer first and foremost, without boxing yourself into a category. This type of mass categorization—as children's author, novelist, non-fiction writer, and so on—will inevitably restrict your options, should cycles change. The same goes even more for genre. If you think of yourself, say, as *only* a writer of fantasy or crime or historical sagas or picture books or self-help books—or whatever it happens to be—you'll have nowhere else to go if your chosen genre runs out of steam on the shelf, or even just for *you*.

Incidentally, this doesn't mean you shouldn't gravitate to a genre; doing so is natural. We all tend to move toward what comes instinctively to our imaginations, and that's important. But remember that there are also many connections between genres: For instance, fantasy fiction and historical sagas share much common ground, and a nimble author can easily skip from one to the other with much enjoyment—and improve her sustainability at the same time.

The writing life may be sedentary, but it is certainly not static. You don't just get one chance; you will certainly be granted second and third and fourth chances. Unexpected opportunities and challenges arise frequently, even for those who apparently have their whole careers worked out. (Trust me, they don't, not really. It just looks that way!) Learning to embrace some changes while steering clear of others are important lessons in a professional career.

KEEP UP WITH WHAT'S AROUND, BUT KEEP THE FAITH

Read industry news: newsletters, magazines, blogs, websites. Ask yourself questions: Which books are getting noticed and why? What's hot right now? What is conspicuously missing?

Being aware of trends doesn't mean having to slavishly follow them. It does, however, mean that you are well-informed, and that, if necessary, you can much more easily discover a new niche for your work in full knowledge of the ecosystem around it, as it were. An added bonus is that it may also bring new books and writers into your reading life.

Now here's a conundrum: You need to be aware of what's going on in the world of books, but you also need to keep true to your writerly core. Chasing fashion is the best way to be unhappy as a writer—plus you run the risk of rapidly becoming, well, unfashionable. Be ready to take risks and be flexible, but be careful not to gamble away your integrity. Does this sound contradictory? It is. In fact, it's the creative tension between flexibility and integrity that gets the sparks flying and ensures that you'll have the magic ingredients for regeneration.

KEEP PROFESSIONAL RELATIONSHIPS IN GOOD CONDITION

The successful writing life is made of healthy relationships, carefully nurtured. It's all too easy to fall out with a publisher or an agent over a disappointing deal or an opportunity that went south. It's also all too easy to fall out with your writing peers over a professional jealousy or conflict or bad review. My best advice? Think twice. Try not to blow up your bridges, no matter what the provocation. Don't send that angry e-mail or unwise text message or put up that inflammatory Facebook post. Express your anger on a piece of paper—and then burn it or tear it to bits. It's amazing what a relief that can be. (I've used this tactic more than once!)

If you have a difference of opinion that truly is too great to bridge, then it's best to just agree to differ and move on gracefully. Who knows? Later on that person may well play a part in your professional life again, and if you've parted on civil terms, then it's much easier to pick up the pieces. Plus you'll have acquired a reputation for being a consummate professional—which is never a bad thing.

On the positive side, make sure you value and nurture good relationships. It's not just about professional etiquette; it's also about recognizing our common interests, indeed our common humanity. And it pays off, always. A book publicist, for instance, is much more likely to actively promote your work if you treat her like a human being rather than a sales robot programmed for your profit.

This all holds true whether you are a traditionally published author or an independent author. Successful self-publishing is all about relationships, too—

whether that is with your production collaborators (such as designers, editors, printers, and distributors) or your readers.

KEEP CONTRIBUTING TO THE WRITING COMMUNITY

We are writers, and writing is a solitary occupation. But if we so choose, we can also be part of a big, supportive, and diverse community—the community of writers. We can become active participants and contributors in that community: by joining local writers' groups and authors' organizations, by joining conversations on writing blogs and websites and social media, and by starting conversations ourselves on our own blogs and websites and social media. Being part of a community doesn't need to take a lot of time—just a willingness to contribute and a generosity of spirit.

In a practical and enjoyable way, it can also help build your profile among your peers, publishers, agents, and other professionals in the industry, as well as readers in general. And even if your publishing career becomes mired in a temporary quicksand, you can still contribute—in fact it's even more important to do so then. People won't forget your name if you remain a presence in the writing conversation, and it also helps in freshening up your résumé once a new publishing opportunity does come your way.

KEEP GOOD RECORDS

This might seem like a rather dull piece of advice, but it really works in creating sustainability and regeneration, and not just in a financial or administrative sense, either. If you maintain good records stretching over many years, not only can you keep track of the shape of your career but you can also see what's worked and what hasn't, and how sometimes over the years these things have changed places.

As well as keeping records of outgoings and incomings, over the last few years, I've also kept a separate literary diary in which I've expanded on things going on in my professional life. These now run to four books, and they are invaluable in helping me with another important aspect of the writer-phoenix life: keeping a sense of proportion. As they are honest snapshots of how I'm feeling about my writing career at a given point in time, they remind me that difficulties pass, new opportunities come to light, and that out of the ashes of a dead project, something new and wonderfully unexpected can arise.

KEEP A SENSE OF HUMOR

Once, at a book signing, someone approached me to say how much she'd enjoyed one of my earlier books. Trouble was, it wasn't my book she was enthusing about but someone else's—and when I gently told her that was the case, she said, "Oh—maybe you could write like that!" and scuttled away without buying a book. This experience could have been crushing—but instead, it tickled my funny bone and inspired a rather rude and bumbling character in a story!

Being able to see the light side of the struggle is part of a writer's capacity for regeneration. By relieving anxiety, it frees the spirit—and helps inspiration soar.

WRITE ON

Why the End of the Book Is Not the End of the Journey

THERESE WALSH

If it seems like it takes a lot of work to write a novel and sustain a career as a novelist, well, it does. It requires ingenuity and dedication; a willingness to hear criticism and develop a gut sense for your story; a hunger for continued growth; a determination to serve the work, even if that means leaving more on the cutting room floor than in your manuscript; and, perhaps most of all, perseverance.

Being a lifelong writer comes with a variety of rewards, but I think one of the most satisfying is recognizing growth over time. Once you've finished a manuscript, step back and look at the trajectory of that story, comparing the final draft to the first. Now look at the first draft of your first scene of your first story attempt, and compare that to where you are now. The evolution you see means you've grown as a writer, and probably substantially. That change doesn't go away when you begin a new work, either; the lessons learned in one manuscript carry over into another.

Now consider that every additional project will come not only with its own challenges but its own rewards, its own unique ways of stretching you as a writer. Over time, you may capture what you want to say in fewer drafts; your ideas may become more experimental and your techniques more polished. Maybe it'll become more difficult to recognize your own growth, but don't doubt that it's happened.

I like to think of the writing process like a ladder, with each stage of a book's creation representing another rung and each new manuscript presenting another full set of those same rungs. Every time you finish one story and start another, every time you complete a hard revision, every time you push yourself to try a new technique, you build self-confidence in both your story-telling abilities and your authorial instinct.

So why would you stop? Keep stretching yourself. Reach for that next rung and then the next. The only limits to this ladder are those you set for yourself, so don't set any at all.

You have become an Author in Progress, after all.

What will your next page be?

Write on.

 **PRO TIP**

Professional novelists grow not just in craft and business savvy; they grow as human beings. Great authors are forever in progress.

—DONALD MAASS

ABOUT THE ESSAYISTS AND CONTRIBUTORS

AUTHOR IN PROGRESS ESSAYISTS

PORTER ANDERSON, BA, MA, MFA, is a journalist, speaker, and consultant specializing in book publishing. Formerly with CNN, the *Village Voice*, the *Dallas Times Herald*, and other media, he is editor in chief of *Publishing Perspectives*, the magazine for the international publishing industry, founded by German Book Office New York. With Jane Friedman, he produces *The Hot Sheet* newsletter, providing publishing industry news expressly for authors in a biweekly e-mail subscription. Anderson also writes the #MusicForWriters series on contemporary composers for Thought Catalog and is the former associate editor of TheFutureBook for London's *The Bookseller*. Learn more about Porter at porteranderson.com and @Porter_Anderson on Twitter.

JULIANNA BAGGOTT is the author of more than twenty books published under her own name as well as two pen names. Her novels *Pure* and *Harriet Wolf's Seventh Book of Wonders* were both chosen by *The New York Times Book Review* for the 100 Notable Books of the Year (2012 and 2015, respectively). Her most recent release, *All of Us and Everything*, written as Bridget Asher, was a Best New Book pick by *People* magazine. Baggott's essays have appeared in *The New York Times* Modern Love column, *The Washington Post*, *The Boston Globe*, *Real Simple*, *Best American Poetry* series, and on NPR. The author of three books of poems, she teaches in the film school at Florida State University and holds the Jenks Chair of Contemporary American Letters at Holy Cross. Learn more about her at juliannabaggott.com.

BRUNONIA BARRY is the *New York Times* and international best-selling author of *The Lace Reader* and *The Map of True Places*. Her work has been translated into more than thirty languages. She was the first American author to win the International Women's Fiction Festival's Baccante Award and was a past recipient of Ragdale Artists' Colony's Strnad Fellowship as well as the winner of New England Book Festival's award for Best Fiction and Amazon's Best of the Month. Her reviews and articles on writing have appeared in *The London Times* and *The Washington Post*. Brunonia co-chairs the Salem Athenaeum's Writers' Committee. She lives in Salem with her husband, Gary Ward, and their dog, Angel. Her new book, *The Fifth Petal*, will be released in January 2017. Learn more about Brunonia and her books at www.brunoniabarry.com.

TOM BENTLEY is a business writer and editor, an essayist, and a fiction writer. (He does not play banjo.) He's published hundreds of freelance pieces—ranging from first-person essays to travel pieces to more journalistic subjects—in newspapers, magazines, and online. His small-press short story collection, *Flowering and Other Stories*, was published in the spring of 2012. His book on finding and cultivating your writer's voice, *Think Like a Writer: How to Write the Stories You See*, was published in June of 2015. He would like you to pour him a Manhattan right at five. Learn more about Tom on his website: www.tombentley.com.

SHARON BIALLY is founder and president of the PR firm BookSavvy Public Relations, where she proudly publicizes fiction and nonfiction authors and their books. A lapsed writer, she's the author of the novel *Veronica's Nap* and an active supporter of Grub Street, Inc., the nation's largest independent writing center. Earlier in life Sharon worked in the field of international economic policy in Paris and has also lived in Aix-en-Provence. A hopeless Francophile, she lives with her French husband and their two teenage sons in the Boston area. Learn more about Sharon on her website: www.sharonbially.com.

DAN BLANK is the founder of WeGrowMedia, where he helps writers share their stories and connect with readers. He has helped hundreds of authors via online courses, events, consulting, and workshops, and has worked with amazing publishing houses and organizations who support writers, such as

Random House, Hachette Book Group, Workman Publishing, Abrams Books, Writers House, *The Kenyon Review*, Writer's Digest, Library Journal, and many others. He is also the author of the forthcoming book *Dabblers vs. Doers*, aimed at helping creative professionals work through risk as they develop their craft and build a meaningful body of work. You can find Dan on his blog at wegrowmedia.com.

 ANNE GREENWOOD BROWN writes young adult (YA) fiction from a quiet cul-de-sac in Minnesota, as well as new adult (NA) fiction under the pen name A.S. Green. She is represented by Jacqueline Flynn of Joëlle Delbourgo Associates Literary Agency. Her titles include the dark paranormal mermaid trilogy, which includes the titles *Lies Beneath*, *Deep Betrayal*, and *Promise Bound* (Random House/Delacorte Press); a co-authored contemporary mystery/suspense novel, *Girl Last Seen* (Albert Whitman Co., 2016); and *Summer Girl* (Entangled Embrace, 2016). Anne has been contributing to Writer Unboxed since 2010. When she's not writing fiction, she's practicing law and watching her children slowly leave the nest. You can learn more about Anne on her website at annegreenwoodbrown.com.

 KIM BULLOCK has an MA in English from Iowa State University, where she taught composition for several years. Though mainly a historical fiction writer, she has contributed nonfiction articles to regional, historical, and Arts and Crafts periodicals in the United States and Canada. In addition to working on her novel-in-progress, a story based on the bohemian and scandalous lives of her artist great-grandparents, Kim has also been a keynote speaker at several recent exhibitions of her great-grandfather's paintings. She is an assistant editor and contributor at Writer Unboxed. Kim lives in Dallas, Texas, with her husband and two daughters. Learn more about Kim at writerunboxed.com/kim.

 SARAH CALLENDER lives in Seattle with her husband and two children. A writer, freelance editor, and tutor, Sarah is also passionate about erasing the stigma of mental illness. While her novels, *Between the Sun and the Oranges* and *Flight of the Birdmen*, are out on submission, she is working on her third book. Learn more about Sarah on her website: sarahrcallender.wordpress.com.

DAVID CORBETT is the author of five novels: *The Devil's Red-head*, *Done for a Dime* (a *New York Times* Notable Book), *Blood of Paradise*, *Do They Know I'm Running*, and *The Mercy of the Night*. His novella, *The Devil Prayed and Darkness Fell*, also appeared in 2015, and his story collection *Thirteen Confessions* was published in 2016. David's book on the craft of characterization, *The Art of Character*, has been called "a writer's bible," and he's written numerous articles on the craft and theory of fiction for *The New York Times*, *Writer's Digest*, *Narrative*, *Bright Ideas*, and numerous other outlets. He has taught at the UCLA Extension's Writers' Program, Litreactor, Book Passage, 826 Valencia, and numerous writing conferences across the United States, Canada, and Mexico. Learn more about David on his website: www.davidcorbett.com.

KATHRYN CRAFT is the author of two novels from Sourcebooks, *The Art of Falling* and *The Far End of Happy*. Her work as a freelance developmental editor at writing-partner.com follows a nineteen-year career as a dance critic. Long a leader in the southeastern Pennsylvania writing scene, she is an active member of the Women's Fiction Writers Association and Tall Poppy Writers. Kathryn leads writing workshops and retreats, and blogs at Writers in the Storm and Writer Unboxed. Learn more about Kathryn on her website, www.kathryncraft.com.

LISA CRON is the author of *Wired for Story: The Writer's Guide to Using Brain Science to Hook Readers from the Very First Sentence* (Ten Speed Press). Her TEDx Talk, "Wired for Story," opened Furman University's 2014 TEDx conference, *Stories: The Common Thread of Our Humanity*, and her video tutorial, "Writing Fundamentals: The Craft of Story," can be found at Lynda.com. Her book *Story Genius: How to Use Brain Science to Crack the Code of Your Novel (Before You Waste Three Years Writing 327 Pages That Go Nowhere)* was published by Ten Speed Press in August 2016. A frequent speaker at writers conferences, schools, and universities, her passion has always been story. She currently works as a story coach, helping writers, nonprofits, educators, and journalists wrangle the story they're telling onto the page. Learn more on her website: wiredforstory.com.

KEITH CRONIN is a corporate speechwriter and professional rock drummer who has performed and recorded with artists including Bruce Springsteen, Clarence Clemons, and Pat Travers. He is also the author of the novels *Me Again*, published by Five Star/Gale, and *Tony Partly Cloudy*, published under his pen name, Nick Rollins. Keith's fiction has appeared in *Carve Magazine*, *Amarillo Bay*, and a University of Phoenix management course. He holds a bachelor's degree in music from Indiana University and an MBA from Florida Atlantic University. A South Florida native, Keith spends his free time serenading local ducks and squirrels with his ukulele. Learn more about Keith on his website: www.keithcronin.com.

MARGARET DILLOWAY is the author of the middle-grade fantasy series Momotoro and the novels *How to Be an American Housewife*, *Sisters of Heart and Snow*, and *The Care and Handling of Roses and Thorns*, which won the 2013 American Library Association's Literary Tastes award for Best Women's Fiction. She lives in San Diego with her family, where she also teaches creative writing at a charter middle school and conducts workshops for adults. Learn more at margaretdilloway.com.

JO EBERHARDT first announced she was a writer when she was four years old but put her career on hold while she learned the alphabet, suffered through teen angst, and held down a series of boringly real jobs. Thirty years later, she traded financial security for creative freedom and hasn't looked back. Jo runs a local writing group, teaches novel writing workshops, and mentors teenagers in creative writing. When she's not living in worlds of her own making, Jo can be found in rural Queensland, Australia. Learn more about Jo on her website: joeberhardt.com.

ANNA ELLIOTT is an author of historical fiction and fantasy. Her first series, the Twilight of Avalon trilogy, is a retelling of the Trystan and Isolde legend. She wrote her second series, the Pride and Prejudice Chronicles, chiefly to satisfy her own curiosity about what might have happened to Elizabeth Bennet, Mr. Darcy, and all the other wonderful cast of characters after the official end of Jane Austen's classic work. She enjoys stories about strong women and loves exploring the multitude of ways women can find their unique strengths.

Anna lives in the Washington DC area with her husband and three children. Learn more about Anna at www.annaelliottbooks.com.

BILL FERRIS is a stand-up comedian who writes mysteries, fantasy, science fiction, and horror, and does not do stand-up. His writing has appeared in publications such as *Unidentified Funny Objects*, *Crowded*, *Opium*, and *Stupefying Stories*. When he's not typing words into a thing, Bill develops online courses at a university his lawyer advised him not to name. He has two sons who asked not to be mentioned in this bio, but Elliott and Wyatt forgot to say "please."

JANE FRIEDMAN has twenty years of experience in the publishing industry, with expertise in digital media strategy for authors and publishers. She's worked with or served a diverse range of organizations and publications, including the *Virginia Quarterly Review*, The Great Courses, *Writer's Digest*, *Publishers Weekly*, and the National Endowment for the Arts; and has a book forthcoming from the University of Chicago Press, *The Business of Being a Writer* (2017). Her essays have been published in collections from Milkweed Editions, McPherson & Co., and Seal Press, among others. Find out more at janefriedman.com.

TRACY HAHN-BURKETT is a writer and former congressional staffer and public policy advocate. She writes the parenting blog, *Uncharted Parent*, contributes regularly to Writer Unboxed, and has published dozens of essays, articles, stories, and reviews. A recipient of a grant from the New Hampshire State Council on the Arts, she is currently revising her first novel. Tracy lives in New Hampshire with her husband and two children. Learn more about Tracy and *Uncharted Parent* on her website: www.tracyhahnburkett.com.

GWEN HERNANDEZ is the author of *Scrivener for Dummies*, *Productivity Tools for Writers*, and the Men of Steele series (military romantic suspense), several of which nearly gave their lives as kindling at one point or another. Formerly a manufacturing engineer and programmer, Gwen teaches Scrivener to writers all over the world through online classes, in-person workshops, and private sessions. In her spare time, she likes to travel, read, run, practice Kung Fu and yoga, and spend time with her family. Learn more at gwenhernandez.com.

 Originally from Houston, Texas, **KRISTAN HOFFMAN** studied creative writing at Carnegie Mellon University and attended the Kenyon Review Writers Workshop. Now she lives with her husband in Cincinnati, Ohio, where she writes both fiction and nonfiction with a focus on contemporary, multicultural stories. Her shorter work has appeared in *Sugar Mule*, *The Citron Review*, and *Switchback*, among others. She is currently at work on a young adult novel and is represented by Tina Wexler of ICM Partners. For more, please visit kristanhoffman.com.

 STEVEN JAMES is the critically acclaimed author of thirteen novels. He serves as a contributing editor to *Writer's Digest* magazine, hosts the biweekly podcast The Story Blender, and has a master's degree in storytelling. *Publishers Weekly* calls him "[a] master storyteller at the peak of his game." Steven's groundbreaking book *Story Trumps Structure: How to Write Unforgettable Fiction by Breaking the Rules* won a Storytelling World award as one of the best resources for storytellers in 2015. When he's not working on his next novel, Steven teaches Novel Writing Intensive retreats across the country with *New York Times* best-selling author Robert Dugoni. Learn more at www.stevenjames.net.

 In addition to editing everything from YA to harrowing memoirs, with romance, mysteries, and historicals in between, **DAVE KING** is the co-author of *Self-Editing for Fiction Writers*, now in its second edition with more than 140,000 sold. He works from a small home in the hills of western Massachusetts that he shares with Ruth Julian, his wife and personal editor. They often watch bears, beaver, deer, ducks, muskrat, fox, wild turkeys, and the occasional bobcat wander around in the yard and pond. In spite of the limits of satellite Internet access, Dave can keep editing without ever having to move away from the wood stove. If you'd like to learn more about Dave and his services, visit his website, www.davekingedits.com.

 JEANNE KISACKY trained to be an architect before going back to her first love: writing. She studied the history of architecture, has written and published nonfiction, and has taught college courses. Her first book-length publication, *The Rise of*

the Modern Hospital: An Architectural History of Health and Healing, was released in the fall of 2016 from the University of Pittsburgh Press. She is also still polishing a long-brewing work of fantasy and fighting valiantly to keep her writing time despite the demands of a day job, a family, and a very particular cat.

ROBIN LAFEVERS is a *New York Times* best-selling author who has written more than sixteen books for young readers. Her most recent young adult trilogy about assassin nuns in medieval France (featuring the titles *Grave Mercy, Dark Triumph*, and *Mortal Heart*) was awarded starred reviews from *School Library Journal, Booklist, Kirkus,* and *Publishers Weekly,* and has been translated into a number of languages. Though she has never trained as an assassin or joined a convent, she has been on a search for answers to life's mysteries for as long as she can remember. She currently lives with her husband in the hills of Southern California. Learn more about Robin on her website: www.robinlafevers.com.

ALLIE LARKIN is the internationally best-selling author of the novels *Stay* and *Why Can't I Be You* (Dutton/Plume). Her work has also been published in the *Summerset Review* and *Slice* magazine. She lives in the San Francisco Bay area with her husband, Jeremy, and their German Shepherd, Stella. Learn more about Allie on her website: allielarkinwrites.com.

ERIKA LIODICE is the author of *Empty Arms: A Novel* (Dreamspire Press) and a regular contributor to the popular fiction writing website Writer Unboxed. She is currently at work on her second novel and an action adventure series for early readers. When she's not writing fiction, you'll find Erika on her blog, Beyond the Gray, where she enjoys inspiring readers to chase their own dreams. Visit erikaliodice.com to learn more.

A literary agent in New York, **DONALD MAASS**'s agency sells more than 150 novels every year to major publishers in the United States and overseas. He is the author of *The Career Novelist* (1996), *Writing the Breakout Novel* (2001) *Writing the Breakout Novel Workbook* (2004), *The Fire in Fiction* (2009) and *Writing 21st Century Fiction* (2012). He is a past president of the Association of Authors' Representatives, Inc. Learn more about Donald and his agency at maassagency.com.

French-Australian writer **SOPHIE MASSON** is the award-winning and internationally published author of sixty-five books for children, young adults, and adults. Her latest adult novel is *Trinity: The False Prince*, (Momentum, 2015) while her latest YA novel is *Hunter's Moon*, (Random House Australia, 2015). Her nonfiction title, *The Adaptable Author: Coping with Change in the Digital Age*, was published by Keesing Press in 2014. Sophie is also a founding partner and director of Christmas Press, a boutique publishing house producing beautiful children's books. Learn more on Sophie's website: www.sophiemasson.org.

Raised in the Midwest, **GREER MACALLISTER** is a poet, short story writer, playwright, and novelist whose work has appeared in publications such as *The North American Review*, *The Missouri Review*, and *The Messenger*. Her plays have been performed at American University, where she earned her MFA in creative writing. She lives with her family on the East Coast. Her debut novel, *The Magician's Lie*, was an Indie Next pick, a Target Book Club selection, and a *USA Today* bestseller. Learn more on her website: www.greermacallister.com.

JULIET MARILLIER was born in New Zealand and now lives in Western Australia. Her historical fantasy novels and short stories for adults and young adults have been published internationally and have won a number of awards. Juliet's lifelong love of folklore, fairy tales, and mythology is a major influence on her writing. She is a member of the Order of Bards, Ovates and Druids (OBOD). Juliet's next novel is *Den of Wolves* (Blackthorn & Grim series, Book 3), to be released in November 2016. When she's not busy writing, Juliet is active in animal rescue. Find out more at www.julietmarillier.com.

JULIA MUNROE MARTIN is truly an author in progress. She is a freelance writer and blogger as well as one of the assistant editors for Writer Unboxed. She lives on the coast of Maine in a very old house in a very small town, where she is happiest at her dining room table working on her latest story or out and about taking photos. She has a lot of experience with waiting, and while she waits, she writes. As J.M. Maison, Julia is the author of the indie mystery novel *Desired to Death*. Learn more on Julia's website: juliamunroemartin.com.

SARAH MCCOY is the *New York Times, USA Today*, and international best-selling author of *The Mapmaker's Children; The Baker's Daughter*, a 2012 Goodreads Choice Award Best Historical Fiction nominee; the novella "The Branch of Hazel" in *Grand Central*; and *The Time It Snowed in Puerto Rico*. Her work has been featured in *Real Simple, The Millions, Your Health Monthly, The Huffington Post*, and other publications. She has taught English writing at Old Dominion University and at the University of Texas at El Paso. She calls Virginia home but presently lives with her husband, an Army orthopedic surgeon, and their dog, Gilly, in Chicago, Illinois. Learn more about Sarah on her website, sarahmccoy.com.

KATHLEEN MCCLEARY is the author of three novels: *House and Home* (2008); *A Simple Thing* (2012), nominated for the Library of Virginia Literary Award in fiction; and *Leaving Haven* (2013), a Target Emerging Author pick. Her nonfiction articles have appeared in *Parade* magazine, *The New York Times, The Washington Post, Good Housekeeping*, and many other publications. She has taught writing as an adjunct professor at American University and is an instructor with Writopia Labs, a nonprofit that teaches creative writing to kids. Learn more about Kathleen on her website: www.kathleenmccleary.com.

JAEL MCHENRY is the author of *The Kitchen Daughter* (Simon & Schuster/Gallery Books, 2011) and an enthusiastic amateur cook, blogging about food and writing at The Simmer Blog. She is also the editor in chief of Intrepid Media. Jael lives in New York City. Learn more on her website: www.jael mchenry.com.

A graduate of McGill University in history and law, **CATHERINE MCKENZIE** practices law in Montreal, where she was born and raised. An avid skier and runner, Catherine's novels, *Spin, Arranged, Forgotten*, and *Hidden*, are all international bestsellers and have been translated into numerous languages. *Hidden* was also a number one Amazon bestseller and a Digital Bookworld bestseller. Her fifth novel, *Smoke*, was published by Lake Union in October 2015. It was named a Best Book of October by Goodreads and one of the Top 100 Books of 2015 by Amazon. Her sixth novel, *Fractured*, was published in October 2016. Learn more on Catherine's website: catherinemckenzie.com.

LIZ MICHALSKI's novel *Evenfall* was published by Penguin Berkley. She's working on her second novel, a fairy tale for adults about all the ways in which wishes can go wrong. She's been a reporter and an editor and once owned a large barn in a small corner of Connecticut. In that previous life, she wrangled with ill-tempered horses and oversized show dogs. She traded it all in for a house in suburbia where she freelances, carpools her children, yells at the dog to stop taking the drainpipe off the house, and reminds her husband to whack back the wisteria before it overtakes civilization. She wouldn't change a thing. Learn more at www.lizmichalski.com.

ANNIE NEUGEBAUER is a short story author, novelist, and award-winning poet. Her work has appeared in more than fifty venues, including *Black Static*, *Apex Magazine*, and *Fireside*. She's the webmaster for the Poetry Society of Texas and an active member of the Horror Writers Association. Annie graduated from the University of Texas at Austin with an English degree and highest university honors. Now she lives in North Texas with her sweet husband and two diabolical cats. Visit her at annieneugebauer.com for blogs, creative works, organizational tools for writers, and more.

Although she knew in grade school she wanted to write fiction, **JAN O'HARA** left her dreams behind for a time to become a family physician. She provided birth-to-death healthcare to her patients and served as an assistant professor at the University of Alberta, teaching residents and medical students about patient-centered care and human sexuality. Jan lives in Alberta, Canada, with her husband and two children and writes a monthly column for Writer Unboxed. Once obsessed with helping people professionally, she has retired from medicine and now spends her days torturing them on paper. See? Win-win scenarios really do exist. Learn more about Jan on her website: janohara.net.

BARBARA O'NEAL has won the highly prestigious RITA award from Romance Writers of America seven times and was inducted into the RWA Hall of Fame in 2012. She published her first novel in her twenties and has written more than fifty books since then, including *The Lost Recipe for Happiness* (Bantam), which went back to print eight times, and *How to Bake a Perfect Life*, which was a Target Club Pick. Her books have been translated into more than a dozen languages, and she is a popular blogger and teacher who loves to travel, teach, and hike. Learn more about Barbara and her many novels on her website: www.barbaraoneal.com.

RAY RHAMEY is an author, freelance fiction editor, and designer of book covers, interiors, and e-books for indie authors and small publishers. He writes the internationally known blog, Flogging the Quill, on creating compelling fiction. His how-to book, *Mastering the Craft of Compelling Storytelling*, has gotten rave reviews from writers. Ray's background includes screenwriting and advertising. Readers call him a "genre-bending" writer—his *The Vampire Kitty-cat Chronicles* is a satirical paranormal adventure, *Gundown* is a speculative thriller, *The Summer Boy* is a coming-of-age mystery set in 1958, and *Hiding Magic* is a blend of science fiction and contemporary fantasy. Learn more about Ray on his website: www.rayrhamey.com.

ERIKA ROBUCK is the best-selling author of *Hemingway's Girl, Call Me Zelda, Fallen Beauty, The House of Hawthorne*, and *Receive Me Falling*. She is also a contributor to the anthology *Grand Central: Postwar Stories of Love and Reunion* and to the Writer Unboxed blog. She has her own blog, Muse, and is a member of the Hawthorne, Historical Novel, Hemingway, and Millay Societies. In 2014, Robuck was named Annapolis' Author of the Year, and she resides there with her husband and three sons. Learn more about Erika on her website: www.erikarobuck.com.

New York Times bestseller **M.J. ROSE** (www.mjrose.com) grew up in New York City, mostly in the labyrinthine galleries of the Metropolitan Museum, the dark tunnels and lush gardens of Central Park, and reading her mother's favorite books before she was allowed. She believes mystery and magic are all around us but that we are often too busy to notice. Rose has written more than a dozen novels; is the creator of www.authorbuzz.com, the first marketing company for authors; is the co-creator of www.1001darknights.com; and is one of the founding board members of International Thriller Writers.

VAUGHN ROYCROFT claims he came to writing later in life, but that's not entirely accurate. In truth the aspiration was kindled much earlier. Before Vaughn moved to the perfect writing cottage, before he built a successful business, even before he married his soul mate, he dreamed of writing his epic. The roots of his stories might actually be traced to the day his sixth-grade teacher told him Tolkien's Rohirrim resemble the Goths. Vaughn is a moderator for the Writer Unboxed community and has been writing about the support he finds there since 2012—support he's certain will see him through to publication. Learn more about Vaughn on his website: www.vaughnroycroft.com.

As a Brooklyn-based author and producer, **LANCELOT SCHAUBERT** continues to cross the borders that hem in the land of tales. He started out selling poetry to small zines like *SP Quill* and *Doxa*. Then he moved on to nonfiction in *Harry Potter for Nerds*, *The World Series Edition of Poker Pro*, *Occupy*, *Poet's Market 2016*, and *McSweeney's*. Later he sold fiction to *Encounter* as well as to *Brink*, *Hatch*, *Scars*, and others. In recent years, his stories crossed into transmedia as he reinvented the photonovel via *Cold Brewed* and *The Joplin Undercurrent*, acted in short films, and recorded an album coinciding with his short stories. His first novel, *Faceless*, is making the rounds with agents. Oh, and his hobbit hair grows longer by the day. So there's that. Learn more about Lance on his website: lanceschaubert.org.

SUSAN SPANN is a California attorney whose practice focuses on business and publishing law; she also writes the Hiro Hattori novels (Shinobi Mysteries), featuring ninja detective Hiro Hattori and his Portuguese Jesuit sidekick, Father Mateo. Her first novel, *Claws of the Cat* (Minotaur, 2013) was a *Library Journal* mystery debut of the month and a finalist for the Silver Falchion Award for Best First Novel. Her fourth novel, *The Ninja's Daughter* (Seventh Street Books), was released in August 2016. Susan founded and curates the Twitter #PubLaw hashtag to provide authors with information about the publishing business and legal issues. When not writing or practicing law, she enjoys traditional archery, reading, and raising seahorses in her marine aquarium. She lives near Sacramento, California. Find her online at www.susanspann.com.

VICTORIA STRAUSS has authored nine novels, including the Way of Arata duology (*The Burning Land* and *The Awakened City*). She has written hundreds of book reviews for magazines and e-zines, and her articles on writing have appeared in *Writer's Digest*. She's co-founder, with Ann Crispin, of Writer Beware, a publishing industry watchdog group sponsored by the Science

Fiction and Fantasy Writers of America. She maintains the Writer Beware website (www.writerbeware.com) and blog (accrispin.blogspot.com), for which she won a 2012 Independent Book Blogger Award. She has also been honored with the SFWA Service Award. Visit her at her website: www.victoria strauss.com.

JOHN VORHAUS is the author of some two dozen books, including the outstanding novels *Lucy in the Sky* and *Poole's Paradise*, the classic comedy writing textbook *The Comic Toolbox*, and the unbelievably conceptual *A Million Random Words*. Strange as that sounds, it's not even the odd part of his résumé, for he has also taught and trained writers in thirty-three countries on five continents (at last count) and created television shows in such exotic locales as Romania and Nicaragua. He tweets for no apparent reason @TrueFactBar Fact, sells all his works at www.amazon.com/author/jv, and secretly controls the world from www.johnvorhaus.com.

THERESE WALSH co-founded Writer Unboxed with Kathleen Bolton in 2006 and is the site's editorial director. Her debut novel, *The Last Will of Moira Leahy*, was nominated for a RITA Award for Best First Book and was a Target Breakout Book. Her second novel, *The Moon Sisters*, received starred reviews from *Library Journal* and *Booklist*, and was named a Best Book of 2014 by *Library Journal*. She has a master's degree in psychology. You can learn more about her on her website, www.theresewalsh.com.

HEATHER WEBB is a historical fiction author, freelance editor, and blogger at the award- winning writing sites Writer Unboxed and Writers in the Storm. Her works have been translated into three languages and have received national starred reviews. Heather is a member of the Historical Novel Society and the Women's Fiction Writers Association, and she may also be found teaching craft-based courses at a local college. Visit her at www.heatherwebb. net for more information.

CATHY YARDLEY sold her first novel to Harlequin in 1999. Since then, she has traditionally published eighteen novels in women's fiction, chick lit, romance, and urban fantasy, and in 2016 she is self-publishing her "geek girl" category rom-com series, *Fandom Hearts*. She's been quoted in the *Chicago*

Tribune, *The Washington Post*, and the *SF Guardian*, among others. In 2011, she started rockyourwriting.com with the mission of helping genre novelists make a living. She has helped hundreds of authors as a developmental editor and writing coach, and through her "plot sessions"—one-on-one calls that get authors from concept to plot points in one hour. She's also written the Rock Your Writing series of reference books, taking authors through the writing cycle, from concept to completion, as well as helping authors figure out the foundation plan for building their brands and marketing their work. To learn more about Cathy, visit cathyyardley.com.

WRITER UNBOXED COMMUNITY CONTRIBUTORS

CG BLAKE has thirty years of writing and editing experience. He published his first novel, *Small Change*, in 2012, and his second novel, *A Prayer for Maura*, is due out in 2016. His interest in family dynamics has led Blake to choose family sagas as his genre. He maintains a blog called A New Fiction Writer's Forum at www.cgblake.wordpress.com. Blake lives outside of Hartford, Connecticut. He is employed as an association management executive in the higher-education sector.

VIJAYA BODACH is a scientist-turned-children's writer. She is the author of the novelty book *Ten Easter Eggs* (Scholastic), fifty supplemental science books for children, and more than sixty articles, stories, and poems in leading children's magazines. She is a former instructor at the Institute of Children's Literature. Vijaya wrangles children, students, pets, and words in beautiful Charleston, South Carolina. To learn more, visit her blog at vijayabodach. blogspot.com.

PAULA CAPPA is the recipient of a Chanticleer Book Award, the prestigious Eric Hoffer Book Award, the Readers' Favorite International Bronze Medal for Supernatural Suspense, and a Gothic Readers Book Club Award. She is the author of *Greylock*, *The Dazzling Darkness*, and *Night Sea Journey*. Her short fiction has appeared in *Dark Gothic Resurrected Magazine*, *Whistling Shade Literary Journal*, *SmokeLong Quarterly*, *Sirens Call Ezine*, *Every Day Fiction*, *Fiction365*, *Twilight Times Ezine*, and in anthologies *Journals of Horror: Found Fiction*, *Mystery Time*, and *Human Writes Literary Journal*. She is a freelance copyeditor and writes a weekly short story blog, Reading Fiction, Tales of Terror at paulacappa.wordpress.com.

 VALERIE P. CHANDLER received her BA in literature from Southwestern University and has been a paralegal and a teacher. The city girl married her cowboy and became a rancher as well as a jill-of-all-trades. The crazy escapades of ranch life and the urge to document the fading history and culture of rural Texas have fueled her lifelong desire to write. She's a member of the Heart of Texas chapter of Sisters in Crime and Austin Mystery Writers, as well as a moderator for the Writer Unboxed Facebook group. Learn more about her on her website, vpchandler.com.

 LJ COHEN is a novelist, poet, blogger, ceramics artist, and relentless optimist. After twenty-five years as a physical therapist, LJ now uses her anatomical knowledge and clinical skills to injure characters in her science fiction and fantasy novels. She lives outside of Boston with her family and her dogs. Her most recent book, *Ithaka Rising*, Book 2 of the Halcyone Space series, represents her fifth novel and was published in the summer of 2015. The third book in the series, *Dreadnought and Shuttle*, will be published in June of 2016. LJ is active in SFWA and Broad Universe. Learn more about her at www.ljcohen.net.

 RON ESTRADA is a young adult and middle-grade author, currently editing the first of his Navy Brats historical novels, *Scorpion Summer*, for submission. His first YA series, *Cherry Hill*, is available on most online retailers. He lives in Michigan with his understanding wife and almost-out-of-the-house children. You can find him at his website, ronestradabooks.com or on Facebook.

 TONIA MARIE HARRIS resides in south-central Illinois with her husband, three children, and three rescue animals. She writes speculative fiction and poetry, aided by her muse, a cross-dressing goblin with a penchant for rum and Kafka novels. Her work has appeared in various anthologies, and she is an administrative assistant for Writer Unboxed. Learn more about Tonia on her website: toniamarieharris.com.

NATALIE HART is a writer of biblical fiction and of picture books for children who were adopted when they were older. Her father was an entrepreneur, so she'd never intended to be one, but she's about to independently publish everything. Learn more about Natalie on her websites: www.nataliehart. com and westolivepress.com.

BARRY KNISTER's first novel, a thriller titled The Dating Service, was published by Berkley. More recently, he has self-published *Just Bill*, a novel about dogs, and two novels in a suspense series, *The Anything Goes Girl* and *Deep North*. He taught for many years at Lawrence Technological University in Southfield, Michigan. He served as the secretary for Detroit Working Writers and as the director of the Cranbrook Summer Writers Conference. He lives north of Detroit with his wife, Barbara, and their Aussie shepherd, Skylar. Learn more about Barry on his website: www.bwknister.com.

BARBARA MORRISON, who writes under the name B. Morrison, is the author of a memoir, *Innocent: Confessions of a Welfare Mother*, and two poetry collections, *Terrarium* and *Here at Least*. Barbara's award-winning work has been published in anthologies and magazines. She conducts writing workshops, provides editing services, and (as the owner of a small press) speaks about publishing and marketing. She has maintained her Monday Morning Books blog since 2006 and tweets regularly about poetry @bmorrison9. For more information, visit her website and blog at www.bmorrison.com.

BERNADETTE PHIPPS-LINCKE says that some of her fondest memories involve picnics in cemeteries as a child, where her eccentric mother taught her to read via tombstone epitaphs and also encouraged the small girl to make up stories about the lives led by those dearly departed. Bernadette still finds inspiration in cemeteries and loves stories that dabble with and dance in the darkness. Her first novel, a paranormal thriller, *Burning Lily*, is scheduled for e-book release soon from Wild Child publishers.

THOMAS HENRY POPE credits a songwriting career in Hollywood for schooling him in the weight of words. The characters in his novels long for home because they chose to leave theirs to worry the bones of injustice. They are hushed by place and the vibrancy of subcultures. They squirm in the face of the very power they seek. The world they inhabit is ours, where passion fuels action and moral ambiguity complicates happy endings. His novels—*The Trouble with Wisdom* (quest) and *Imperfect Burials* (thriller)—bind the genres of crime, adventure, and magical realism with a literary thread. More are in the pipeline. Learn more about Tom at www.thomashenrypope.com.

ALISHA ROHDE writes stories that weave together past and present, history, and myth, seeking the magic in the ordinary. She's taught college-level English, done administrative work in a range of industries, and managed projects and licensing for a small video/multimedia company. Alisha has a PhD in English literature from The Ohio State University and a BA in theatre from Kalamazoo College. She's a member of the Women's Fiction Writer's Association. When not writing or reading, she enjoys knitting and yoga. Alisha lives in Evanston, Illinois, with her husband and one chatty tuxedo cat. You can find her online at alisharohde.com.

SUSAN SETTEDUCATO grew up in a family of storytellers of both the Irish and the Italian variety. She also grew up in the heyday of fairytales being brought to life on the screen by Walt Disney. These influences have resulted in Susan's desire to blend myth, legend, and magic into the fabric of her novels. Although trained as a painter, Susan has been writing all her life and is nearing completion of *Luminous*, the first novel in the McCool Saga. She lives in Bucks County with her husband, Peter; three sheep; and two barn cats. Visit her website at susansetteducato.com.

M.L. SWIFT is a lover of words who squanders away his afternoons arranging them into sentences that, when combined, resemble fiction. He has written articles for Writer Unboxed and The Alzheimer's Reading Room, and, as a caregiver for ten years, is writing a novel based on his experience. He lives in the Florida panhandle with his two dogs, Rameses and Buster, and spends his nights fighting a losing battle to reclaim his side of the bed. Visit him online at mlswift.me.

 DEE WILLSON felt the writer's call at fifteen, when she penned her first novel and received her first rejection to go with it. More than twenty years later, she has published short stories and interviews, contributed to blogs, and wrote the novel *A Keeper's Truth*, followed by *GOT* (*Gift of Travel*). She currently resides in Burlington, Ontario, with her husband and their two daughters. Visit her online at www.deewillson.com.

 GRACE WYNTER is a copyeditor, blogger, and writer of romantic women's fiction. Her blogs have been featured on CNN.com, the Huffington Post, and More.com. In 2010, she was voted by *WE Magazine for Women* as a Woman Blogger to Watch. She spends much of her time writing and helping other writers on her blog, The Writer's Station, and when she's not alternating between the Marvel and DC universes, she resides in Atlanta, Georgia. You can connect with Grace on her blog (thewritersstation.com) and on her author website, ggwynter.com.

INDEX

professional, 235–242

surface-level, 239–240

Eliot, T.S., 69, 263

Emerson, Ralph Waldo, 48

empathy, 109

Empty Writer's Nest, 304–306

envy, 256–258

Epic of Gilgamesh, 103

Erhard, Werner, 200

espresso book machines, 150

exercise, 261–262, 267–268

family, as beta readers, 150

A Farewell to Arms (Hemingway), 209

feedback, 305–306. *See also* critique

Fellowship of the Ring (Tolkien), 79

Fenton, Liz, 165

first draft, 61–63, 92

Fisher, M.F.K., 90

Fitzgerald, F. Scott, 263

flashbacks, 72–73. *See also* backstory

Fleming, Ian, 263

Flight Behavior (Kingsolver), 182

Flight Patterns (White), 164

Flynn, Gillian, 45–46, 152

focus groups, 144–145

Ford, G.M., 52

Fowles, John, 103

Fractured (McKenzie), 213

Francis (pope), 200

Frank, Rob, 184

Frey, James N., 182

Friedman, Jane, 202

friends, as beta readers, 150

Gable, Michelle, 17

Gardner, Rachelle, 205

Gerritsen, Tess, 78–79

Gingerbread (Dinsdale), 111

Girl Lost Seen (Anne Greenwood Brown), 87

Gladwell, Malcolm, 45

Glass, Ira, 61

GMC: Goal, Motivation and Conflict (Dixon), 182

goal, motivation and conflict (GMC), 230–231

goal setting, 10–13, 82–83, 189, 193

The God of Small Things (Roy), 111

Goethe, Johann Wolfgang von, 31

The Goldfinch (Tartt), 15

Gone Girl (Flynn), 45–46, 152, 308

Grafton, Sue, 101

The Great Gatsby (Fitzgerald), 263

Green, Jane, 164

Groff, Lauren, 101

Grub Street conference, 190, 191, 202

Gruen, Sara, 173

Hammett, Dashiell, 263

Hannah, Kristin, 180–181

Harry Potter series, 15

health, 259–265

and diet, 260–261

and drinking, 262–263

and exercise, 261–261, 267–268

and smoking, 263–264

Hedgebrook (Washington), 16

The Help (Stockett), 118

Hemingway, Ernest, 93, 196–197, 209, 217

Here Comes Everybody (Shirky), 203

The Hero's Journey, 177

Hiding Magic (Ray Rhamey), 87

Holmes, Oliver Wendell, 105

How to Tell a Story: The Secrets of Writing Captivating Tales (Rubie and Provost), 182

The Hunger Games (Collins), 152

I Am a Camera (Van Druten), 75

Iceland Writers Retreat, 16

idea selection, 35–36

imitation, 180–185

the Writer Unboxed community on, 185–188

imposter syndrome, 126–127

inspiration, 35, 103

false muses, 98–102

from memories, 105–107

from quotes, 122

true muses, 102–104

Internet

avoiding, 94, 116

positive use of, 167–168, 190, 203

interviews, 52–53

Isherwood, Christopher, 75

Ivey, Eowyn, 111

Jabr, Ferris, 210

James, Henry, 216

James, Steven, 80

Jewel (Ray Rhamey), 88

Jobs, Steve, 269

Johnson, Bill, 183

Journal of a Novel: The East of Eden Letters (Steinbeck), 181

journaling, 119

Kaputt (Malaparte), 52

Kent, Hannah, 111

The Key: How to Write Damn Good Fiction Using the Power of Myth (Frey), 182

Killer Nashville, 190

King, Stephen, 36, 79

Kingsolver, Barbara, 111, 182

Kinsey Millhone books (Sue Grafton), 101

The Knight (James), 224

Kowal, Mary Robinette, 196

Kress, Nancy, 182

L'Engle, Madeleine, 118

The Lace Reader (Barry), 143

language, sound of, 215–217

Larkin, Allie, 213

Larson, Jonathan, 184

Lehane, Dennis, 52

Leonard, Elmore, 78, 80, 177

Lessing, Doris, 48

Levin, Donna, 52

Lewis-Stempel, John, 111

Liadis, Paul, 77

Lies Beneath (Anne Greenwood Brown), 87

Lipskar, Simon, 308

Logical Marketing, 205

The Lost Wife (Richman), 310

Lystra, Karen, 50

Maass, Donald, 182

MacLeish, Archibald, 196